Praise for *ADHD in Sport*

It's an excellent book which is so easy to read and find the appropriate chapters. It has great psychological strategies and techniques for example, strength audits, pots of power, habit stacking and goal setting which can help athletes with inattention and also strategies to manage impulsivity and emotional dysregulation. I would honestly recommend this book in my post-diagnosis psychology sessions with clients who have an interest in sport and exercise.

Sabina Bedi, Counselling Psychologist

This book is essential reading for coaches, parents, practitioners and athletes who are interested in better understanding ADHD within the sporting context. Not only will this enhance your knowledge, but the practical and actionable guidance contained throughout will help you better support yourself, or the neurodiverse athletes you work with.

Dr Ross Shand, Sport and Exercise Psychologist

I think the book is an incredible resource, and one I wish I had access to during my time as an athlete!
Caragh McMurtry, Former Olympic Rower and CEO of Neurodiverse Sport

This is a vital resource for athletes, coaches and parents. This book empowers athletes with ADHD to unlock their potential in sports, and provides coaches and parents with effective strategies to help them thrive. A must-read for anyone involved in supporting neurodiverse athletes.

Dr Darren Britton, Sport and Performance Psychologist

This book is informative, easy to follow and helped me reflect on my own coaching and practice. It will be such a huge help to so many. All future PE teachers and coaches should read this. The stories really bring this book to life, bringing the theory into light. The practical tips for use throughout the book are excellent as sometimes, as coaches, we fail to look beyond the physical.

Phil Greenway, Education and Sport Consultant

Another brilliant book from Dr Josie Perry. ADHD in Sport *is insightful, practical and a must-read for athletes and coaches alike.*
Jenny Coe, Performance Well-being Lead, Women's Professional Football

As a Consultant Clinical Psychologist and mum of a neurodiverse child athlete, I found this book to be an excellent resource. It provides in-depth evidence-based yet accessible up-to-date information and helpful practical advice. I would highly recommend it to professionals, coaches, athletes and parents alike.
Dr Rachel Skippon, Consultant Clinical Psychologist

ADHD in Sport

ADHD in Sport

Strategies for Success

Josephine Perry

Every possible effort has been made to ensure that the information contained in this book is accurate at the time of going to press. The publishers and author(s) cannot accept responsibility for any errors and omissions, however caused. No responsibility for loss or damage occasioned to any person acting, or refraining from action, as a result of the material contained in this publication can be accepted by the editor, the publisher or the author.

First published in 2025 by Sequoia Books

Apart from fair dealing for the purposes of research or private study, or criticism or review, as permitted under the Copyright, Designs and Patents act 1988, this publication may only be reproduced, stored or transmitted, in any form or by any means, with the prior permission in writing of the publisher, or in the case of reprographic reproduction in accordance with the terms and licenses issued by the CLA. Enquiries concerning reproduction outside these terms should be sent to the publisher using the details on the website www.sequoia-books.com

©Josephine Perry 2025

The right of Josephine Perry to be identified as author of this work has been asserted in accordance with the Copyright, Designs and Patents act 1988.

ISBN
Print: 9781914110481
EPUB: 9781914110498

A CIP record for this book is available from the British Library

Library of Congress Cataloguing-In-Publication Data

Name: Josephine Perry
Title: ADHD In Sport/Perry
Description: 1st Edition, Sequoia Books UK 2025
Print: 9781914110481
EPUB: 9781914110-498

Print and Electronic production managed by Deanta Global

Dedication: *To Paul and Henry*

Contents

Introduction		1
	Are athletes more likely to have ADHD?	5
	Impact of ADHD in sport	6
	How to use this book	8
1	Understanding the sporting brain	11
	Key brain functions for high performance	12
	Habit function	12
	Logical decision function	13
	Survival function	14
	Threat responses	17
	Physical impact of the threat response	19
	Cognitive impact of the threat response	20
	Threat system sensitivity	21
	Why the logical decision-making function and threat system are so influenced by ADHD	22
	Hannah's story	24
2	The impact of sport on your ADHD	28
	Cognitive benefits	29
	Benefits for behaviour	32
	Motor skill development	32
	Emotional and social benefits	33
	Brooke's story	36
3	How ADHD influences sporting performance	40
	Executive dysfunction	40
	Self-regulation difficulties	41
	Emotional deregulation	42
	Benefits of ADHD on athletes	43

	The A-Z of the individual issues where your ADHD might impact your sporting performance…	44
	Tom's story	62
4	**Wellbeing strategies**	65
	Nutrition	65
	Hydration	74
	Sleep	75
	Stress management	79
	Rachel's story	87
5	**Training strategies**	90
	Coins	90
	Earn Dopamine	92
	Daily scaffolding	93
	Goal setting	96
	Chunking down	97
	Creating a communication passport	98
	Prioritizing preparation	99
	Building habits and routines	100
	Become an expert in you	101
	Body doubling	103
	Behavioural skills training	104
	Reducing procrastination	105
	James' story	106
6	**Competition strategies for ADHD athletes**	109
	Control mapping	109
	Strengths audit	111
	Surround yourself with the right people	112
	Pot of Power	113
	Know your triggers	116
	Dealing with waiting mode	117
	Task-focused goal setting	119
	If…then planning	119
	Panoramic perspective	121
	Senses ladder	121
	Colourful breathing	121

	Alien breathing	122
	Give visual reminders	122
	Fuel up	123
	Coach on a shoulder	123
	Reframing	124
	STOP approach	125
	Analysis	126
	Curious questions	127
	Jen's story	129
7	Common ADHD co-occurring conditions	133
	Autism Spectrum Disorder (ASD)	134
	Dyspraxia/Developmental Co-ordination Disorder	135
	Dyslexia	136
	Alexithymia	136
	Hypermobility	137
	Behavioural disorders	138
	Anxiety-based disorders	139
	Depression	140
	Bipolar	141
	Rejection Sensitive Dysphoria (RSD)	142
	Seasonal Affective Disorder (SAD)	143
	Burnout	144
	Eating Disorders and obesity	145
	Accidents, injuries and illness	145
	Physical co-occurring conditions in ADHD	146
	Olivia's story	147
8	Medication	150
	How stimulant medications work…	150
	Benefits of medication for general functioning	152
	Benefits of medication for athletes	152
	Risks of stimulant medication in daily life	153
	Specific side effects to be aware of as an athlete or a coach…	154
	Mitigating the risks	156
	The ethics of medication in sport	157
	WADA Guideline summary	159
	Isla's story	161

9	**Coaching an athlete with ADHD**	165
	Disorganization	167
	Emotional dysregulation	168
	Forgetfulness	170
	Hyperactivity	171
	Hyperfocus	171
	Impulsivity	172
	Inattention	173
	Lack of perseverance	174
	Low self-esteem	174
	Motor skill development delays	175
	Processing difficulties	176
	Procrastination	177
	Rejecting routine and structure	177
	Sensation seeking	178
	Unhelpful training behaviours	178
	Jess' story	181
10	**Supporting an athlete with ADHD**	185
	Supporting children	189
	Supporting a teenager	191
	Supporting an adult	194
	Louise's story	200

Final reflections	205
Glossary	207
Acknowledgements	218

Introduction

Three athletes at the Paris 2024 Olympics stood on podiums having bounced back from difficult and public setbacks: Gymnast Simone Biles, Sprinter Noah Lyles and Swimmer Adam Peaty. They are all multi-medal-winning athletes. They all inspire us. They all entertain us. They have also all talked about having Attention Deficit Hyperactivity Disorder (ADHD).

Biles, Lyles and Peaty are not alone. Other athletes you'll have watched over the years such as Michael Jordan (Basketball), Michael Phelps (Swimming), Greg le Mond (Cycling), James Guy (Swimming), Shaquille O'Neal (Basketball), Louis Smith (Gymnastics), Nicola Adams (Boxing) and Charlie Hull (Golf) have all talked about their ADHD diagnoses, too. Perhaps this is because, alongside hard work, dedication, confidence and investment, traits from ADHD can sometimes be helpful in sport making sport an excellent way for neurodiverse athletes to feel good and thrive. They can channel excess energy to emotionally regulate, use their creativity to see opportunities where others wouldn't and use their hyperfocus to get exceptionally good at new skills. In a neurotypical world, when you don't usually feel you fit in, are constantly told you are not living up to your academic or intellectual potential or reprimanded that 'if you could only focus you might actually learn something', life can feel hard – and sport can feel like your safe place.

It won't have been easy. Over time, these amazing athletes will have had to figure out how to work with their brain, when often it might have felt like it was working against them and do so within a sporting world that isn't designed with their brain in mind.

As a Sport Psychologist specializing in helping athletes perform under pressure, I have worked with many athletes with diagnosed or suspected ADHD. I have not yet found a sport-specific book to direct them towards – so this has been written with them in mind. This is the book that I hope any ADHD athlete will be able to read and find some solace within. If you have ADHD, then this strengths-based toolkit is designed to help you deepen your understanding of yourself and your symptoms so you can use more of your strengths and pick the right strategies to thrive. I hope it feels accessible for both teenage and adult athletes and their coaches and supporters. It includes athlete stories so you can see if their experiences resonate with yours and, if they do, I hope you might consider some of the tools and techniques they find worked for them.

You might have already received an ADHD diagnosis, you might be on a waiting list for an assessment or you might have noticed specific traits that suggest you would be likely to receive a diagnosis if you reached out for one. This book is not designed to label you or scare you or patronize you with knowledge you have probably read many times before. What I hope the book will do is give you a greater understanding of how your ADHD brain works in competitive environments and some strategies and tools to manage your traits effectively so that you thrive within your sport.

First, let's look at ADHD in the context of sport. ADHD is considered to be present when someone has persistent patterns of inattention, hyperactivity or impulsivity (or a combination) which causes significant dysfunction and challenges in their lives. ADHD has previously been characterized by attention deficit, but increasingly evidence suggests that there may also be a reward and motivation deficit, too, so maybe it would be better to consider ADHD as a condition that causes some deficits in some cognitive functions. Cognitive functions, the ways we monitor and regulate our goal-directed behaviours, can impact our behaviours, emotions, performance, relationships and motivation, allowing us to work things out to rationalize, find solutions, contextualize, problem solve, learn and feel safe – all of which are essential in sport.

The symptoms that tend to show up if you have ADHD might be:

- Inattention – difficulties in focusing and getting distracted easily. You might struggle to listen to a coach giving instructions.
- Impulsivity in behaviour and emotions – quick to anger, easily excitable, get frustrated and find it hard to self-soothe. In sport, you might lose your temper with a coach or referee.
- Slow information processing speed – you may take longer than others to take in information, interpret the meaning of that information and respond to it. This means you might be slower to start a drill or respond to a mid-training or competition instruction.
- Risk taking – doing activities that have the potential to be dangerous or harmful and not considering the consequences. You might ignore some of the rules in place.
- Difficulties in switching tasks – any transitions feel hard as the brain pushes back against switching from one activity to another.

- Impaired response inhibition – unable to hold back from doing inappropriate actions or saying inappropriate things, even when doing so might harm your goals or plans. This might see you tell a referee or umpire what you really think of their decision making!
- Hyperactivity – unusually or abnormally active. Unable to sit or stand still. A coach may see you constantly fiddling, moving about or dancing when they think you need to be still to listen.
- Poor working memory – unable to hold information for short periods of time so forget what you are supposed to be focusing on. This might mean you switch off and don't keep on practising what you have been asked.
- Planning difficulties – struggling to anticipate and consider the future and see time in a binary way (so there is only now or 'the future') making organization poor and showing up late to practise or meetings.
- Lack of cognitive flexibility – difficulty adapting and changing behaviour to match the situation or environment you are in. You might carry on with a competitive approach when everyone else has switched to being friendly.
- Deficits in motor abilities – delayed motor coordination, sluggish gross motor movements and poor graphomotor (writing) ability.
- A love of novelty – in sport, this might look like you constantly looking for the 'next big thing' and trying new exciting sounding treatments or equipment that you hope could make all the difference.

The most common form of ADHD is known as the 'Combined' type. If you are given this diagnosis, you are most likely to have problems with sustaining attention; maintaining persistence; resisting distractions; feeling hyperactive; acting impulsively; struggling to find the right actions, words, thoughts and emotions that are appropriate for the situation; and finding it hard to stay on target towards longer-term goals and wellbeing plans.

If you get diagnosed with the predominantly 'Inattentive' type, then you will exhibit the symptoms of inattention: having difficulty in focusing, getting easily distracted, forgetting lots of things and being disorganized. This type is often known as ADD – dropping the H as there is no hyperactivity showing up.

The 'Hyperactive-Impulsive' diagnosis will be given to those who need constant movement. If you receive this type of diagnosis, it is likely to be because you constantly fidget and wriggle around, struggle to stay seated or still and you move about excessively. It may seem like you talk non-stop, interrupt lots, blurt out answers and struggle with self-control.

You are likely to already know about the diagnostic journey for ADHD. It requires a clinical diagnosis that includes a medical evaluation with information obtained from the patient (child or adult), parents and other family members or partners, teachers and work colleagues. A difficulty for adults is that for diagnosis, several symptoms must be present before the age of 12 and it can be hard to find the evidence required to support that if you no longer have parents alive or copies of school reports. For diagnosis, your ADHD traits must be present in more than one setting (usually home, school or work) but if you have managed to choose a work or sporting environment that is flexible or even suits your ADHD traits, then it may not show up so strongly there. What you may not know yet, and is worth keeping in mind, is that in some sports, the requirements to be allowed to use ADHD stimulant medications are higher than they would be for regular diagnosis and may need more information provided.

Over the last 20 years, there has been a big rise in awareness of the condition. This rising awareness is one of the reasons that diagnosis levels have increased significantly and now ADHD is considered to be one of the most common neurodevelopmental conditions of childhood. Estimates of the prevalence of ADHD for children and adults worldwide vary widely due to different types of diagnostic criteria, educational expectations, awareness, opportunities for diagnosis, waiting list times and availability/acceptability of medication. While a 2015 study suggests 11% of children in the United States have ADHD, in general, the figure is usually thought to be around 5–8% of under 18s.

More boys than girls are currently diagnosed but this is thought to be because they will often present differently and that teachers (who generally trigger the assessment process) will be looking for it in boys (who more often externalize their behaviours) and not girls (who more often internalize theirs). The stereotype of an ADHD child (as a highly excitable, distracted boy) overlooks the specific characteristics that so often show up for women and girls such as anxiety and masking. As we will see in Louise's story, many girls with ADHD are able to function well until they hit puberty where the hormonal changes and the additional organizational requirements of school cause them psychological collapse. This suggests then that actual prevalence levels in children may be much higher.

Between 65% and 85% of those diagnosed as children will still meet the diagnostic criteria when they become teens but some of the traits change, in particular, hyperactivity, may become less visible. As these teens become adults, the diagnosis would still fit but again externally noticeable elements might change as some learn coping mechanisms and tools to handle the factors that are hindering their abilities to function well. A meta-analysis (a study which pulls together and examines lots of earlier studies) of ADHD studies which followed those diagnosed into adulthood found that 15% of all cases persist fully but up to 75% of those diagnosed will still continue to have significant ADHD-related impairments as an adult. As a result, the stats would suggest that at least 4–6% of the adult population will have ADHD. Although the contextual elements suggest that the numbers are likely to be higher, it could be that their ADHD was missed as a child when awareness levels were far lower or if they had learnt to mask well, had good scaffolding from parents or teachers or they internalized their struggles.

ARE ATHLETES MORE LIKELY TO HAVE ADHD?

Studies suggest the elite athlete population may present with ADHD at greater rates than that seen in the general population and, as a result, it is thought in the United States that at least 10% of athletes have ADHD. To start to understand this, we can investigate the numbers of athletes who are using Therapeutic Use Exemptions (TUE) for ADHD medication. A study at a US university in 2010 found 7.1% of their elite athletes had a relevant TUE. In the 2018 season, the USA Major League Baseball (MLB) reported that 8.4% were granted a TUE. Considering only around 60% of those with ADHD take medication (some don't like how it feels and others have medical issues which would be exacerbated by a stimulant) and the clinical standards required to get a TUE within the MLB are much higher than the standards required in the community to get a diagnosis, the actual rates in athletes would then be expected to be much higher.

Why would rates be higher in athletes? We will investigate this in chapter 3 but one theory is that those with the hyperactive or combined type are pushed towards physical activity and sports by parents/carers keen to use up their energy. Another is that those with ADHD are drawn to activity to gain positive reinforcement through chasing the Dopamine buzz that comes from doing something well and feeling a sense of achievement, as a way to self-medicate. Others suggest that when someone with ADHD uses their hyperfocus towards their sport they can become very good at it very quickly and so will commit to it for far longer and with more dedication than others might.

IMPACT OF ADHD IN SPORT

Models for understanding the development of sport performance tend to focus on five factors: physiology, biomechanics, psychology, tactics and overall wellbeing. ADHD can impact most of these: biomechanics (those with ADHD reportedly have more accidents due to distraction and motor function issues), tactics (especially when impulsivity is involved), wellbeing (particularly around emotions and relationships) and psychology (behaviours and motivation) which when not managed well can diminish potential performance.

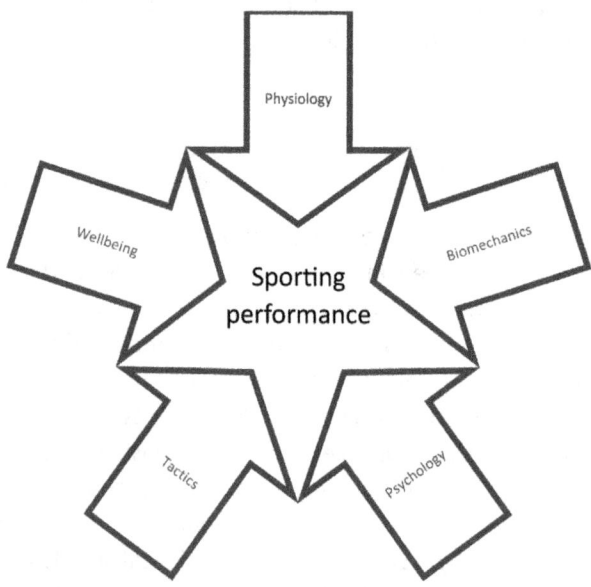

Two specific areas worth considering here are wellbeing and psychology – in particular, relationships and behaviours.

Relationships (whether it is a coach-athlete, family or peer-to-peer), when an athlete has ADHD, can be fractious at times. Relationships will be specifically tackled in chapters 9 and 10 because studies have found that the inattentive, hyperactive and impulsive behaviours within ADHD can socially disadvantage children and adults as intrusive interpersonal styles break unwritten codes of social life if they disturb others, interrupt conversations or blurt out inappropriate comments. This can mean difficulties with friendships as a child and higher divorce rates as an adult. One element of this is that those with ADHD have a higher likelihood of Rejection Sensitive Dysphoria (RSD) where neutral comments or actions are interpreted as critical or attacking and can feel physically painful. A coach who is trying to feed back a critique of a sporting performance is going to struggle to have a valuable conversation about this.

On top of that, the symptoms of ADHD might show up in some behaviours that feel hard to handle when you have a large group of people to manage. Hyperactivity, impulsivity and risk-taking may make it difficult to sit still or follow rules that are designed for safety or order. Risky behaviour might increase Dopamine levels to soothe an athlete's brain after a day in school or work fighting to focus but will cause friction with others. The athlete might also have low tolerance for frustration so instead of being able to sit with discomfort or unpredictability they will have a temper out-burst or mentally beat themselves up. In children, these elements might mean constantly fidgeting in coaching sessions, disrupting others trying to focus, shouting at a team-mate or running off the sports pitch without reason. Adults may interrupt team meetings, seem unable to plan or complete projects, ignore team rules (like not partying ahead of matches or talking to the media) and driving recklessly, putting their own health and club reputation at risk. They might seem like they are not thinking about the consequences of their actions (which is true – they are not because they cannot) and this can cause frustration from coaches and peers.

Practice sessions require an athlete to concentrate on a coach's instructions. Without this, it becomes significantly harder to learn skills or deliver the required moves. When you add in the potential to show up late (time management is covered in chapter 3) or not well organized (again chapter 3) and you also have a lack of concentration, poor attention to detail, slower processing speed, forgetfulness, a brain going off on tangents and emotional dysregulation, then performance is far harder to do well. We will look at some behavioural tactics in chapters 4–6 to help handle some of these issues.

The behavioural and relationship aspects and their impact on performance ultimately harm an athlete's confidence. Studies suggest adults with ADHD may not rise to the level within their occupation that their intelligence might suggest they should, have fewer years of schooling, are more likely to be unemployed, earn less and have lower productivity. The impact of these means that the person with ADHD can get labelled as lazy or disinterested which doesn't just reduce opportunities for them but also exacerbates the likelihood of a mental health problem like anxiety or depression as self-esteem falls and relationships fade. These can lead the athlete to feel shame and powerlessness – often causing a huge amount of stress.

Stress is essential for athletes to have a handle on as it has such a strong response on our psychology and physiology (as we will see in chapter 1). As a psychologist working in high performance, I often support performers who are suffering fromstress and burnout. When we look at the list of symptoms that indicate chronic stress, we see a strong replication of all of the same issues expressed daily by athletes with ADHD:

- Procrastination
- Degraded concentration levels
- Feelings of anxiety around work or relationships
- Difficulties in decision making
- Constant feelings of fatigue and exhaustion
- Physical stress symptoms; poor gut health, weight gain, skill disorders and increased sickness
- Trouble switching off at home and feeling unable to be present with loved ones.

These elements suggest then that living with unmanaged ADHD can feel incredibly stressful and mirror burnout. Stress management solutions are then essential. There are a number of approaches that can be used: psychotherapy, psychoeducation, neurofeedback, counselling, behavioural management, family support and exercise. In this book, we will focus on psychoeducation (chapters 1, 3, 7 and 8), behavioural management (chapters 4–6), external support (chapters 9 and 10) and exercise (chapter 2).

HOW TO USE THIS BOOK

In chapter 1, we learn about the brain in sport and how it behaves when you are trying to perform at a high level. We focus on the threat system within the brain, and how, when we mix ADHD with the unpredictability of sport, this can become highly combustible and ready to trigger for a wide range of reasons. Understanding your threat system and what triggers it can help you plan for better training and competition strategies and ensure that you are better able to look after your own wellbeing.

Louise, the parent who shares her story in our book, tells us how she felt her daughter's sporty childhood acted as self-medication for her later discovered ADHD. Athletes often mention this too; so, in chapter 2, we consider the benefits of sport and exercise for ADHD.

Chapter 3 looks more in detail at the specific traits and issues that might show up with ADHD and how they can impact sport. Some of these, such as hyperfocus, reactive decision making and creativity, might help sporting performance, others might hinder it. In understanding these though we can work on strategies and tactics to better handle them within life, training and competition.

In sport, we tend to consider the athlete in three phases and so the tactical section of this book is split the same way: as a person with wellbeing requirements (chapter 4) in training; needing to practise and develop skills, strengths and fitness (chapter 5) and in competition; and needing to perform under pressure (chapter 6).

Chapter 7 will look at the co-occurring conditions that can be common alongside ADHD. This is important because some of these will impact the sporting journey too. Hypermobility can seem beneficial in some sports but can also bring physical and psychological risks. Anxiety and depression can be more common in those with ADHD due to the additional mental energy requirements of trying to fit into a neurotypical environment. Athletes with Rrejection Sensitivity can struggle with losing, competitors being unkind or feedback being given. Knowing your co-occurring conditions can help you better protect yourself – both from injury and psychological sporting threats.

In chapter 8, we learn about ADHD medications. As we will see in the stories, some athletes really value their medication and feel it makes their sporting ambitions more sustainable, some have conditions which mean they are unable to take them and others have tried it but found it hinders their sporting abilities. This chapter highlights all the pros and cons so you can consider how or if you use them.

For those working or living with athletes with ADHD, there are two chapters: one specifically for coaches (chapter 9) and one for those supporting the athlete (chapter 10) like a parent, carer or partner. Here, we will show how to help scaffold around some of the areas of cognitive deficit to support an ADHD athlete to function optimally.

Between every chapter, we have someone to learn from. We have the stories of Jen, Tom, Hannah, Brooke, James, Isla, Olivia and Rachel. We also hear from Louise (a parent) and Jess (a coach) on their experiences of supporting athletes with ADHD.

To make it more accessible and shorter (always a bonus), there are no references as we go along but if you head to my website (www.performanceinmind.co.uk/books), you will find direct links to all the studies and statistics cited within these pages.

The athletes whose stories are included have all spent time trying to understand their brains and how they work best when playing their sport. My hope for this book is that if you have ADHD, or spend time with athletes who do, it will help you understand the ADHD brain and amplify all the benefits that exercise and high-performance working can bring so you can manage the difficulties while using your strengths to maximize success in your sport.

CHAPTER 1

Understanding the sporting brain

Imagine you are a 17-year-old Hockey player. You have worked hard all year, turned up to every training session, been at the gym religiously for your strength and conditioning work, done all your fitness whatever the weather and kept your school work up to standard, getting great predicted grades. Your reward is a place on the GB Under-18s team. This is your dream come true. You head off to your first training weekend with the team hoping to wow the coaches. On the way, your club hockey WhatsApp group constantly pings with messages showing how proud and excited everyone is for you. Once the warm-up is done, you finally get to play a match. And then everything goes wrong. You are playing like a novice. None of your shots are going where you intend. Your legs are heavy and slow. You don't respond fast enough and you feel sick the whole time. You feel like a total fraud. What on earth is going on?

It feels like your brain is out to sabotage you, destroying everything you have worked for. You have now branded yourself a failure and cannot stop ruminating about how poor your performance is. You are embarrassed and certain that everyone will be judging you. You want to explain to the coaches how hard you have worked and how much you want this but you fear gabbling and saying something stupid so you skulk away to hide, hoping no one notices you.

This situation replicates itself in thousands of situations to thousands of us every single day: driving tests, work presentations, school speeches, stage work, sporting events, sales meetings or even Monday morning team catch-ups. Any time we are in a situation that matters to us and we could be judged or fail, we can feel a huge amount of anxiety.

Clients I see in my clinic who come in following this sort of situation have occasionally asked if their brain is broken. No, I always reassure. Definitely not broken. In fact, that super complex 1.4 kg lump of 86 billion neurons inside your head is doing exactly the right thing; working incredibly hard to make continuous connections, reconnections and even regenerate. The problem is that brains are not designed to make us brilliant in sport. They, at their very core, have a much more important role; your survival. And survival and high performance require our brains to do very different things which manifests very obviously when you are under pressure. When you are under pressure and throw ADHD into the mix, it can turn into total overwhelm and burnout.

KEY BRAIN FUNCTIONS FOR HIGH PERFORMANCE

There are three key functions of our brains that come into use when we are aiming to perform at a high level. Two of those functions are incredibly helpful; habit and logical decisions. The other function (survival) is more variable; it can be very helpful when we are at risk of physical threat, but very unhelpful when it is psychological threat that is taunting us. When you understand how each function works and what prevents them working effectively, you can adapt your attitude and your environment to develop far more helpful behaviours to limit underperformance.

HABIT FUNCTION

Since research from Donald Hebb in the 1940s discovered that when 'neurons fire together they wire together', we have been able to see how the brain can make stronger connections. We call this neuroplasticity; neurons that respond to the same stimulus connect to form neuronal ensembles so that eventually, just activating a few select neurons can trigger the whole ensemble, making memory recall far faster and less energy intensive. This makes our brain far more efficient and effective.

This is handy because, on average, we each make around 35,000 micro decisions a day and if we had to actively think about each of them then we'd never get anything significant done. Having to repeatedly figure things out time and time again, or doing lots of new things uses up lots of energy so we would become fatigued.

Imagine the fatigue a runner would suffer from if they had to consciously, constantly think about HOW to run. Their brain would be full of where do my arms go and how high do I lift my leg? They would tire incredibly quickly. Or consider an accountant who had to use a calculator for every simple sum, it would quadruple the amount of time each calculation took and use up both calculator battery and physical energy; both highly inefficient. The runner and the accountant, once they have learnt the basics of their trade, develop these into habits so that they can fly through basic calculations or around the track. Their habit function does the basics for them, saving time, energy and stress.

We can think of our habit function like a storage unit; holding all our values, skills, strengths and techniques, working away in the background using all the stored information to make automatic decisions based on pre-programmed thoughts and behaviours that you have developed over years of practice. Once you know about your habit function you can use it to help you perform well; practising new skills or techniques not until you get them right but until you find it difficult to get them wrong. This is particularly important with ADHD as your brain knows WHAT to do, just doesn't always DO it. Once something is habitual the process of one part of your brain telling the other part what to do becomes redundant and your body just acts automatically. Additionally, having your habits work away in the background, making thousands of unconscious decisions for you means you have more headspace left over for the decisions and actions which do require more strategy or tactical knowledge.

LOGICAL DECISION FUNCTION

When something is too complex, happens too irregularly to become a habit, or if you are still learning a skill or routine, then your logical decision function comes into play. It is made up of the networks in your brain that help you make great choices, specifically those based in the pre-frontal cortex (involved in decision making, executive functioning, behaviours and planning – but also the area where ADHD creates deficits – you'll find more on these in chapter 3) and hippocampus (where all your knowledge, learning and experiences are stored). When a choice needs to be made your brain searches through the knowledge and evidence you have on offer with the aim of figuring out the best option to take and tells your body how to do it.

For example, surgeons often have to make very quick decisions that will change someone's length or quality of life. They need their executive function to be working brilliantly, their hippocampus to be full of the most relevant, up-to-date knowledge (which is why medical training processes are so intense and so long) and to be able to filter through all the information quickly to make the best possible decision for their patient. An eye surgeon doing something like cataract surgery (which is bread and butter work for them) will pretty much be working through the habit function. In more unusual surgery, something they may only do every few months, there will be far more decisions to make that would fall outside their usual habitual actions and the surgeon would need to make best guess decisions based on years of experience and lots of knowledge about what will give someone the best quality of life.

With the habit and logical decision functions working well you should be able to get focused and perform brilliantly. You should be able to practise until key skills become habits and use all your additional energy on the efforts that need logical decision making. You would then expect your results to match up to the level of preparation you have invested and your overall potential. However (and isn't there always a however) as our brains are not really designed for high performance, and are instead designed to keep us alive, there is another function to consider; the survival function. This is what causes overthinking, underperforming and, when you have ADHD, may see you over-react in an attempt to keep you psychologically safe.

SURVIVAL FUNCTION

As your brain is designed to ensure your survival it has developed four incredible ways to do so; helping you predict possible outcomes, body budgeting so you run efficiently, prioritizing negative memories and activating a threat system in emergencies. All these together aim to keep you as comfortable as possible and ensure your survival. When they combine they push you towards staying in your comfort zone (for safety) and so you don't get to stretch yourself or try new things and this limits your ability to perform at a high level.

Prediction

One way for your brain to keep you safe is to be able to figure out all the possible outcomes of a specific situation in advance and decide the least risky thing for you to do. It does this through prediction. It is officially known as 'allostasis' where we automatically predict our needs before they arise; saving headspace and speeding up reaction times.

Your brain is making constant predictions based on external elements (like the sensations you notice) and internal elements (like things you have learnt or previous experiences) and amalgamates them into a best-guess prediction. That becomes your sensory experience – most of the time it is right – but not always – and from that experience your brain tells your body how to act, and itself how to feel.

The element of prediction doesn't just help us feel safe; it also helps us feel good and rewarded. Being able to figure out the answers before the actual thing has happened makes you feel great. When we spot a pattern and see some kind of puzzle come together we get a Dopamine buzz. Dopamine plays a big role in your brain's reward system where it helps you to feel pleasure or joy when you achieve something giving you heightened arousal and ability to learn. As you will see throughout this book, Dopamine is also thought to be significant in the craving associated with ADHD and is a neurochemical you will come to think about more so you can use it to handle your ADHD effectively.

Body budgeting

The second survival function that your brain relies upon is budgeting. Your brain is constantly trying to figure out what resources you do and don't need to use. As an athlete your brain needs to balance out your daily physical energy needs so that it can use energy for the essential elements but conserves resources when they are not needed. Every action you take will be one that your brain will have assessed is a worthwhile action. It sounds fairly simple but it can be an incredibly difficult balancing act and when you get it wrong and use too much energy receiving too little back in return or don't build in enough time for rest and recovery you end up with burnout, long-term injury, illness or chronic fatigue. This is a big risk when you have the hyperactive element of ADHD and you do too much or the hyperfocus element and work too intensely on a sporting problem and put your body budget out of whack.

Unlike an accountant using a few pages on Excel, the spreadsheet our brain would use would be vast. We pay in a deposit to our body budget in the form of food, drink, sleep, friendships and nurturing. We withdraw from it each time we exercise, we focus, we care for others, we argue or we work too hard. This giant mental spreadsheet needs to balance out the use these deposits and withdrawals. The withdrawals will be significant involving our muscles (over 650 of them), all our neurotransmitters (over 100 types of these) and our hormones (best guess is that there are between 50 and 70 types of these). The brain is also directing your heart to beat around 100,000 times a day (pumping around 8 pints of blood through 60,000 miles of blood vessels), to digest and excrete food and liquid and to constantly fight off any illnesses, bugs or viruses that come within reach. When we are adding in high-performance activities the brain needs to figure out how to do that without too much of a deficit on any of these other essential things. It is a tough job!

It means that sometimes our body might behave in a way we find holds us back from what we believe we want, but it is doing so for a very good reason. If our body balance is depleted, it is going to crave more sleep so will talk you out of getting up early for the gym. If you have been really focused on a project for hours it will crave Dopamine and movement before it will allow you to move on to another intense task. It means we need to be incredibly motivated to act when we are trying to do tasks that take resources away from the essentials. But, as you will have read in the introduction, one of the issues with ADHD is that it can give you a motivation deficit.

Negative amplification

A third element of the survival function comes from thousands of years ago when human survival was constantly threatened by physical risks. To handle this our brains developed a negativity bias. It came about because, in order to survive, you need to remember very clearly all the things which can harm you; our caveman cousins needed to know that a big animal with sharp teeth might well eat them so that they should stay away from it. They needed to know the tribe in the next-door village was more likely to steal their food than share so they should hide their supplies. This knowledge is very helpful for physical survival but a negativity bias around psychological elements (friendships, confidence, esteem, belonging) can really hamper our pursuit of happiness or success. Over time this negative bias has developed so that neuroscientists now believe that for every negative thought you have about yourself, you require five positive things to stay in a good place.

Threat system

Finally, the most dramatic (but sometimes helpful) function that our brain has to keep us safe is a tiny, almond-shaped part of our brain buried deep in the cerebrum known as the Amgydala (there are actually two so maybe should be called amygdalae). It is basically your threat function, an alarm system for the body., constantly on alert looking out for things that could physically or psychologically harm you.

This threat response is our base instinct. It needs to be speedy to protect us (in fact it works five times faster than our decision function) and of course, it uses that prediction element so jumps very quickly to conclusions. It needs to be paranoid to ensure we are safe so it can push us into thinking a little (sometimes a lot) irrationally. It means the decisions it makes are based not on evidence but on feelings so can be rather emotional and impulsive.

This threat system is incredibly helpful when there is a physical threat. If you have ever walked home late at night and noticed someone walking too closely behind you then you may feel the hairs on the back of your neck stand up on end and a gut ache telling you to do something to get away; call a friend, cross the road, speed up your walking. This is your amygdala trying to keep you safe. It is a very helpful action following a rational physical threat.

Fortunately, most of us these days don't have much physical threat in our lives. What we might have a lot of though is psychological threat; usually some kind of threat to our identity. We fear doing something that harms our self-image. As our amygdalae are pretty rubbish at distinguishing a physical threat from an identity-driven one, when something looks like it could threaten our sense of self; losing a competition, looking inept, embarrassing ourselves, not being in control, feeling like we are a failure, being judged by others or screwing up something we have worked really hard to achieve, then the threat system triggers. The bigger or more important something is to us, the more likely it is to trigger. When it triggers you can no longer access the logical decision making function in your brain so everything becomes emotional and dramatic. You overthink and performance plummets.

THREAT RESPONSES

When the amygdala's threat system perceives some sort of threat (physical or psychological) it releases two chemicals (adrenaline and cortisol) and sends them off to flood your body; facilitating you to do one of four things; fight, flight, freeze or fawn.

The fight response may seem more common on a Saturday night after pub kick-out time or after a really close football match between local rivals but in day-to-day life most of us turn our fight response into something more socially acceptable; talking. You can spot it easily on the start line of races or in the changing rooms of team sports – the people who find themselves scanning around for others to chat to, hoping to find conversation in their vicinity, have a fight response and are trying to talk out their nerves.

Those with a flight response will be seen far less often because when it comes to situations where they will feel under threat they will not show up. Their body budgeting element will have made the decision that the event or activity confronting them was not worth the fatigue and stress it was causing and so they refuse to engage. They turn down opportunities, put others forward in their place and find all sorts of reasons to justify this to themselves, and others.

The fawn response is one I see in two groups of people; those who have a psychologically or physically unsafe home life or those who have been bullied or abused in school, work or sport. In this situation as soon as someone comes across threat they show a trauma response; they either yield and tip toe (as if on eggshells) around the person causing the threat or they totally shut down and disassociate with the situation. This is people pleasing taken to the extreme to avoid conflict or rejection and in order to appease and gain approval. They are doing whatever it takes to survive.

If someone doesn't get support or therapy this fawn response can last a lifetime. A young gymnast may have spent a number of years in a club with what we used to cowardly call an 'old school coach' and now, more honestly, label 'abusive'. Weekly weigh-ins with the numbers written up on the wall. A refusal to allow anyone to drink or go to the toilet in sessions that last hours. An atmosphere of punishment rather than reward. Their threat system would notice a coach and switch to fawn mode; treading on eggshells, hiding their real personality and tiptoeing around them. Even if a parent pulls their child from that club and finds another with nourishing, positive coaching the fawning continues as their brain has now been wired in a way that expects coaches to be harsh and unforgiving. One missed jump on a vault and they flinch, waiting for a tirade; a threat system on hyperalert.

Finally, we come to the freeze response. I left this response till last because it is the one I see most often in those with ADHD. It comes from the primal idea that if you are in survival mode and have no control over a situation you may as well play dead, hope the threat doesn't see you, and goes away. It leaves you immobile in the face of threat. You feel forced to pause and assess the situation – but do it so much that you can get stuck there. You go quiet, want to find space away from others; you do not want the fight people in your face. You won't take in the encouragement, you just want to get lost inside your head until you are forced to take on that challenge.

Whatever your 'go to' threat response, the more we anticipate potential harm, the earlier your survival systems get activated and the more resources you use up. This creates an unbalanced body budget with both harmful physical and cognitive impacts.

> "Another rider was diagnosed with ADHD last year and he said something in an interview which I could relate very strongly too. He said 'I feel like I'm working so much harder than everybody else but getting less reward.'" Isla, Cyclist

PHYSICAL IMPACT OF THE THREAT RESPONSE

The adrenaline and cortisol that flood the body can have a really strong impact on us physically. 'You can always spot a scared gymnast', says Alex, my gymnastics coach, 'they get smaller and faster. A confident gymnast stretches out, owns their space. They slow down.' He is spot on. In so many sports when I ask athletes what their coach tells them they need to do in order to improve they roll their eyes (from being told so often) and tell me they need to be 'patient'. You will see it yourself when you see someone who is nervous; they speak really fast, as if the quicker they talk the faster they can get out of there. So, while patience isn't usually a word we connect with high-performance sport, it is those who are patient who have time to assess a situation and respond to it. The fearful ones react. Reactions hold us back. It is well-thought-through responses that move us forward.

We don't just get smaller and speedier when nervous though. There are five clear physical signs that your threat system has been triggered:

- A nauseous tummy: causing sickness, diarrhoea or battling butterflies.
- Increased breathing rate: Rises from around 13 breaths a minute up to around 21. This means you only fill the top of your lungs and so develop shallow breathing, reducing the amount of oxygen circulating in your body.
- Higher heart rate. This can harm concentration and limit endurance.
- Tight muscles. This can cause injury or poor movement patterns.
- Loss of senses: This could be your touch, taste, smell, hearing and in particular your peripheral vision.

The big issue is that our threat surveillance system doesn't just scan the external world for potential risks, it also scans internally within our bodies. When our heart and breathing rates are elevated then the amygdalae notices and releases more adrenaline and cortisol to flood the body. It becomes a very unhelpful feedback loop.

Each of us tends to have a different mix of these anxiety signs. How many of these signs do you recognize in yourself? Once you know your main responses they can act like an early warning system – helping you to handle your anxiety before it gets too enmeshed in the feedback loop. It is important though to realize that different activities are impacted differently by these physiological responses.

Let's consider an Olympic archer. They may be ok with a nauseous stomach but will be really badly impacted by the increased heart rate when what they ideally need is a slow, steady rhythm. This is backed by a study in the American Economic Review looking at the heart rates of 122 of the 128 archers in the Tokyo Olympics found that those with higher heart rates performed worse. The stage of the competition also had an impact – as the rounds went on, and got closer to the possibility of winning a medal, the relationship was even stronger. The more they wanted success, and the closer they got to it, the harder their own body and brain made it for them.

Or we could consider the gymnast Simone Biles. In the 2021 Tokyo Olympics, she pulled out of the Beam competition citing The Twisties; a movement disorder that comes from anxiety. When your muscles get super tight and tense and you are unable to feel where you are in the air (the proprioception sense) as you do an extremely complicated risky move then you are struggling with not just the psychological threat of not winning but a physical threat of breaking your neck. Competing with this level of anxiety would be incredibly dangerous for her and so it was clear why she needed to withdraw.

COGNITIVE IMPACT OF THE THREAT RESPONSE

There isn't just a physical impact on our body when our threat system is triggered – there is a cognitive impact too as what the amygdala wants when the threat system has been triggered is persuade you to head back towards comfort. It does not want you to try and do something difficult; like shooting arrows, a back somersault on the beam or to shoot the final penalty. It wants to find some way of getting you safely in your comfort zone and this often involves your head chatter becoming very negative; lots of catastrophic thinking, rumination and far too much attention based on embarrassment or fear so you develop lots of excuses, procrastinate, lower your ambitions, finish it as quickly as possible or completely stop trying.

In addition, with all this going on it becomes much harder to focus on what will help you to do well in your upcoming performance so your preparation is poorer. In fact, recent research in the Journal *Psychological Science* found that having anxiety about taking a test doesn't just make it harder to do well in the exam but also makes it harder to absorb the information we need for it. The researchers studied 309 German medical students using a digital learning platform to prepare for their finals and found that students with the highest levels test anxiety went into the final exam with less knowledge. This suggests that the that cognitive test anxiety doesn't simply impair performance during an exam, but actually makes it harder to even acquire the knowledge you need in the first place. If you are constantly living with that anxiety when training for your sport then you take in far less information and imbed fewer of the skills you need. And then with ADHD you have the cognitive difficulties too which makes it harder to focus and retain the information that you do learn.

THREAT SYSTEM SENSITIVITY

Our amygdala's sensitivity to threats will be impacted by a huge number of things; things we are born with like personality traits (such perfectionism or sensitivity) can ramp it up, as can high intelligence (as your brain becomes very good at predicting the worst) or lots of external pressures that can come when you have done well in the past. Alongside this will be previous experiences (like having been bullied or publicly criticized) or possible future experiences (knowing that people around you are very judgemental). ADHD will not only amplify many of these elements but if you are neurodiverse living in a neurotypical culture everything will feel a little more threatening.

One thing I see regularly impacting high performers is a mono-identity; having one thing in your life that is much more important than everything else. The stronger that mono-identity is then the more threatened their brain feels when they attempt to do that thing. Someone who feels like they are 20% father/husband/son and 80% footballer will find every match threatening. Someone who is totally dedicated to their Rugby will see every match as a threat to their identity, even if it is supposed to just be their hobby. With ADHD you may have spent lots of time being told to work hard, focus more or stay still, making sport, the one area you can thrive, as your safety zone. While this is great it can make it become overly important to you and this can create a mono-identity.

When you attempt to do something important to you within that identity area (lets imagine a newly qualified coach taking on their first session with athletes) then their need to be successful in it will feel fraught and take on extra significance. If our coach has wanted to work in their sport since primary school and everyone knows this was their future vocation then if they fail at it they have not just failed in their first choice of career but they will feel they have failed as a human. The mono-identity might not just relate to a career or sport but it can also relate to a personality trait. If someone has an identity of someone who is 'resilient' or does everything 'perfectly' then whenever they are in a position for this to be tested it can be really anxiety-inducing and their threat system becomes very sensitive to it.

WHY THE LOGICAL DECISION-MAKING FUNCTION AND THREAT SYSTEM ARE SO INFLUENCED BY ADHD

As ADHD is highly heritable (estimated to be over 70% genetic) we know there will be some strong neurobiological causes of it. This doesn't mean that there may not be environmental aspects too but while we don't necessarily need to know the causes at a detailed, neurological level, some understanding can be helpful in terms of figuring our approaches to use and comprehension of why an athlete with ADHD might struggle in certain areas when it comes to making the right decisions at the right time and handling the threat that can come from being in a sporting environment.

The most common perspective is that ADHD comes from a dysfunction in the Catecholamine System. This system involves three key neurotransmitters (Norepinephrine, Epinephrine and Dopamine) that scientists believe are involved in ADHD. This theory is supported by the fact that the stimulants used successfully to help many of those with ADHD are medications which act as agonists; activating the Catecholamine receptors in the brain to allow more of that type of Catecholamine to be released.

One specifical neurotransmitter you will read about in this book is Dopamine. The Dopaminergic system is associated with motor control, reward, motivation and affect. It is thought that the Prefrontal Cortex (PFC) and the Dopaminergic systems interact and that this interaction impacts cognitive and behavioural control. Dysregulated Dopamine in the PFC has been shown to play an important role in ADHD. An example of this is that experimental studies have found that when Dopamine receptors in the PFC are obstructed, then deficits in working memory are found. It is also suggested that attentional impairments may be due to overactivity of Dopamine within the PFC.

Another neurotransmitter that seems to play a part in ADHD is Norepinephrine which impacts how you regulate your attention, inhibit your behaviours and effects your working memory, again all of these are modulated through the PFC. Low concentrations of Norepinephrine in the PFC have been associated with impairments in working memory and executive functioning.

And Epinephrine, well that is also known as Adrenaline, which, as you just read, plays a big part in the threat system and keeping us safe, but also excited and driven.

To support these ideas, neuroimaging studies of the brain have found a number of neurobiological abnormalities associated with ADHD, particularly, as we would expect, in the PFC suggesting neurological differences in both its structure and function. This area of the brain is responsible for the performance of a set of higher order cognitive tasks that require response inhibition, planning, working memory, updating and task switching.

A simpler way to think about it though is that ADHD significantly impacts the PFC in the brain, the part of our brain which controls our thoughts, emotions and actions. In those with ADHD, the PFC develops in a way that can create difficulties in controlling emotions and behaviour. This may mean the person with it struggles with emotional dysregulation, behavioural issues, low mood, sleep issues, low impulse control and has to put more effort into developing new skills or knowledge. Most importantly though these elements mean that you will know what to do but often can't do it because the part of the brain that holds the knowledge doesn't talk effectively to the part of the brain that creates action. This means there may well be time blindness (an inability to track the passage of time so you may be late for training or unable to stick to timings), executive function deficits (meaning you have poorly controlled emotions, difficulty solving problems or struggle to plan and organize yourself) and an inability to action what you know is required. This can be incredibly frustrating which can cause anger issues.

So, let's head back to the GB Hockey player we met at the start of this chapter. With our knowledge of the three brain functions we can see that all that the pressure, expectation, investment and importance of it all has triggered his threat system. His decision-making will have become impaired, he's become cognitively frozen and his body has been flooded with cortisol and adrenaline so he can't perform in the way he has practised. He is frustrated so feeling angry. His expertise has left him and he's behaving like a novice. Now he should understand why and beat himself up less. The next step for him is to something about it, which we will tackle in chapters 4–6 in the book.

HANNAH'S STORY

Hannah is a professional Rugby player and PhD student.

'I was always flagged as being neurodivergent; from probably three or four. I was very hyperactive. I got diagnosed with dyslexia when I was doing my GCSEs and then I went to uni and they said we're 99.9% sure that you've also got ADHD.'

'My mum would say I was a bull in a china shop; so hyperactive, always wanting to be busy doing stuff. I couldn't sit down and do something for more than ten minutes. I was always wanting to do something new and different. I was a very sporty kid, probably because I had loads of energy. I very much had slow processing but then in other areas I'd shock people and come top of the class, and then something else, I'd come bottom of the class.'

'In primary school, I was a pretty good kid. I was chatty, very chatty. It was the same in senior school when the school weren't interested in me because I wasn't going to get As or A*s. Then in year 11, I realized my teachers genuinely thought I'm not going to get back into the school for sixth form and then I was like "oh, I'll work my butt off." So, I worked my butt off doing that, and then the behaviour kind of settled down. I became very studious, and ten years down the line, I'm doing my PhD.'

'I did athletics from the age of four. It was a sport that my mum could get me to do where I came home and I was tired and didn't necessarily require a lot of attention. So that was pretty much athletics from the get-go. I went on to compete at like a national level in the Heptathlon and then moved into the hammer throw from 14 up to 19.'

'There were so many coaches that I had as a multi-eventer that were shocking and didn't give two hoots about whether you understood it or didn't process it, or you were just slow or didn't pick up on the instructions. When I was training for the other events, I'd be high jumping with 10 other people and I'd piss about all the time as I didn't understand, so thought "I'll just have a giggle or have a chit-chat."'

'My Hammer coach, Ted, though was an absolute legend. When I started working with him I think he was 79 - we had such an interesting relationship as you would do as a 17/18-year-old and a 79/80-year-old. In Hammer you work in a one-to-one scenario which suited me a lot better and Ted was so personable. Obviously, we would have bickers where I was like I don't get what you're saying and he would talk whilst I was doing, and I'd be like "you can't do that." For example, I'm swinging a hammer round, he'll say "think about your low point," or "needs to be more 45/45" and I'd then stop and be like, "what do you want? You need to chill and figure out when you're going to give me information, because I can't take information when I'm doing." I think that was pretty much the only challenge I had with him.'

'Ted very much learnt straight away that I was a visual learner. He always used to carry round chalk, so if for example, he'd spend five minutes telling me what to do and I don't understand what he's saying, so he'd draw it on the floor. He would draw a lot. Then when he would be like "45/45," I could look at the floor, and could tell what he meant by 45 and I knew exactly what to do.'

'I came to uni and started rugby at 20. And I'm still there at 25. Now, with rugby, especially at the level that I'm at, you can't hide. If I don't understand something and there's lots of people, I take myself to the edge of the game scenario where I can watch and observe and figure that out. And then, when I feel comfortable, I'll go get myself more involved. In larger groups the information feels a lot harder to process, especially if it's all verbal. Verbal I find really hard. I'm very much a doer.'

'When I started I had a coach called Abbie and she was phenomenal at being able to coach it one way, coach it another, coach it another. She knew she had quite a few athletes who were neurodiverse. You don't necessarily require specific information all the time but she was very good at noticing when I didn't know what I was doing.'

'Last year I moved into playing at a Premiership club and that was hard. I didn't feel I could disclose my ADHD there. I don't know if it's because it was the first time I was in an elite environment, or if it was just that team in general but the way that they went about it at the club was tough. I've come away from it being able to outline my flaws but not being able to tell you where I could show strengths. With ADHD and the way I process, if you say something to me it hits and it sticks, and it stays, and you become so fixated on it. For example, I'm a hooker so I throw the ball into the lineout and I struggle to reach back ball because I'm so tense and I know that I need to reach it and when I do it by myself, I reach it all the time, but because you get such bad feedback when you're playing, I've come out of that year and I'm like, "I can't hit back ball, I can't do it. I'm not gonna get picked, I'm never gonna get picked because I can't hit back ball." I know I can but because they were so quick to tell you what is wrong, I become so fixated on it and then it's all you can think about. I can go and I can do it 100 times a day, but as soon as I do it in front of somebody, I can't do it.'

'I have just moved to another Premiership club, and already I feel accepted and at home. You can tell that the coaches predominantly want to do well but at the end of the day, they're like we've got 40 athletes, we need to make sure that all these athletes are okay. We had a meeting of the newbies with the defence coach where he clipped loads of areas where we'd gone wrong or off-pace and hadn't followed the system and he took us through each of those scenarios which was really good. Whilst my skills and physicality can be there, I have only been playing for five years and sometimes I do just need it really, really, really stripped back.'

'Time for me is either "here and now," or it's an 'in the future' problem and I find bringing the "in the future" problems to light very difficult because I've got five to-do lists going. It is like the ADHD paralysis; If I know I had something to do, or it was on my to-do list, I couldn't do anything else besides that, even if it was something that I couldn't do at that period of time.'

'I get so funny about medication. I feel like if I was to medicate myself for ADHD, I'm allowing it to win. I'm so stubborn, I'm like, "I'm fine, I've worked this hard already, I don't need that." I get so nervous about how it would actually make me feel inside and there's also a part of me that's like, "other people have got it worse." Like I've got ADHD, but I don't feel like I'm massively impacted by it.'

'Sleep for me is so important. I could nap pretty much anywhere. As long as I was flat, I could nap anywhere. I had an MRI yesterday, and it was 20 minutes, and I napped for the full 20 minutes. But I still get the 9 o'clock zoomies when I know I'm meant to go to bed, I've just got so much energy. Sleep is pretty much the one time I can't feel my brain working. But then you get up, and it's 500 things at once. So, I love sleep when the brain's quiet, but if it isn't being quiet, it's hard. To help with switching off I read a book, it takes your brain away from everything that's going on in your head to the problems that are in the book. It's the one other time that your brain switches off, and I like doing that and do that before bed as and when I can.'

'I do use lots of To Do lists but if I see a small task on there I will think "I can do it just before I go to bed," it then becomes a pain. Or I'll leave it and forget it. So, it's like, "I've made my strategy, I've made a To Do list, I'll stick it on my door so I can see it when I wake up," and I just walk past it because it doesn't correlate with how important everything on it was last night.'

'Talking to people about my ADHD is probably one of the most beneficial things I've done. I resonate a lot with the athletes who have ADHD and definitely academics who struggle with learning difficulties, I find them really interesting to talk to.'

'What also helps is clarity. If you are feeling overstimulated or you're unsure on how to do things. I think clarity is ideal. But, any time anyone gives a whiff of not necessarily having the confidence in what I'm doing, I move towards autonomy; 'I'm gonna do this, I'm gonna do this my way. I'll figure a way round it. I'll make it work'. So, in some instances, I really, really like it when people tell me what to do and in others I want to do it my way.'

'I'd say that I struggle with ADHD more than I find positives in it, but I think that's because I'm quite a negative fixator as a person. There are so many benefits to being neurodiverse and being in an elite training environment. Like the fixations. I find with my ADHD it's a lot easier to keep going when the radar of stimulation is on the perfect point because your brain is like, "you haven't finished your job yet, you keep going." I think that if you can get it right, and you get your processes right, then you can feel a bit more bulletproof because you just go for it. I think that that sometimes it acts like an additional energy that other people don't necessarily have.'

'There are obviously multiple struggles and challenges and hurdles to overcome but if I didn't have the weird, nuanced things I have, I never would have gone into sport or be where I am.'

CHAPTER 2

The impact of sport on your ADHD

Research is clear that, for everyone, being physically active can reduce cognitive deficits (improving your concentration, executive functioning and motor skills), help control inappropriate behaviours, act as an anti-depressant with anti-anxiety properties and provides a place to get positive feedback, build friendships and grow confidence. These are all areas though where you might struggle more if you have ADHD. So exercise is thought to be particularly effective, and can have brilliant benefits on reducing some of the symptoms of ADHD.

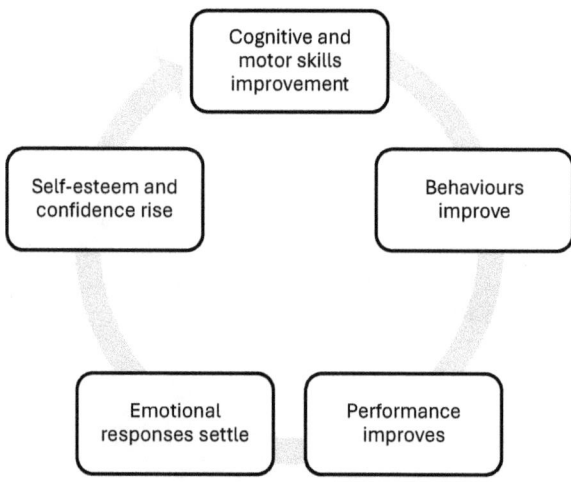

COGNITIVE BENEFITS

In a wide range of research on children and adults, short physical activity breaks have been found to help with cognitive functioning, in particular improving ability to focus and stay on task. As cognitive functions are impaired in those with ADHD, it follows that exercise could help to improve these then and this is what a large number of studies in this area are now finding. In fact, in some studies, the effect of exercise on those with ADHD is actually higher than it is for children or adults without it. This means it can be a really safe method of symptom relief with benefits far beyond the ADHD cognitive symptom reduction.

The specific cognitive improvements that research finds exercise can support:

- Overall cognitive functioning – all of the different skills that involve learning and problem-solving.
- Attention – the ability to focus on the right things at the right time.
- Set shifting – the ability to move between different tasks.
- Cognitive flexibility – the ability to adapt our behaviour and ways we think depending on the environment we are in.
- Planning – being able to solve problems.
- Information processing – the way we gather, manipulate, store and retrieve information within the brain.
- Reducing impulsivity – not acting before considering the consequences.
- Response inhibition – being able to prevent yourself doing behaviours or actions that might harm your long-term goals.
- Improved organization – put in place the systems and logistics to get what we want done.
- Improved working memory – ability to hold onto the information we need for the current task we are on.
- Cognitive control – the thought processes which allow us to make the right choices for the goals we have.

- Processing speed – how fast your brain can take in, assess and choose what to do with new information.
- Vigilance – keeping watch for danger.

The benefits seem to be strongest when it is cardio (exercise that raises your heart and breathing rate repetitively using your large muscle groups, like running, jumping, dancing or cycling) exercise and specific types that demand cognitive engagement (i.e. you need to be alert and decision making – not just mindlessly pedalling), like using co-operation, awareness, anticipation, task-demands and team-sport strategic thinking. The acute and chronic effects of non-cardio exercise seem to be more questionable but those studies that have been published are positive, and physically it will be beneficial for the non-cardio exercise to back up the harder more intensive heart rate lifting exercise to reduce injury and enhance overall performance.

How exercise helps

Everyone benefits from exercise. The simple explanation is that there is a positive influence of exercise on the structure, function and growth of the brain. The act of movement facilitates changes within the brain: in neurotransmitter levels, enhanced cerebral capillary growth and blood flow to the brain, promotion of neurogenesis (the process of creating new neurons in the brain) and growth in brain tissue volume. These are all changes that can enhance our cognitive function. It is thought that those with the greatest deficits in cognitive function will benefit the most from exercise, so it will be especially beneficial to those with ADHD.

If we want to go more in depth then the three main theories as to why exercise helps reduce the cognitive symptoms of ADHD are based on the catecholamines hypothesis (that we read about in chapter 1), the impact of the movement on growth factors and that exercise increases blood flow to the prefrontal cortex, a key part of the brain for cognitive function. You will see how these build on the ideas discussed in chapter 1 on how ADHD influences the brain.

> The catecholamine hypothesis: We just learnt about how the catecholamine system is involved in ADHD in chapter 1. Well, the same elements are involved in exercise. We think exercise may be

advantageous in managing the symptoms of ADHD because it increases the availability and responses of catecholamines in the brain. Some specific catecholamines (those neurotransmitters used within our brains to send messages to tell parts of our body to take action or other parts of our brain to feel) that tend to have a deficit in ADHD are Dopamine (a chemical involved in pleasure and allows us to think and plan, striving, focusing and getting us interested in things), Norepinephrine (involved in your executive operations, helps you reduce distractibility, modulates your arousal levels and enhances your memory) and Serotonin (helps regulate mood and sleep) and they are all important for cognitive function. Exercise has been found to be a powerful stimulus to catecholamines, creating higher availability of Dopamine, Norepinephrine and Serotonin in three key parts of the brain (the PFC, hippocampus and striatum) which then positively affect cognitive functioning and mood.

BDNF impact: A second theory is based on the belief that ADHD is also associated with disruptions of brain-derived neurotrophic factor (BDNF) levels so the positive effects of exercise on specific cognitive processes may also be attributed to an increase of BDNF. BDNF plays a key role in the way your hippocampus (the area where your memory is stored) functions, cell proliferation and also creates a greater long-term effectiveness of your learning and memory. Exercise has been found to increase the levels of hippocampal BDNF and some suggest that these exercise-induced increases in BDNF may allow for improvements in attention, inhibiting unhelpful behaviours and learning.

Increased blood flow: The third theory is that each individual session of exercise sees increased arousal and greater blood flow in the PFC ensuring that oxygen and nutrients are delivered to the brain, enhancing attention, speeding up information processing, improving decision-making and enhancing short-term memory and motor learning. While our body and brain feel more aroused due to exercise, memory processes may be altered to allow the retention of information and figure out how to respond to new or unexpected stimuli. It has been argued that persistently focusing on exercise, beginning at an early age, could have the potential to change the trajectory of ADHD by permanently altering the brain's physiology. Therefore, it is thought it is especially important to exercise at the ages where brain development is taking place.

BENEFITS FOR BEHAVIOUR

Studies looking at the behavioural elements of ADHD tend to focus on children and so are assessed by parent or teacher observation and feedback. When parent or teacher observation is used the studies show beneficial effects on several symptoms. Sometimes these studies will be based on long-term interventions (something like 30 minutes of cardio exercise at least three times a week) and sometimes these will be short exercise breaks in classrooms between subjects. These exercise 'breaks' don't even need to be particularly long to have an impact on behaviour; 10 minutes of 'energiser activities' can be enough for immediate behaviour change. One study had children running around and found straight afterwards their attention span and impulse control improved and the number of times they disrupted the classroom reduced by half, for 2 to 4 hours after the exercise. Longer-term changes have been found from low heart rate exercise in lowered levels of anxiety, reduced hyperactivity, inappropriate emotions and daydreaming.

Why does exercise improve inattentive, impulsive, and hyperactive behaviours? Again, it is thought that the underlying low levels of catecholamine neurotransmitters (like Dopamine and Adrenaline) leave those with ADHD constantly trying to reach optimal stimulation when there is insufficient sensory stimulation or under-arousal. When tasks are boring or monotonous, novel and active tasks (like exercise breaks) dissipate poor behaviour and improve performance.

Never limit exercise as a punishment

The behavioural findings about the importance of exercise highlight why it is so vital for children with ADHD not to be punished in school for ADHD behaviours by having breaktimes taken away or forced to sit and watch in PE lessons. Similarly, for adults who become stressed due to overload in work and study, it can be tempting to avoid exercise as 'too much' but it can actually be an excellent coping mechanism and a way to soothe the brain to improve both cognitive and behavioural functions.

MOTOR SKILL DEVELOPMENT

A specific symptom of ADHD can be diminished motor skill proficiency. This is a real issue for those who want to excel in a sporting environment. Fortunately, a number of studies suggest that exercise can benefit poor motor skill proficiency:

- Locomotor skills (the skills that help us move from one place to another like walking, marching, running, jumping, hopping, galloping, skipping or climbing which may be impaired in children with ADHD). A study over 10 weeks of 45 minutes of moderate-to-vigorous exercise three times per week found improved locomotor skills.
- Dexterity (fine motor skills to do small, precise movements and valuable in sports that involve hand-eye co-ordination). In a study of boys with ADHD, exercise appears to improve manual dexterity.
- Overarching motor skills: Researchers who set boys with ADHD 9 × 30 minute HIIT sessions over a three-week period found that, as well as physical fitness, motor skills (including dexterity and ball skills) and scores focused on self-esteem and friends.

EMOTIONAL AND SOCIAL BENEFITS

Exercise can support emotional improvements through two routes; the exercise itself making brain changes which trigger fewer negative emotional responses and the cognitive and behavioural responses to exercise mean that those with ADHD have fewer social issues, less moments where they feel they have failed and not feeling they are being told off or nagged. All this can boost self-esteem and social functions. A range of studies can bring these elements to life.

> Stress: Low heart rate exercise (like Yoga or Tai Chi) can help those with ADHD cope better with stressful situations, be more mentally flexible (so able to cope with changing situations or environments) and place attention in the right places at the right time. One study reported improved anxiety and conduct as well as less hyperactivity, inappropriate emotions and daydreaming in children with ADHD following tai chi sessions.
>
> Anxiety: As we will see in chapter 7 on co-occurring conditions, those with ADHD have a higher-than-average risk of anxiety. While there may well be neurological reasons for this, it also seems rational to consider that if you are living with a neurodiversity in a world that is designed for neurotypicals, life will be harder. You may need to mask your natural behaviours, you may be constantly being told off or struggling to listen to instructions when your brain has ideas of its own and is noisily shouting at you. That can cause anxiety, because living on the edge of your nerves or waiting to get in trouble for doing something 'wrong'

is not a relaxing way to live. Exercise has been found to lower the risk of anxiety and depression in everyone but a lovely study looking at those with and without ADHD found children with ADHD who regularly participated in sports showed fewer anxiety-related symptoms compared to those participating less.

Physical ailments: When our threat system is triggered adrenaline and cortisol flood our body strongly physically impact us. This physical manifestation of our worries is called somatic anxiety. The first place we tend to notice its impact is in our stomach, causing tummy ache. Exercise has been found to reduce these somatic anxiety symptoms. It may be related to exercise lowering levels of stress in general or it may be that exercise is working well as a coping mechanism.

Positive mood: A study looking at ADHD adults using exercise found that almost all of them proactively used exercise to lift their mood. They reported that being physically active increased mental clarity and attention and that two-thirds said when they were less physically active their mood dropped and they felt their mental health suffered.

Confidence: A third of ADHD participants in a study on the value of exercise reported that seeing progress at the gym helped them feel they had increased their competence, confidence, and self-esteem.

Motivation: A 20-minute cycling activity in adult men with ADHD symptoms found their motivation and energy increased and their feelings of confusion, depression, and fatigue decreased.

Sense of belonging: A core human need is to feel that we belong. Exercising with others can serve as a way to facilitate positive social and peer interactions. These can be lacking in those with ADHD if they have spent a significant amount of time being 'told off' or shamed for disruptive behaviours. Exercising has been found to improve social skills and enjoyment of being able to work well with others.

Again, some of the same neurotransmitters come up for discussion when we look at why exercise might reduce the emotional symptoms related to ADHD: serotonin and endorphins. Serotonin is the neurotransmitter that regulates mood, sleep and your digestive system. Endorphins are neurotransmitters released when you feel pain or stress and are designed to reduce those feelings; imagine them to be like a natural pain killer. It is assumed that exercise provides an increase in both serotonin and endorphins so that your mood improves and you flood your body with a natural painkiller improving your sense of wellbeing.

More widely on the social side it is thought that the more exercise you do the more your sporting competence levels improve and this can connect you to peers and improve your relationships with them. Additionally, the physical health outcomes of exercise; improved fitness, a strong body, relaxation and coping mechanisms means that you not only feel better but also engage in other positive health behaviours like having a good health routine, sleeping well and eating healthier foods.

The ADHD exercise prescription

Prescription to use exercise to improve ADHD symptoms:

10-minute energy boosters for immediate changes to reduce hyperactivity, improve attention and lower stress.
Regular cardio exercise (that makes you out of breath and sweaty) between 20 and 30 minutes at least five times a week to improve cognitive functions and motivation, curb some disruptive behaviours, lower impulsivity, emotional stressors, intrusive and worrying thoughts and reduces confusion and fatigue). These benefits are often found to extend beyond the day the exercise took place.
Aim to take part in at least three different physical activities to significantly reduce symptoms of anxiety or depression.
Low heart rate exercise (like stretching or yoga) can help with longer-term anxiety reduction or hyperactivity.
Amp up this prescription any time significant brain development is taking place.

As well as the numerous physical benefits we all know of, exercise does seem to have good ADHD symptom relief; improving cognitive functioning, day-to-day behaviours and, longer term, as cognitive and behavioural functions improve, then individuals achieve better outcomes, make stronger friendships and handle emotional issues better which builds their self-esteem and confidence.

Exercise is cheap, non-invasive and easy to set up. As athletes (especially if your sport involves cardio exercise) you are already doing lots to manage your ADHD symptoms. There are risks though if you sustain an injury or illness and are unable to exercise so having a range of options can be helpful. While the gold standard from an ADHD symptom management perspective seems to be exercise combined with stimulant medication, studies have found that children with ADHD who performed lots of physical exercises were able to reduce their medication levels.

BROOKE'S STORY

Brooke is a footballer from the United States. She has played for West Ham (WSL) where she played in the FA cup, Reading Women FC (WSL) where she won player of the season and a team in Italy playing in the Champions League. She is now playing for Tampa Bay Sun (USL Super League).

'My mom is a teacher [who focuses on gifted students], teaching a lot of the high-IQ children so she knew a lot of the signs for ADHD. Growing up I was textbook; very active, I was mannerly, but I had my own way of doing things. My mom helped me with a lot of coping mechanisms as otherwise I would show up to school with no shoes on sometimes, not because I forgot, but because I was focusing on other things. We ended up having a very detailed list with times and everything and I had to really stick to that list. She made it more like a game for me to make it a little more engaging, like I wanted to do it so it really helped me. From there, I would have other lists. Basically, I was dealing with a lot of lists!'

'In middle school (13–14 years old) I was struggling a little bit and losing lapses of time so I got a brain test. It came back that I wasn't having seizures, it was just pretty hard to deal with the ADHD and so I would just be zoning out and not even realize I was zoning out. That is when I started to get testing to see about ADHD. It was like a week-long test where I ended up being diagnosed with ADHD and social anxiety.'

'I was in a lot of advanced classes because I was gifted, and I had a high IQ, but my peers made it look so easy to get all of these things done and I couldn't figure it out. When you're growing up, especially when you're going through puberty, you already feel different than everyone else, so then having the ADHD on top of it and not being able to concentrate in class was frustrating. Once I got diagnosed, it was really helpful cos, not only did my mum recognize it but then the school was able to help me too. It showed because my grades improved. It was really helpful to finally understand, "okay, nothing's wrong with me, I just have to learn differently".'

'I have a heart condition so I wasn't allowed to have a stimulant medication. I've had to do everything through coping tools and strategies.'

'I got started in soccer because of my ADHD. I was bad at ballet, very bad. I couldn't remember the routine, the choreography, all that stuff, that was when I was like 3 or 4. I was a very rambunctious child so I would be running up and down the hallways, never taking naps. And my parents were like, "oh my gosh. We need to get some energy out. How do we do this?" My mom was like, "I saw some kids playing soccer, they were running around for like a whole hour every day. Maybe this will help her" so she put me in soccer and then I just stuck with it ever since. It was always my outlet.'

'The ADHD means you are hyperfocused on things you're very interested in. And soccer had me hooked. I would be outside for hours and hours kicking the ball against the wall or into my little net I had and it became kind of like an obsession for me, so it was a positive outlet. It actually helped me in school too because I had something to strive for, look forward to, gave me like goals and a structure, which is what I needed I think.'

'I think why I like soccer so much is in the game, it's so free flowing. You're allowed to make your own decisions and you're allowed to just do what you need to do and make things work. I think I actually work better under pressure because my brain's able to work pretty quickly, so it's almost calming to be active the whole time and constantly having a new decision to make.'

'It helped that my dad was my coach until I was 15 so he was able to understand and know "just give Brooke a task and she'll do it. But if we're talking in a group, she's not going to listen to the speech. Just go let her pick up all the cones." As I got older and didn't have my dad as a coach, I had to learn for myself. I realized "it's okay if I'm not listening, it's okay if I'm doing my own thing, but try to at least pretend" so I would just pick different things to look at near the coach and just kind of make a game for myself. Like, how many hairs are placed on his head, or freckles on his face, then I wasn't disturbing anyone else and I was just in my own mind. And then after I'd be like "okay, what are the bullet points of that speech that I need to know".'

'I didn't really disclose my ADHD. At that age you're so afraid of everyone judging you. I didn't want coaches to treat me differently, especially in an America, there's always an understood rule about sports that you don't complain, you just do what you're asked and you don't admit your weaknesses, so I decided 'I'll keep it to myself. I'll work really hard, I'll just use my coping mechanisms'. As I got older and into the professional game, I've recently started talking about it. Professionally it is quite hard as you are expected to be perfect, and it's your job.'

'In training sometimes with drills when you have certain rules and I can't remember the rules, or I can't remember where I'm supposed to pass next or how many touches I'm supposed to take, when it's very structured, I find it very difficult. If you don't tell your coaches that too it's also hard, because then they're like why are you always messing up, and you're like, "I'm not dumb I promise, I know how to play soccer, I'm just I struggle with the recollection of what I'm supposed to be doing." I don't think coaches really know what to say about ADHD a lot of times. When I first told the coach last year it was after a drill that I just kept messing up, and I just went up to him and was like, I haven't had a chance to talk to you before, but I have ADHD and I struggle with remembering rules and patterns He was like "oh, don't worry about it," and moved on. So I was like, "okay, we'll leave it at that then."'

'A lot of coaches are very verbal, so they're like, "you're going to pass from here, to here, then pass from here" and that is my absolute worst way to learn. Like I really need to either do it or see it. and most likely see it and do it! In my recent team I coped by finding a friend that was good at passing patterns and then I'd go behind them or I ask them questions. That way I didn't have to go to the coaches about it. My team in Reading were really helpful and they were all like "Brooke, go here, go here, and like pass here, the next one's here." They were really patient with me.'

'When I've had a coach that liked to basically be a play-station controller on the sideline saying "pass here! Do this, do this," I can't function like that because I don't think I saw a game the way he saw it. I saw the space, I saw where the ball needed to go next, but he wanted me to go, let's say, to the person in the midfield and then go there. Whereas I saw it, I should go on the outside and go in. Whenever he would do that I ended up messing up the pass I wanted to, because in my brain, instead of being able to decipher, pick one or the other, my brain decided to do both so I kick it in the middle of it. I had another coach who would just be "alright, I trust you, go do what you want to do" and then we would just be able to talk about it after and he would show me things then, rather than in the moment. That was much better because in the moment, my brain's already going "I already see the answer" so once another answer is brought into the equation, my brain just basically goes *bang* and I just can't do it.'

'The sensory issues I have to deal with are usually how my uniform fits and the moving screens at the bottom of the pitch. That is what is distracting. With women's soccer there's not usually too many crowds but when I played in the FA cup final at Wembley, and there was a big crowd. I actually found the noise suited me because it sounded more like a murmur and you can't hear individual voices, which I find more distracting and overwhelming because I'm picking up all these other conversations that I don't wanna pick up. The big crowd becomes a white noise, and cos you're not in the crowd, you're away from it, it's almost a distant noise, which is nice.'

'We visited Wembley the day before the FA cup so we got to walk onto the pitch but obviously it's empty, so there's not really anything going on. When we got there on the day you're in the changing room and you have warm-ups and stuff, but it wasn't too bad, but when we came back out to walk out, there was a red carpet, these balloon things, these flame throwers, the bubble machines, it was crazy. I wasn't prepared for that, I didn't know anything about it. That was a bit of a shock. It feels overwhelming until the whistle blows. And when all that is gone, it's just the hum of the people, and just the football, that's when I get back to being more soothed.'

'What I like about soccer is that there's never just one answer; there are so many different ways to get to the same point and you just have to go off the person before you. Whatever decision they made, your decision becomes different after what they've done. We all make the story together and at the end, hopefully you've won the game with all of you contributing.'

CHAPTER **3**

How ADHD influences sporting performance

There are no good or bad traits or characteristics in life but there are traits or characteristics that are helpful or unhelpful in different contexts and environments. Even within sport, even within the same sports, there might be traits which help the athlete at some times and hinder them at others. And some traits will be harder to handle in a sporting environment that has been designed for neurotypical athletes. So, while the definitions of ADHD will explain that it covers an executive dysfunction and sometimes also inattention, hyperactivity, impulsivity or emotional dysregulation it is worth understanding all the facets so you can work out which elements impact you, and how they impact your sporting performance. You might see some elements as a benefit to your sport; I have worked with athletes who are very clear that they consider their ADHD their strength and others who feel it holds them back. This chapter is designed to help you figure out what helps and what hinders.

The three areas of deficit within ADHD to really focus attention on are executive dysfunction, self-regulation and emotional dysregulation. A number of clinicians argue they are actually very similar deficits and most certainly intertwined, suggesting then that ADHD is fundamentally a disorder of the way our brain processes help us function day to day.

EXECUTIVE DYSFUNCTION

Our executive functions are all the brain processes that whir away in the background helping us to problem solve (plan, organize and execute the things we need to do) so we can achieve our goals. They figure out what we need to do to get stuff done, and then tell us to do it. With ADHD they get applied inconsistently so even though you will often know what to do you find yourself not doing it. The inconsistency is often related to attention so if something is interesting or novel your executive functions can allow you to hyperfocus and when it is routine or dull then they will be much harder to activate.

The first area we notice this impacting is in managing time, remembering details of things and being able to switch focus. When we struggle with these (because we have forgotten we were supposed to, we have run out of time or we have got obsessed with something else) it becomes hard to organize tasks and follow through. When this happens in an organization where we need to perform; school, sport or work then it can mean our performance looks poorer than others and our progress can become stifled.

SELF-REGULATION DIFFICULTIES

One of the key functions we use to get stuff done is self-regulation (these are behaviours like inhibition, working memory, planning, self-talk) which mean we can ignore distractions or boredom and stay focused on our goals. Self-regulation is required extensively in sporting life. ADHD involves deficits in self-restraint and our self-awareness, internal head chatter, reading of our own senses, emotional control and motivation can all be impacted. ADHD is therefore not you lacking knowledge or skill; but sometimes not being able to connect those to your performance. When you are trying to perform at a high level and have the knowledge and skills to do this but your regulatory functions have not developed enough to make this happen it can be incredibly frustrating.

Imagine if your coach has said to you that you have a big game coming up and that means you need to recover well from every session and get lots of sleep. You get home, look around your living room and there is a Playstation, a half-done jigsaw puzzle, a pile of Lego that has been left out, the TV and your phone with lots of new WhatsApp messages highlighted. All of these are temptations which might harm your chances of an early night. If you have good levels of self-regulation you would be able to employ a number of strategies to ensure you don't get excited by the toys and tech and instead can go to bed to sleep; you might leave the living room and go into a room without temptation, have an internal head chat with yourself about how good you'll feel for the game if you feel refreshed in the morning, make an agreement with yourself you can play as much Playstation as you want after the game and finally, you might visualize yourself waking up all bouncy and ready to compete because you had lots of sleep. In doing this you have used several different self-regulation abilities; self-awareness of the potential for distraction, inhibition of an urge to go play, attentional management to move into another room, verbal self-instruction to remind yourself of your goals, willpower to negotiate and visual imagery of how it will feel when you achieve your goal. If you don't have many of these tools you can't self-regulate well and your immediate wants and needs will block your longer-term goals and ambitions causing frustration and an inability to achieve your potential.

EMOTIONAL DEREGULATION

The final element that will really influence your athletic journey is emotional deregulation. We learnt about the three functions of the brain (habit, logical decision making and survival) in chapter 1 so that we can now see how emotional deregulation can stifle your sporting ambitions. Research is finding that ADHD brains appear more likely to experience amygdala hijack (this is where the threat system 'flips the lid' because the brain is more sensitive to threat). Some think this is because an ADHD brain may have a larger amygdala (this has specifically been identified in those who have hypermobility (a condition found in around 50% of those with ADHD). Others suggest that the ADHD brain struggles to switch off emotional processing which means the brain (and body) is constantly flooded with stress prompting emotional dysregulation so it becomes far harder to access the rational, logical decision-making part of the brain.

Everyone can become emotionally dysregulated but in ADHD emotional deregulation can last longer and be felt more intensely. It comes when your emotions are too loud for you to manage so you feel overwhelmed, uncomfortable or even in pain and struggle to recover from them. As children we are often very poor at regulating our emotions but over time our brains learn how to regulate the signals coming from different areas of our brain (handling memories, emotions, input from senses, awareness of others) to be able to mostly keep them at manageable levels. If your brain development in this area has become stalled for any reason then you may feel these emotions more intensely and struggle to turn down the volume.

BENEFITS OF ADHD ON ATHLETES

We saw in the introduction that the prevalence of those with ADHD in sport is disproportionately higher than we would see in the general population. This suggests that perhaps ADHD may offer some benefits to the athlete and there are several suggestions as to why this might be.

One of the areas considered to be in deficit with ADHD is explicit memory and learning which is needed extensively in an academic environment but less so in sport which requires <u>implicit memory</u>. Those with ADHD who have not been able to work around these difficulties in academic environments will find themselves being far more successful and thriving in environments which require implicit memory (like sport) and so it becomes a popular career choice.

Parents of those with <u>hyperactive</u> ADHD may well encourage their children into lots of sports to 'tire them out' and use up excess energy. If they find a sport they love then their ability to <u>hyperfocus</u> can mean they have both the energy required and the intense engagement to work hard and improve at that sport, getting them to an elite level and able to do well in it. Additionally, the hyperfocus allows athletes to be highly stimulated and still able to ignore other distractions which in some sports can be really beneficial. Alongside the hyperfocus, the ability to react quickly to changing stimuli can be valuable in many sports.

Another element of ADHD which can be used really effectively in sport is <u>novelty seeking</u>. This can be beneficial in sport as the athlete becomes creative about looking to do things differently, less predictably or taking more risks in order to feed that craving, all elements that can set one athlete above others.

Finally, the demands of competitive sport (such as structure, routine, dedication, and effort levels) could have a protective role for those with ADHD as it gives a safe energy outlet and fulfils the need for routine, hyperfocus and high energy. When you feel <u>safe</u> in an environment you achieve great results and flourish, something that, for some, might have been missing in an academic environment.

So, while it doesn't seem like ADHD traits can uniformly offer any significant advantage (though in some specific sports there may be some helpful elements) it does start to make sense as to why there are higher numbers of those who have a diagnosis in sport than in the general population. This acceptance is important as while some traits might help some athletes some of the time, the idea that ADHD is some kind of sporting 'superpower' can frustrate athletes who find their traits holding them back.

THE A-Z OF THE INDIVIDUAL ISSUES WHERE YOUR ADHD MIGHT IMPACT YOUR SPORTING PERFORMANCE…

Ants in your pants…

One of the phrases often used describing those with the hyperactive form of ADHD is that they have ants in their pants; not able to sit still or focus who fear unstructured, unplanned time. This may well have been why parents or carers but them into sports in the first place. But, many athletes who have gone into difficulties in their sporting careers often say the unhelpful habits began when they went professional and then had too much time on their hands they felt a compulsion to fill. When the unhelpful habits that get taken up are gambling, drinking or excessive gaming then their sporting performance can dive.

Behavioural inhibition

Behavioural inhibition focuses on how well we can control our responses to the things that happen to us. Do we react or respond? Research suggests that those with ADHD will be more influenced by immediate consequences (i.e. reacting to something that has annoyed them – usually driven by threat or emotion) than longer-term or delayed consequences (responding thoughtfully considering the implications of what is said or done). This tends to mean that 'good' sporting behaviour might be reduced with ADHD as the focus is on the specific moment in a game or competition, not on how they would like to be seen as an athlete or long-term career aspirations. This issue arises regularly in sports with a referee or umpire where an athlete with ADHD might rally against the ref for an unfair or unjust decision, mid match. It can harm their flow, cause their threat system to trigger and can get them a poor reputation as the athlete with a short fuse.

Boredom

ADHD athletes can work incredibly hard when they are interested in a subject, but struggle when something doesn't hold their interest and get bored. This is often the cause of disruptive behaviour in sport, particularly when it comes to the essential but less exciting elements of sport like strength and conditioning, team tactics, or physio rehab. The disruption isn't intentional but a side effect of the distraction that can occur and it requires significant levels of motivation or structure to handle the more boring elements of elite sporting life.

> *I'm pathologically impatient, obviously because my brain is working on a different schedule, in a different order, in a different pattern.'* Jen, Runner

Brain fog and headaches

To help medics support athletes who receive a concussion in their sport many student athletes in the USA have pre-season cognitive testing. One element of this is to report if they have any concussion-like symptoms (headache, dizziness, difficulty concentrating, and 'fogginess') at the start of the season to set a baseline so that if they do sustain a concussion they can be re-tested and results can be compared to their baseline performance. A large study of over 39,000 college athletes found that those with ADHD reported more concussion like symptoms in their baseline testing than those without it suggesting that, day to day, athletes with ADHD are experiencing higher levels of headache, dizziness, difficulty concentrating, and 'fogginess'.

Concussion

As we have seen above, ADHD symptoms can overlap with concussion symptoms, but there is also emerging research that having ADHD can make concussion symptoms worse. This is clearly an issue in sports where the athlete with ADHD is already at higher risk of injury and may assume the concussion symptoms are related to their ADHD not the injury and return to play without having fully recovered. In a 2023 study it was found that ADHD was associated with 1.2 times greater risk of a concussion and those using medication were at 1.5 times greater risk of a concussion – we don't yet know why. The study found that those with ADHD had more severe concussion symptoms, took longer to recover (on average three days longer) and had worsened ADHD symptoms after concussions. So, it is important as an athlete with ADHD to take this into account if you suffer from a concussion and to share your diagnosis with the clinician that treats you so more recovery time can be factored in.

Disordered eating

Disordered eating is more common in those with ADHD. Some of this will be explained by the medication reducing appetite (see chapter 8) so that you develop a habit of going long periods without fuelling your activity and then either not making up for the calories you need or binge eating because you are so incredibly hungry when the medication wears off. Some elements of disordered eating may be explained by anxiety from trying to mask and concentrate to fit in and 'behave' causing constant nausea making it hard to eat the right foods. The issue of course is that with reduced energy levels sporting performance becomes physically harder and when the body has low blood sugar levels the threat system is far more likely to kick off, causing your performance to drop.

Disruptive behaviours

If you are driven by novelty and immediate reward then a number of aspects of sport might well be very boring and you are unlikely to be motivated to engage. In these periods, particularly with the ease of which you get distracted, you may display some disruptive behaviours. Disrupting others is not your intention, there is no malice, it is just that your brain was unable to maintain focus on the person leading the session or the task you were set. Research has found though that these disruptive and inattentive behaviours in recreational activities (like sport) can not only impact actual performance but also mean those athletes are more likely to be penalized or suspended during game-play.

Distraction

One of the biggest issues for an athlete with ADHD will be distraction whenever they are not hyperfocused. ADHD can feel like a disorder of contradictions with hyperfocus at one end and distraction at the other – but it is the level of interest in a subject that directs which end the athlete is sitting at; an area they love and are keen to excel then hyperfocus, an area that might be essential but is considered boring and routine; distraction. In sporting environments this becomes very difficult when the athlete becomes distracted so they are not following instructions or joining in the same activities as others. It can cause them to be singled out by coaches or to frustrate their peers. On their own in the gym the risk of distraction means it can take an ADHD athlete far longer to get through a workout as they focus on the equipment or their phone instead of just heading through the prescribed set.

Energy levels and fatigue

With poor sleep, a brain that it feels like it never shuts down and the efforts of masking and handling emotional dysregulation and executive dysfunctions it isn't surprising that athletes with ADHD will spend more time with fatigue than other athletes. In particular you might notice the fatigue kicking in after a long period of hyperfocus. This means while chronic tiredness is not a frequently listed symptom in those with ADHD (in fact for those with the hyperactive type it might seem surprising) but it can impact concentration, motivation, mood and quality of life.

> *"I wake up in the morning very high functioning. I can sit and do an hour of uni work before having breakfast but I get to lunchtime and I'm totally useless. I always used to fight that, and would feel quite down on self esteem because like I couldn't get off the sofa and make myself do anything. The diagnosis has really helped me understand that it's totally normal as an ADHDer to have these very varying energy levels throughout the day."* Isla, Cyclist

Focus (or attention or concentration) difficulties

The inability to concentrate on what you need to in order to make your intentions a reality is one of the biggest challenges with ADHD. It is not that you don't know what to do or how to do it, it is that you cannot focus for long enough, or focus on the right things, to bring it to fruition. It is thought to be because an ADHD brain tends to have lower levels of Dopamine and Norepinephrine, two neurotransmitters which affect attention. It does this in two ways; by making it harder for the brain to switch activities and by constantly craving more Dopamine, meaning the brain is constantly looking for activities to provide that.

Hyperactivity

The hyperactivity symptom is thought to show up in around 70% of children's cases and to reduce within adult ADHD. The hyperactivity will be seen as being unable to sit still (the ants in the pants covered earlier), constant fidgeting, excessive physical movement, excessive talking, not being able to take turns or show patience when needed. The hyperactivity is often cited as the reason there are so many athletes with ADHD. Parents wanting to find a way to tire out their hyperactive children put them into sporting classes and the hyperfocus (next) means they work incredibly hard at the sport, eventually for those with talent and the right body type, becoming elite.

At its base level, having high levels of energy, lots of creativity and thinking imaginatively can be really valuable in sport. However, the impact of hyperactivity in sport actually goes far deeper, when we consider the psychological impact of being in an environment where your traits can finally support your success.

Athletes with hyperactive ADHD can spend a huge amount of effort trying to contain their energy in environments where conformity is required (like a classroom or office-based environment) which can be exhausting. When they are unable to contain it then it can frustrate both their peers and teachers and bosses and make relationships difficult. It can be liberating to find that in sporting environments hyperactivity can be beneficial. For someone who gets bored easily having positive movements to focus on between organized activities can be brilliant and allows better interactions. Additionally, sport provides an environment where judgement is made on elements which include effort, focus, speed of movement and speed of decision making. Unlike in school, the ADHD athlete is often able to show up on the same terms, or better than others. If these positive interactions have been missing in other parts of life then an athlete will be keen to thrive in their sport and put additional efforts in, offering protection from some of the social difficulties that ADHD can cause. Self-esteem improves as you receive positive reinforcement which can help keep you motivated and stick with the sport even when you face really difficult challenges.

> "Being hyperactive I think helps in triathlon. I am pretty much always energetic. Obviously, I get tired when I'm in a huge training block but I'm just one of those people that is very excitable and always hyperactive and always have been. Probably always will be." Tom, Triathlete

Hyperfocus

Considered to be a state of heightened, intense focus (usually when doing something that you intrinsically enjoy) where you might lose track of time, fail to notice what is going on around you, get totally engrossed in a task, so much so you struggle to stop something to move onto another task, and can get 'stuck' fixating on small details. It can be considered both a strength and a weakness. Some definitions of ADHD suggest that there is a not an attention deficit, but instead a maldistribution of attention, highlighting that some things can be given a plethora of attention when considered intrinsically rewarding.

Hyperfocus is helpful for giving you the motivation to work incredibly hard on areas you love and enjoy (like participating in your sport) but it can also cause issues if we are so focused on one area that we neglect other needs, even elements like self-care and health. Performance wise, it can also mean you ignore the areas you find boring but are essential for long term viability in your sport so you might work really hard on the pitch or court but ignore the strength and conditioning work in the gym that you need to do to stay injury free. The positives come when your hyperfocus means you are unencumbered by distractions from other hobbies and able to give all your attention to daily sports practices. In competition it means you can focus better on the sporting activity itself (once playing) rather than noticing or become overwhelmed by competition type distractions.

Hypervigilance

As our brain's primary job is to keep us alive it incorporates a threat function focused on maintaining our safety. This considers both our physical, psychological and physiological safety and is constantly scanning for anything externally within the environment or internally within our body that might be of threat to us. Scanning too much for too long is known as hypervigilance. Some of the psychological threats which will be amplified in ADHD will be uncertainty, fear of failure and rejection; all common threats in a sporting environment. When you are in a state of hypervigilance you feel on edge, have heightened senses and a mind racing, even though you should feel you are fairly safe. When the threat system has found something to trigger it then you notice even more symptoms; rumination, negative head chatter, a nauseous stomach, sped up heart and breathing rate, tight muscles and senses which switch off. It can really harm performance and make us feel rubbish. It can impact sleep too so you don't recover from your training well. Athletes with ADHD tend to scan situations very quickly for cues and then draw conclusions based on a few details. This can be very effective in a sporting environment. But sometimes a misjudged or misread situation can trigger the threat system unnecessarily. It might mean you start to totally avoid some situations which can restrict your physical and social interactions and opportunities to thrive.

Impulsivity

Impulsivity (a reduced sense of danger, acting without thinking, excessive talking and lots of interrupting) has pros and cons. In sport, impulsivity can prompt you to have moments of brilliance as you take a shot that no-one else would dare to or it will allow you to go with a breakaway in a bike race that might mean you to win an unexpected sprint finish. But it can also place you in situations of significant harm like reacting without thought to someone driving badly (and getting angry behind the wheel) or behaving disrespectfully to a referee (yelling at them) if they have made a call against you. Impulsivity also means you may take things too far and find yourself with burnout, poor wellbeing or underfuelling. Additionally, impulsivity can lead to risk-taking behaviour and when this goes wrong and an athlete looks like they have been negligent or extreme in their behaviours; especially in team sports where the whole team might be affected and the risk of peer rejection increases. It is also important to remember that supressing impulsivity can be fatiguing and frustrating so will cause overall discomfort when it needs to be reined in for the sake of your sport.

Injury

Injuries in athletes with ADHD are thought to be more common. A study in Japan found that adults with ADHD visited the emergency room 10 times more than non-ADHD adults and were hospitalized three times more than non-ADHD adults. A further study in Denmark found that those with ADHD had a lower life expectancy and double the risk of death compared with non-ADHD adults. Other studies find those with ADHD may drive cars more recklessly, have a higher incidence of traffic citations and more car accidents. One of the biggest issues about injuries for an athlete with ADHD is that injuries can stop you exercising for a while which doesn't just take away your coping mechanism for dealing with the hyperactivity but it also removes lots of the structures you have in place for handling day to day difficulties and have come to depend upon. This can make your ADHD symptoms get, and feel, worse.

Insight and performance awareness

The way that our brains monitor our environments and our behaviours for performance errors is vital in sport if we want to learn from each mistake and improve for the future. In ADHD there is thought to be a loss of insight which leads to diminished awareness of performance errors and this will limit the extent to which you can correct your behaviours. When we align this with some of the explicit learning deficits that also show up in ADHD it means your coach might feel like they are repeating the same advice over and over again and that you are not acting upon it which will be frustrating for both of you. However, coaches who work with ADHD say that they are sometimes blown away by the ability of an athlete with ADHD to see the match or competition in a very different way which can lead to a great ability to problem solve. The athlete may not be able to explain how they did it or 'show their working' as we would ask when doing a maths problem but often have a unique but effective way to see problems and resolve them.

Masking

Masking is where you spend your time with anyone you don't feel totally comfortable with having to pretend you match their 'normal'. With ADHD this means you are adopting neurotypical traits to adapt to the environment you are in. While masking is an effective social compensation or coping strategy to avoid stigma or bullying and works well in environments where neurodivergent behaviours are not accepted or understood, it is incredibly fatiguing and the cognitive and emotional efforts of masking have been associated with stress, anxiety and depression.

Memory

ADHD can impact both working memory and long-term memory. Working memory is our brain's short-term storage. When we take in a piece of information it is firstly held in our working memory and then, if it is deemed useful, encoded in our long term-memory. Up to 85% of those with ADHD are thought to have working memory issues and the worse the severity of the ADHD issues the worse the working memory issues. Working memory can impact how well we do in school, how we organize ourselves and how we interact with others. Athletes with ADHD might notice they forget daily tasks like training session timings, gym schedules, and bringing the right equipment. This can limit their ability to improve and cause difficulties with others who might feel let down.

Motivation

ADHD disrupts Dopamine which is the neurotransmitter that has an impact on our mood and motivation. When we lack Dopamine it becomes harder to achieve things. When we are craving Dopamine from something we find exciting we struggle to do the boring but essential activities which can cause us to leave projects half-way through or lose momentum and leave key elements undone.

Motor skills

In a study of 28 adults, graphomotor skills (those needed to write) were studied in those with ADHD (a mix of those on and off medication) and those without. Those without ADHD and the participants on ADHD medication were able to improve their fluency of writing the more they practised. Those off medication could not. This suggests ADHD reduces the type of skills needed for coding, planning and execution of motor movements. Other studies have also found that ADHD individuals can exhibit motor deficits which might influence their abilities for control over balance, dexterity and coordination meaning they may make jerky or imprecise movements or difficulties in controlling (like catching or throwing) objects; like balls. They have also found some general inefficiencies in motor control and timing. These issues within motor skills development and usage suggest that some with ADHD will find it takes much longer to develop the skills required in a large number of sports. Many will overcome this with a hyperfocus on practising those movements until they have mastered them but it can be off-putting when an athlete starts out if it feels like it takes them longer to learn new skills than it takes others.

Novelty-seeking

An element of ADHD which can be used really effectively in sport is novelty seeking. The neurotransmitter we keep referencing comes up again here; Dopamine. It plays an important role in our drive to seek out new experiences and rewards. Our motivation goes up if we think we are getting a reward at the end of it. Stimulating and exciting activities (something new and different rather than routine and mundane) will release more Dopamine so the ADHD brain learns to seek out these exciting opportunities. shunning the day-to-day requirements that are needed to succeed in something. This brings benefits in sport as the athlete becomes creative about looking to do things differently, less predictably or taking more risks in order to feed that craving, all elements that can set one athlete above others. Learning how to bring novelty into their everyday activities is usually a good tactic for athletes if they are to excel. A note of caution is also needed as novelty-seeking may mean an athlete shuns the day-to-day requirements that are needed to develop really good skills and strength in sport.

Organizational management

Organizational skills are the set of cognitive abilities which allow us to work towards our goals; whether that is having an effective training session or starting and finishing a project. A number of elements that are impacted by ADHD impact organizational skills; poor working memory, difficulties in information encoding, learning, reasoning and distractions therefore it is not surprising that a large number of studies have identified that those with a diagnosis of ADHD have fewer organizational skills. The deficit in these skills means an ADHD athlete might well forget essential kit or equipment, be unable to find the things they need, lose their belongings regularly and leave bookings to the last minute. They may also find they procrastinate in getting anything done. Effective strategies have been found to balance out those deficits but it has been found that some will struggle to use those strategies in a consistent manner.

> *"Running is the easy bit. If I could be somehow fed by sort of osmosis and watered by osmosis and dressed and then teleported to the running track and have the session put on my watch I'd be a champion. But that's not how life works."* Jen, Runner

Over-investment in sport

The hyperfocus which can come from ADHD can sometimes be very helpful for an athlete to really invest their time and energy on improving but it can also mean that you become over-invested and develop a mono-identity. When you over-invest and develop a mono-identity you give the sport a lot of power to influence your mood, confidence and sense of achievement. There are two big issues with this. Firstly, sport is uncontrollable, many things will happen to us in sport we have no control over and judging our worth on these elements is harmful to our wellbeing. Secondly, it can mean you start to expect back a level of commitment from your sport that you are not yet at the right level to achieve. Sometimes sport development needs more than hours physically invested – it needs understanding, maturity and time. This can't be sped up through hyperfocus even though often ADHD athlete will develop all-in thinking and create very strict rules around participation (i.e. I must never take a rest day). These might be helpful to developing your potential (to begin with) but will harm your overall wellbeing and development in the sport.

Overwhelm

There are three types of overwhelm that come up within ADHD. There are the daily moments where tasks can feel too much (due to lack of time, sensory overload, boredom, emotional stress or being asked to switch between tasks too quickly) and this leads to procrastination or self-sabotage. There is a difficulty in saying no to things that get you excited (but then come with a dose of reality that time and energy are limited) and then there is big picture overwhelm (feeling that you are mentally and emotionally overloaded without any capacity to handle your stressors). Everyone can struggle with this at times causing us to be unable to focus, complete tasks or manage daily life. The issue with ADHD is that not only does having ADHD increase your likelihood of overwhelm but if you are already struggling to focus, complete tasks or manage daily life then you will either be totally paralysed with inaction and feel frustration, fatigue and exhaustion or totally overreact to situations which arise around you.

Pain regulation

Research has found that in those suffering with chronic pain (headaches, tummy ache, migraine) levels of ADHD are higher, and other research finding that those with ADHD have more physical conditions associated with pain, suggesting there is a link between ADHD and pain. One theory is that both ADHD and pain are linked to Dopamine dysregulation (because Dopamine plays a part in the processing of pain) altering pain sensitivity in those with ADHD.

Procrastivity

Sometimes known as 'productive procrastination' this is where we stay busy by doing less important tasks (because we fear starting the ones we really need to do) but still end up feeling unproductive and stressed because the big, real task is still hanging over you. We tend to head towards manual, hands-on activities that will give us an easy Dopamine buzz like mowing the lawn instead of filling in a tax form or stretching instead of completing competition entry forms.

> *"I'm a big procrastinator. Unless I'm on a deadline, then I'm actually pretty good at getting stuff done. If you have to be at a pool at a certain time, or it's going to be dark, so you have to be out for your ride at a certain time, or you're meeting someone for a run, then I'm really good at being there on time. If it's just me though I'm not very good at it."* Tom, Triathlete

Relationships issues (family, friends, coaches and peers)

A number of elements within ADHD can make social connections with others more difficult. Within the family some of the more difficult externalized behaviours that some athletes with ADHD might display (like aggression, risk taking, novelty seeking, distraction and time blindness) can strain family relationships. In friendships, particularly for those where the ADHD tends to externalize, the frustrations and annoyances it can have a big, negative impact on your relationships. Your peers can tolerate the inattentiveness and 'fizziness' but they struggle to cope with your anger and frustration. When they realize they can't interact or manage you, and that you might be difficult to predict they may pull away leaving you suffering from social rejection.

Within friendships the motivational issues mean that putting attention into friendships to sustain them must feel worth the effort. If it doesn't, particularly when a friend is out of sight (and thus also out of mind), then contact may drop. This isn't intentional but friendships need regular contact and investment to grow and this is hard if you are constantly behind on everything, late to show up to events or you have got into a shame cycle where, if you haven't seen someone for a while, you then feel shamed and guilty for not being in touch so you then hold off even longer. Additionally, the impulsivity element can lead you to misjudge social cues or break social contracts as you act prematurely or interrupt others. All these elements mean that sometimes an athlete with

ADHD will feel like their only safe place is alone. This flies in the face of our fundamental needs as humans to belong and to engage which can leave an athlete feeling isolated, sad and lonely, often battling symptoms of depression. Positively, environments where ADHD traits can bring benefits (like sport) can help to mitigate some of the issues, offering a helpful way to then build friendships as peer relationships become centred around structured routines and clear routes to engaging with and supporting teammates.

Quality of life

Within my practice as a sport psychologist I am often heard repeating: 'A happy athlete is a successful athlete'. It is cheesy but true. It is much easier to perform well when you feel psychologically and physically safe and secure. When you are happier you are better able to push yourself. Yet an issue that comes up regularly in the research is that having to live with the issues that arise from having ADHD can reduce your quality of life. A systematic review of studies on ADHD concluded that ADHD, particularly unmanaged ADHD, is associated with a lower quality of life and in an analysis of 23 different studies it was found students with ADHD had lower grade point averages, reported more academic problems and would be less likely to graduate – even though their IQ levels were exactly the same as their neurotypical peers. Negative life events (which are more common with ADHD like academic underachievement, occupational difficulties and problems with relationships) also lower the quality of life that might be expected. Elements that can also lower quality of life (like smoking, alcohol or drug use) were also used much more in those diagnosed with ADHD and this was unrelated to the likelihood of also having anxiety or depression. These elements are often considered to be self-medicating processes, helping the ADHD individual cope better with their difficulties but over time reduce their quality of life and ability to perform well in sport. With an overall lower quality of life it is harder for the ADHD athlete to thrive.

Reaction time

With quick movement patterns and reactive decision-making due to impulsivity some athletes with ADHD naturally excel in sports like baseball and basketball. Athletes with ADHD are also thought to excel in using visual feedback which can help them improve some of the required motor skill movements. These fast reaction times are often heralded as a benefit in sport; 'straight off the blocks' on the track, 'jumped on the back of a breakaway' in cycling or a 'brilliant defensive action' on the tennis court. However, we don't always want great reactions – what we want are speedy responses – and there is a difference. Reacting happens in the moment and is often driven by threat or emotion. It happens without thought. Responding is slower, more thoughtful and often based on an assessment of longer-term consequences so will be slightly slower but effective. Some studies have found there is a speed–accuracy trade-off in children with ADHD so that their reaction time might be super-fast but that may be to the detriment of accuracy.

Risk-taking behaviour

Risk-taking behaviours will be driven by impulsivity, novelty seeking and difficulties in seeing long term consequences. This can be effective in sport where athletes will take shots others would be too timid or risk-averse to try but can cause difficulties in life outside of sport where the statistics suggest adolescents (who are at a period of life when risk taking is already higher) with ADHD are at increased risk of academic failure, teenage pregnancy, substance misuse and criminal behaviour.

Sensory impacts

With ADHD can come difficulties in processing information from your senses. This might contribute to sensory sensitivity where you become overwhelmed quickly if there are loud noises going on, too bright lights or lots of sudden changes. When the brain is unable to process all of this information, it can lead to feelings of confusion, anxiety, and even physical symptoms such as headaches or fatigue. There can however also be underwhelm where you don't feel you are getting enough sensory input and this will be where you seek it out; stimming; jiggling about, constantly moving.

Task management

Many elements of ADHD interplay when it comes to 'getting stuff done'. The poor organizational skills, the impulsivity, the ease of distraction, time blindness (there is either now or the whole of the future) and the novelty-seeking all combine to mean it either becomes very difficult to start a task or hard to finish it. The issue here is that ADHD is a difficulty in converting intentions into actions. It is hard to do the right thing at the right time. You totally know what to do but it is the doing it that is problematic. You might actually have lots of the skills needed to do what you need to do – but there is a disconnect between knowing and doing. When complexity or boredom are thrown into the mix it becomes significantly harder. With ADHD your decisions about what to work on will be assessed by whether they have an effect now (this very moment) or the future (out of sight, out of mind). If you don't take 'the future' into mind your decisions will be about immediate rewards and excitement, not potential long-term hardships or requirements. If something piques your interest then starting a task will feel easy, you'll get super excited, buy all the equipment, read up on it, but then you might get bored or distracted and the task (or sport) gets dropped. If the task you need to do doesn't pique your interest then even starting the task will feel incredibly difficult.

Time management

The difficulties with staying on task, poor organization and only seeing 'now' or 'the future' mean that time management can be really difficult. Within ADHD the brain areas associated with time perception are those impacted by the ADHD which can cause time blindness; a lack of perception of time so you have difficulty estimating how long a task will take or how long you have spent on a task. This means you may underestimate how long it may take to get somewhere (so you arrive late), how long you might need to do something (so book a court for an hour but actually need two) or miss significant deadlines. When you mix time blindness with the hyperactivity you can encounter waiting mode. Waiting mode is when you can't get anything done because you're distracted by the awareness that you have something important (like a match or training session) planned for later on. When you are in waiting mode you might feel anxious, impatient and sometimes overwhelmed as you enter a state of mental paralysis.

Help or hinder list (sometimes it might be both)…

	Helps my sport	Hinders my sport	Don't notice this	Tools to try if hindering
Constantly moving				Relaxation tools (Ch4)
Use disruptive behaviours				Behavioural Skills Training (Ch5)
Easily bored				Earn Dopamine (Ch5) Strengths Audit (Ch6)
Regular brain fog or headaches				Task focused goal setting (Ch6)
Suffered a concussion				Rest and follow sport specific Return to Play guidelines
Have disordered eating				Nutrition (Ch4)
Get easily distracted				Daily scaffolding (Ch5) Building habits and routines (Ch5) Body Doubling (Ch5) Reducing procrastination (Ch5)
Become emotionally deregulated easily				Coins (Ch6) Naming sporting emotions (Ch6) Emotional regulation tools (Ch6)
Have low energy levels				Nutrition (Ch4) Sleep (Ch4) Fuel up (Ch6)
Struggle to focus				Goal setting (Ch5) Visual reminders (Ch6) Coach on a Shoulder (Ch6)
Hypervigilant				Know your triggers (Ch6) Emotional regulation tools (Ch6) Control mapping (Ch6)
Hyperactive				Stress management (Ch4) Coins (Ch5) Task focused goal setting (Ch6) Control mapping (Ch6)
Hyperfocused				Coins (Ch5) Dealing with waiting mode (Ch6) If…Then planning (Ch6)

(Continued)

	Helps my sport	Hinders my sport	Don't notice this	Tools to try if hindering
Impulsive actions				Chunking down (Ch5) Prioritizing Preparation (Ch5) Control mapping (Ch6)
Regular injuries				Goal setting (Ch5) Communication passport (Ch5) Prioritizing preparation (Ch5)
Low levels of insight				Communications passport (Ch5) Become a self-expert (Ch5) Common sporting emotions (Ch6) Analysis (Ch6)
Masking				Communications passport (Ch5) Pot of Power (Ch6) Strengths Audit (Ch6)
Poor memory				Visual reminders (Ch6) Building habits and routines (Ch5) Daily scaffolding (Ch5)
Low motivation				Goal setting (Ch5) Body doubling (Ch5) Reframing (Ch6) Strengths Audit (Ch6)
Low level of motor skills				Skills sheet (Ch 9) Task focused goal setting (Ch6) Chunking down (Ch5)
Constantly seeking novelty				Coins (Ch5) Goal setting (Ch5) Know your triggers (Ch6)
Poor organization				Coins (Ch5) Daily scaffolding (Ch5) Prioritizing preparation (Ch5) Building habits and routines (Ch5)
Over-investment in sport				Emotional regulation (Ch6) Curious questions (Ch6) STOP approach (Ch6)

(Continued)

	Helps my sport	Hinders my sport	Don't notice this	Tools to try if hindering
Overwhelm				Stress management (Ch4) Chunking down (Ch5) Emotional regulation (Ch6) Control mapping (Ch6)
Low levels of pain regulation				Emotional regulation (Ch6) Name sporting emotions (Ch6)
Procrastivity				Reducing procrastination (Ch5) Goal setting (Ch5)
Rapid reaction times				
Relationships issues – family				Chapter 10 Surround self with right people (Ch6)
Relationship issues – peers				Surround self with right people (Ch6)
Relationship issues – coaches				Chapter 9 Surround self with right people (Ch6)
Risk-taking behaviours				Goal setting (Ch5) Chunking down (Ch5) Prioritizing Preparation (Ch5)
Self-regulating difficulties				Emotional regulation (Ch6) Name sporting emotions (Ch6) Control mapping (Ch6)
Sensory issues				Communications passport (Ch5) Becoming self-expert (Ch5) Know your triggers (Ch6) Emotional regulation tools (Ch6)
Task management				Goal setting (Ch5) Chunking down (Ch5) Task focused goal setting (Ch6) If…then planning (Ch6)
Time management				Dealing with waiting mode (Ch6) Daily scaffolding (Ch5) Coins (Ch5)

TOM'S STORY

Tom is a professional triathlete racing middle distance triathlons.

'I was very, very badly behaved at school at times but always extremely capable academically which kind of made the behaviour worse because I never saw any pay off for concentrating in lessons. I was always bored, messing around, doing stupid things and would still get good grades and I'd know the answers and didn't have to try very hard.'

'I was excluded from my first school when I was 7, got diagnosed and put on medication. I went through a series of regular state primary schools and then I went to a series of private schools. Excluded from one in year 5. Then went to another private school for a year and got to the end of year 6. Not incident free, but got there! Then went to a Royal Navy School in year 7 and that did not work out well because it was an environment where I just didn't get on, got excluded, suspended and excluded a bunch of times and eventually permanently excluded. There was one time a PE teacher said something really, really nasty to one of my friends, and I just booted a basketball straight at him. Didn't even cross my mind that that was may be not a good thing to do.'

'After that I went to a local comprehensive and the headteacher there was really good. I wasn't without problems there, I still got suspended, but they very quickly understood that shouting at me to behave better is not going to work. They allowed me to have a space and just got me to the end of GCSEs. I actually stayed there for sixth form which was much better for me because you don't really have to go to lessons and you're going from studying 12 subjects that you have absolutely no interest in, to doing three subjects that you have chosen and you really like. I found a ginormous shift in how much energy I had for lessons and found it very easy to do work. I then went onto study Physics at uni and began a PhD until the triathlon took over.'

'I stopped taking my medication when I was 16. I think it was having an environment conducive to being able to be myself that helped. The medication for me was neither here nor there, really. It definitely stunted my growth and stopped me eating. There was a very, very marked change in appetite. The period where the medication was acting during the day, I would not really eat. And that comes as a big shock to people that know me now because I am always eating.'

'I did a bit of swimming and cross country when I was younger and then played football. That was up until I was 18 and went to university. I just got a bit sick of the football culture so I joined the triathlon club after getting a bit unfit from not doing sport for a year and then, you know how it is, you just get really into it, don't you!'

'When I first started doing local races and age group races it was great because with my swimming I basically just had a head-start at every single race. That is no longer true now because racing professionally everyone's a bit better.'

'I really like a full calendar of training. When I was playing football, I was playing on a Saturday for the senior men's team and I was also playing Sunday league football and playing five a side three times a week and training twice a week with my Saturday team. And before that I was swimming, which is well known for having a lot of training. I've always like doing a lot of sport and I'm quite fond of swimming, cycling and running all of the time.'

'At the start I got into it because the people at the university triathlon club were nice, and then they became friends, and then you get into doing the training sessions, and then you suddenly get to the point where it's the summer and everyone goes home from university and I'm still doing the training sessions even though I'm on my own and then it just sort of creeps into being your lifestyle.'

'I am now completely obsessed with triathlon. I don't think about anything else. I wasn't like this with swimming but I was with football. My problem with football was a severe lack of talent, but I tried very hard. Triathlon is a sport that really rewards that hard work which I like. And there's so much in triathlon that's measurable.'

'My self-esteem has never been attached to what anyone else thinks of me but I don't think that that's anything to do with any condition. I think it's more to do with the environment that I have grown up in at home, which has always been an entirely supportive one. My parents have always been both extremely encouraging and have always told me that I am good enough.'

'I have a coach. He's my friend as well. He's actually a cancer scientist. I'm his only athlete and we talk a lot together and obviously I trust his opinion. We have loads of spirited arguments about what to do, and it's really, really good to have someone that I can argue with about those things. And then we decide what we're doing together and how we're going to approach things.'

'I used to get excited about all new training ideas. I would read an article on say "three run sessions to increase your VO2 max," I would then go and do one. When you spend time in the sport you realize that that's not a particularly smart thing to do so now what I would do is I would read pretty much the entire literature, certainly from the last 3-5 years on a particular topic, before I even thought about putting it in my training.'

'One thing I learned from being around really top, top pros is no one's doing anything special. And that's quite reassuring, because there's not something you're missing out on. The thing everyone has in common is that they basically do the same boring thing for ten years, and then they get good. You just have to train a thousand hours a year for 5-8 years before you even become remotely competitive at the top of the sport. And to do that you have to be very consistent all year.'

'Impulsivity does show up sometimes. I had a mid-race argument with a marshal in the penalty tent the other day because I got a 1-minute penalty for racking my bike wrong. I spent that one minute bickering with the marshal which now I get home and think about it I see maybe I wouldn't have bonked on the second part of that run if I spent that one minute eating the gels that were in my pocket! There definitely is a larger instance of things going wrong for me than other people, but I very rarely make the same mistake twice. And again, a lot of that is I think still inexperience in the sport. Because I've only been in the sport for five years.'

'I sleep really well when I'm training because I am really tired. Which makes it a lot easier to sleep. I can get to a point though where I'm so tired that my sleep is all messed up and I don't sleep very well, I wake up in the night, things like that. As soon as I've stopped training I don't sleep well. I end up staying up really late and waking up very early and my sleep suddenly drops from 9 hours a night to like 5 or 6.'

'Then, in the morning I feel like shit and in the middle of the day I get all sleepy and I drink 5x much coffee as I normally do and I definitely eat less healthily as well when I'm not training, and it does not take very long for all of the things that I normally do in my life that are regular healthy habits to all go to shit. So I need that structure, as long as it's not structure imposed on me by someone else. In which case, I don't like structure. I like to have 100% control over my own life on a day-to-day basis.'

'I don't really like really like having structure imposed upon me, but if I remove my own structure from myself, which sometimes I do because, you know, sometimes it's actually nice to do that for 3 or 4 days, it can go wrong. When I get back into training suddenly I feel a lot better, I sleep a lot better and everything feels a bit more normal, everything's a bit more regulated, eating becomes normal again and I do everything without really thinking about it.'

CHAPTER **4**

Wellbeing strategies

While the physical side of sport can feel at times like it is a form of self-medication for ADHD and can bring us the joy of movement and achievement, we don't actually get stronger at the time we train. It is while we rest, recover and sleep that our strength and skills actually develop within our body and brain. They will only develop effectively if we are fuelled, hydrated and have the headspace to take in new knowledge. This means that we need to ensure we sleep, recover, eat and drink well and handle stress effectively to grow as an athlete. We all know this in theory however, some of the ADHD symptoms can make it harder to put the wellbeing approaches into practice. In this chapter we discuss some tools and strategies to manage the different elements of wellbeing as an athlete with ADHD and aim to reduce some of the difficulties.

NUTRITION

Our brains are about 3-5% of our body weight but they suck up about 20% of the fuel we put into our body – in particular they love glucose. When they are underfuelled the threat system is much more explosive and we stop thinking with the rational, logical decision making part of our brain and instead think more dramatically, using lots of black and white emotionally driven thinking. This can often get us into difficulties as we either switch off and lose focus or we get the red mist when someone annoys us and we react irrationally because now we have reduced emotional regulation. This means maintaining good nutrition and fuelling our sport well becomes incredibly important.

Unfortunately nutrition is a tricky area with ADHD because (a) there are a number of different symptoms that make it hard to maintain, (b) medication can reduce appetite, (c) symptoms can prompt disordered eating and eating disorders and (d) weight or aesthetic based sports can negatively impact nutrition goals. This last point is really important for athletes. If you are in a sport that maintains a 'lighter is faster' culture (running, cycling, climbing), requires you to be 'aesthetically pleasing' (gymnastics, trampolining, diving) or you compete in weight classes (rowing, judo, boxing) then you will be at an additional risk of disordered eating.

Reasons for higher levels of disordered eating in athletes with ADHD:

- Feel hungry but lack the motivation to get up and make something to eat.
- The texture, smell, shape of some food feels uncomfortable.
- Night owls (up to 80% of those with ADHD) will struggle to eat early in the day when their brain and body would prefer them to still be asleep.
- If you get distracted or hyperfocused on a task you can forget to eat.
- If you have forgotten to eat in the day (hyperfocus or medication reducing appetite) you may binge when you notice huger at night.
- If you get distracted you will eat slowly which becomes frustrating.
- Aversive consequences of eating like regular stomach upsets (often caused by the anxiety that might sit alongside ADHD) or a fear of chocking can make food feel like a threat.
- Hyper focusing on food needing to be prepared a certain way.
- Requiring a specific routine when it comes to food (i.e. the same thing every day).
- Hyper focusing on trends or diets which can limiting the variety or regularity of food.
- ADHD medication reducing appetite.

Nutritional strategies to fuel training well

Reflecting on the macro nutrients you need

- Ensure you get lots of protein – foods that are rich in protein are used by the body to make neurotransmitters. Proteins have also been found to tone down blood sugar surges and this can reduce hyperactivity and the risk of the threat system triggering. Protein is also used to rebuild muscle after exercise so good for helping for athletes wanting to build strength.

- Balanced macros (protein, fat and carbohydrates) help keep your body in sync which can help you better manage the ADHD symptoms. A meal plate would ideally be about 50% full of vegetables, 25% of protein and 25% carbohydrate. Where athletes might also need to add to this though would be additional carbohydrates before and during exercise (especially if endurance based) and additional protein afterwards to help with strength and recovery.

> *"I know when I have a lot of sugar my ADHD is worse so I try not to eat too much sugar cos it makes my energy levels go up and down really fast. I try to have more of a whole foods diet."* Brooke, Footballer

Nutrients to prioritize with ADHD

- A 2016 study in the *Journal of the Royal College of Psychiatrists* found that concentrations of vitamins B2, B6 and B9 were associated with ADHD, and that low levels of B2 and B6 impacted symptom severity. For this reason B6 is suggested as a helpful supplement or dietary priority for those with ADHD.
- A 2010 study in *Child Psychiatry & Human Development* Journal found Zinc levels to be lower in children with ADHD and that supplements could reduce hyperactivity and impulsivity.
- Optimal Iron levels are essential for athletes to feel energetic and strong. Due to losing blood each month through their periods, a significant number of female athletes find themselves with low Iron levels (one study found nearly a third of female athletes and up to half of adolescent female athletes were low) and some men will too due to the physical micro traumas of repeated movements on the ground. Specifically in ADHD, one small study looked at Ferritin levels (this measures iron stores) and found that 84% of children with ADHD were low in it, compared to 18% of children without it so researchers suggest that iron deficiencies may contribute to ADHD symptoms. Studies have found improvement in ADHD symptoms of taking iron supplements. If you are considering Iron supplementation though you need blood

tests and to speak to a medical professional first as having too high an iron level can be dangerous for your health.
- It is suggested the <u>Magnesium</u> can help to calm hyperactivity and agitation – when these levels are lower it becomes easier to focus on the task in front of you.
- A meta-analysis of <u>Omega-3 Fatty Acid</u> Supplementation (The *Journal of the American Academy of Child & Adolescent Psychiatry* in 2011) suggested that omega-3 fatty acids can improve symptoms of ADHD, specifically cognitive skills, attention and behaviour.

Increase emotional literacy around food

Food and our feelings can be closely linked. I have often had athletes tell me that they 'eat their feelings'. Instead of fighting this, we can use this knowledge to get to know which feelings are impacting our diet. You can do this though widening your emotional vocabulary so you use more specific words to describe how you feel. This helps you communicate worries or stresses better. Specifically, try to notice if you ever say the phrase: 'I feel fat.' Fat is not a feeling so if you notice yourself doing this the goal is to figure out what you actually mean. What emotion are you hiding with the word 'fat'? You can find a list of emotions at the end of the chapter. The more specific you are in your descriptions and naming of how you actually feel the more likely you are to find the right strategy to handle it.

Take easy options (without guilt)

Fuelling well for training is essential so if food is something you regularly forget about and you don't notice your appetite then build up a list of foods that are easy for you to eat, portable (so they can travel with you) and accessible so you can eat them without much effort. Buying these in bulk and freezing them if perishable or storing near your desk or in your kit bag if they don't go off for a while means you are more likely to eat. Social media ADHD nutritionists often have some good examples of meals you can put together easily giving you the marcos you need without lots of effort when motivation is low.

> "On medication I could eat breakfast, then I wouldn't eat anything until at night. And that's no good when you're training 8 hours a day." Olivia, Cricketer

Incorporate food into daily plans

If you are following a training plan for your sport then building in the nutritional elements can help remind you when to eat to enhance your training. Carbs an hour or so before a hard session and protein straight afterwards will be commonly seen on a training plan.

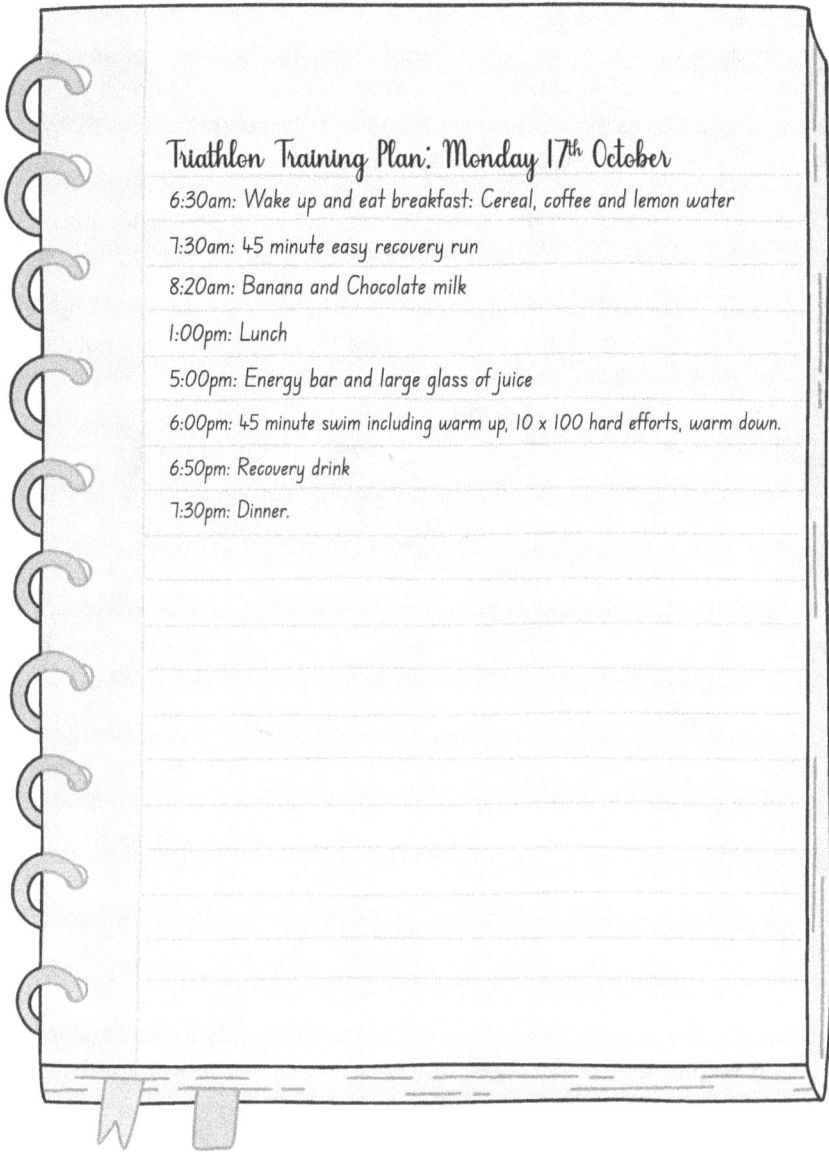

Triathlon Training Plan: Monday 17th October

6:30am: Wake up and eat breakfast: Cereal, coffee and lemon water

7:30am: 45 minute easy recovery run

8:20am: Banana and Chocolate milk

1:00pm: Lunch

5:00pm: Energy bar and large glass of juice

6:00pm: 45 minute swim including warm up, 10 x 100 hard efforts, warm down.

6:50pm: Recovery drink

7:30pm: Dinner.

> *"Quite often if will be the time designated to do my run, and because I've been focused on something else, I won't have eaten or drunk enough to fuel an intense training session. I'm trying to perform at a high level and that takes a lot of fuel."* Jen, Runner

Nutritional strategies for competition day

The biggest nutritional issues for competition day for ADHDers tend to be how to handle the lack of appetite if you are on medication, getting so into the zone you forget to eat or feeling so anxious about the competition so that your stomach feels too churned up to eat. A number of tools to try:

Nutritional prompts – Having alarms set on your phone in the hours before competition can help you remember that you need to fuel the competition ahead of you.

Medication holiday – Some athletes choose to take a medication holiday on competition day (see chapter 8) so they feel able to fuel well enough. You must discuss this with your medication prescriber first though as missing medication may have negative issues for you.

Front load food – Some athletes (like Rachel below) will eat lots of breakfast before taking medication however this can be difficult if you are anxious about the upcoming competition (as we read in chapter 1, anxiety can upset your tummy) and you don't feel hungry. Emotional regulation tools (chapter 6) can help you to reduce the threat response within your body so you feel better able to eat and front load your food for the day.

Sneak calories into your drink – We tend to notice thirst more than hunger so if you have a drink bottle with electrolyte and carbohydrate drink in it then you will be better fuelling your activity without actively having to remember to eat.

Make eating easy – Have lots of very easy to eat snacks in your kit bag or the kit box (see chapter 5) so you don't have to feel motivated to go and find something. Ideally you would eat the healthiest food as an athlete but sometimes it is more important you are fuelled for performance so, if you are struggling, eat whatever your stomach feels it can cope with.

Competition nutrition plan – Just like the example training and nutrition plan (above) try to incorporate nutrition and hydration into your competition plan too.

Consider caffeine – There are a number of theories as to how caffeine can help in sport and with ADHD but the current thinking is that it can block the action of adenosine (a chemical which blocks dopamine release – which is what is already low in ADHD) so caffeine will help the athlete feel they are doing well and the effort and attention being given is worth it. Caffeine also speeds up response times, helping you focus when fatigued. For those with inattentive ADHD this could be beneficial as it improves alertness, concentration and reduces error rate in complex cognitive tasks.

> "In the first two to three weeks that I started taking my medication I lost 4 or 5 kilos cos as soon as I took it I couldn't eat, and I felt sick at the thought of food. If I am struggling with that, I'll just try and have a big breakfast before I take my medication, and then take it, and see if it can either just have small snacks or maybe have like small snacks or maybe have like a liquid, like a smoothie or a protein shake during the day, and then, like around 9, 10 o'clock at night, when I get my appetite back, I'd have a massive meal again." Rachel, Cricketer

Dealing with eating disorders

Alongside the disordered eating that can come with ADHD there are also specific eating disorders that have been found to be more common in those with ADHD. A study in the USA found that adults with ADHD are nearly three times more likely to have been diagnosed with an eating disorder at some point in their life than non-ADHD adults. Eating disorders are also more common in athletes; in studies used by UK Sport in their guidance on Eating Disorders in Sport, it was found that about 13.5% of all athletes have some kind of eating disorder and in sports like distance running that was higher at 16%. This means when we put ADHD and sport together we need to be particularly careful.

There are four eating disorders we tend to see most within athletes: RED-S (Relative Energy Deficiency in Sport), Anorexia, Bulimia and Binge Eating Disorder.

- Binge Eating Disorder – Binge eating disorder will be diagnosed if someone has recurrent binge eating episodes where they consume large quantities of food in a short amount of time and feel they can't stop. With ADHD, this can occur because they have become incredibly hungry without noticing: either due to stimulant medication reducing appetite during the day or being hyperfocused and forgetting to eat. To fill this hunger they might eat far more than they needed in a way that can feel frantic. They know this is not a healthy way to be and may hide some of the binging but feel unable to stop.

- Anorexia – If an athlete has anorexia they will want to keep their weight as low as possible. There won't really be a figure in mind, they always just always want to weigh less. The athlete may well feel they are actually overweight (unable to see their body as others might), have a real fear of gaining weight, weigh themselves obsessively, restrict food, weigh food, lie about what they are eating and obsessively focus on following the anorexic voice within their brain. Anorexia is a really serious illness and it is incredibly important to get help as early as possible.

- RED-S – RED-S stands for Relative Energy Deficiency in Sport where the athlete does not have enough energy to fuel all the exercise they are doing. The nutrition they take in is not enough to cover the energy needed by their body (to fuel day to day demands) and by their sport. It can sometimes come because the athlete is trying to reduce their weight to improve performance but can also be because they haven't realized how much more food they need to eat to fuel all the exercise they are doing.

- Bulimia – Bulimia comes when we binge (eating much more food than we need) and then purge it to stop ourselves gaining weight. Some people will make themselves vomit, others take laxatives or over exercise. Some people with bulimia will lose weight but many will not as actually the calories will be absorbed into the body before they throw up. Athletes who over-exercise as their approach to purging will struggle because they will be very fatigued, over trained, and much more susceptible to injury.

The impact of an eating disorder on day-to-day life is huge. It takes over your thoughts so you are unable to focus on anything else and become obsessed by food. You want to work out how to get the most enjoyment out of the tiny amounts of food you will eat. You will also feel weak and afraid of what is happening to you and realize you are losing control but don't know how to handle it. You will be exhausted and lack energy to do even basic things and get very angry, very quickly. Those with anorexia can hear their anorexic voice talking to them – telling them they have failed if they eat so they are in a constant battle in their own heads. Those vomiting regularly may notice worn away teeth, damage to the lining of the throat, issues with the heart, kidney, stomach or bowel which can cause things like constipation, intense pain, bloating or constant reflux. In sport these elements don't just harm your performance, they harm the relationships with others, your short- and long-term health and suck away your happiness.

Spot the triggers of disordered eating

It is important to know if you are at risk of an Eating Disorder:

1. Do you have a personality type (anxious, sensitive, perfectionistic, kind) which might mean you are more susceptible to disordered eating behaviours?
2. Do you compete in a sport where weight or body shape and size are discussed?
3. Do you care a lot what other people think about you?
4. Do you set really high goals for yourself and expect to achieve them?

If you answer yes to a number of these then keeping an eye on your fuelling patterns becomes really important – you can use the ABCDE tool to do this.

- Absence – Are you avoiding any food related activities, being secretive around food, lying about what has been eaten, hiding food or missing social occasions or activities which involve eating?
- Body – Do you feel weak, have lost muscle strength and get dizzy and cold? Is hair falling out of your head but growing on your arms and legs as your body tries to keep you warm? You might find it really hard to sleep. If you are female have your periods stopped? If you are male have you lost your morning erection?
- Control – Feeling that you need to extensively control what you eat and when. It may feel like you have a voice in your head directing you to follow controlling behaviours: restricting, purging or binging and making you develop 'food rules' that you cannot break. Are you spending more time than normal exercising or doing exercises which

won't help you get better at your sport, but help you feel like you are 'burning calories'?
- Diet – Changing your diet, cutting out whole food groups (meat, dairy products, carbs, gluten, sugar), counting calories, not eating anything seen to be fattening and having lots of rules around food would all be red flags to look out for.
- Emotions – When you have an eating disorder it becomes very hard to concentrate and think clearly and your mood will drop significantly as eating disorder moods mirror depression.

If you spot any of these signs it is really important to reach out for support. You would start with your doctor and if they think you have an eating disorder they will refer you to specialist services. This might involve seeing a dietician (who can advise how to get your weight back to a healthy level if weight is too low), a psychologist (who will help you understand why you took on these behaviours and help you to learn more beneficial coping strategies) and an endocrinologist (who will be able to help you work on recovering any hormonal damage).

HYDRATION

ADHD symptoms can make you less likely to stay hydrated (you either don't tune into your thirst signals, ignore them if you are in the zone or forget to regularly drink if in sporting environments) and the symptoms of dehydration can make your ADHD symptoms worse. A very unfair catch 22 situation.

Dehydration can impact your executive functioning, attention and memory, all issues you may already struggle with if you have ADHD. In addition, stimulant medications can also lead to dehydration as, in the process of increasing the amount of Dopamine in the brain, they also activate the sympathetic nervous system and the side effects of this are those we warn of in chapter 8: increased heart rate, overheating (and so excessive sweating) and dry mouth. This means if you are not drinking regularly you will become dehydrated and suffer more. Dehydration will show up in worsening brain fog, difficulties in concentrating, forgetfulness, slower than usual processing times and you may also be clumsier. All limiting factors in high performance sport. This means it is essential for athletes to scaffold hydration with tools and strategies so you don't expect your body to remind you when to drink but have external reminders instead.

The base line of hydration should be around two litres of liquid a day but add on more if:

- You are doing lots of exercise that day
- You are training in a hot environment
- Your body feels it is fighting off any illness
- You have had alcohol in the last 24 hours.

Ten tips to drink more…

- Add flavours to drinks – it doesn't have to be water.
- Have a water bottle next to your kit, in your bag or leave it by the front door.
- Use the habit stacking concept (chapter 5) to drink before or after a snack or meal.
- Find a water bottle with visual reminders on it – such as a line at half way to have reached by a certain time.
- Get the biggest water bottle you can – then you won't need to remember to refill so often.
- Set a 30 minute alarm on your phone to remind you to drink.
- Some research suggests using a straw can help you drink more.
- Put a pitcher of water on to the dinner table so you subconsciously keep filling your glass.
- If you need to take protein after training then drink that protein (most often in the form of milk).
- Drink a glass of water as soon as you wake up – it gets you off to a good start.

SLEEP

We know sleep is really important as an athlete as it is when your body develops the strength from the training you have done that day. ADHD and sleep is an interesting area as some athletes with it really struggle to sleep, others find they drop off within seconds and are constantly craving more. Both can cause problems for our wellbeing as when we live out of sync with normal sleep patterns we can get a form of jet lag and become unable to perform at our best.

It is estimated that 70% to 80% of adults with ADHD have one or more sleep problems and this is an issue because ADHD and sleep problems can exacerbate each other. An analysis of 16 studies found children with ADHD were more likely to have difficulty with sleep initiation (i.e. trouble falling asleep) fragmented sleep, poor sleep efficiency, sleep disordered breathing and excessive daytime sleepiness. Poor or inadequate sleep can prompt behavioural and learning difficulties in the daytime and exacerbates inattention, distractibility, and irritability.

The biggest sleep issue that tends to arise with ADHD is social jetlag and the resulting sleep debt. Sleep debt means we can get we get sleepiness, less focus, lower cognitive functioning, impaired memory function, irritable, low mood and you increase risk of binge eating (see above) as if you do not get energy from sleep you binge eat instead in an attempt to get more energy. These can cause increased inattentiveness (which is hardly fair when you already have ADHD), social issues and reduce ability to perform in sport.

At the core of many sleep issues is a hormone called Melatonin. Melatonin is naturally occurring in our bodies. Our levels rise at night (helping us to feel tired and fall asleep) and lower in the daytime, making us feel awake. It is thought that ADHD can delay the onset of melatonin release – for up to 105 minutes later than for those without ADHD meaning it can take much longer to fall asleep and you feel energetic at night when others are winding down. Sometimes athletes call this the 9pm zoomies. It is estimated that about 80% of those with ADHD are night owls; they like to go to sleep late and would prefer to wake late too. When you can't wake late due to school, work or training then you get into sleep debt as you end up getting only around 5-6 hours sleep. This can be really hard as an athlete if you are trying to sleep the night before a competition and know you need to be well rested, if you have inflexible training times (like swimmers or ice skaters who have to be in training before school or office hours) or if you are having to share a room with another athlete on tours or away matches.

> Tips to improve sleep for athletes with ADHD:
>
> - Get as much light and sunshine in the day as possible – we need the sunlight to pass through our eyes to improve sleep pressure so make sure you go outside every day. Those with ADHD can be more sensitive to light (68% say this is an issue for them) and so they wear sunglasses but limiting the amount of time in sunglasses when outside can help build your sleep pressure so it becomes easier to sleep earlier.

- Make your bedroom as dark as possible: Black out blinds, eye mask, chargers and phones in a different room (this helps trigger the release of Melatonin)
- Reduce drinks after 8pm (so you don't wake needing the toilet)
- No screens for an hour before bed.
- Aim to wake up at same time every day – even at the weekend – this can really help regulate your sleep patterns.

"When I wake up, I'm awake. Like, brain's on and that's it. I remember in my younger years, just having a brain that wouldn't stop. And I wouldn't get to sleep for ages. And then I would get to sleep, I couldn't get up. And I probably wasn't getting the quality of sleep that I should have done either." James, Equestrian

Circadian rhythm awareness

Our bodies follow a circadian rhythm. It sets out when we will fall asleep, feel hungry, thirsty, feel tired or alert and be able to focus and it follows a very predictable 24-hour cycle. When we expose the body to light in the morning the clock resets. If we don't get enough light early on the clock can start to reset later and later so you end up with delayed sleep.

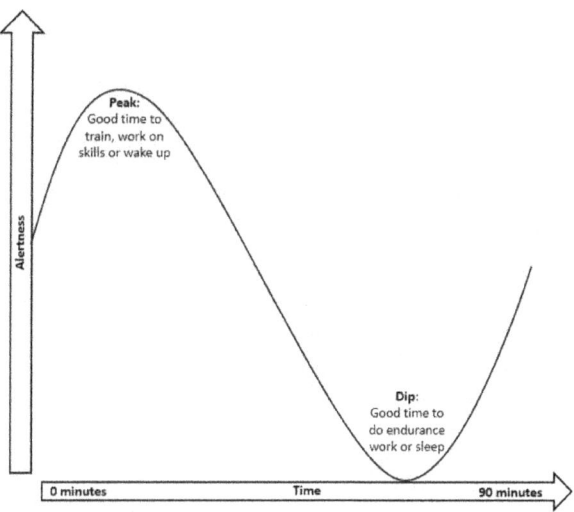

Each cycle within the circadian rhythm is about 90 minutes long and in that time we will have one peak (when we feel alert) and 45 minutes later a dip (when we feel lethargic). If we understand when our peaks and troughs are we can use them in our sport; in particular giving ourselves things to counteract the dips. When we try to do things in the wrong part of the 90 minutes (like go to sleep earlier when we have a peak because we have an early training) we usually fail. We need to move things in blocks of 90 minutes. We can spot our dips by noting down the times we start yawning. Any time we yawn during the day we take a note of the time and we can see the pattern by jotting up each set of 90 minutes.

If you figure out your circadian rhythm and make the dip between 9:30 and 11 pm your bedtime and then work out five and a half cycles later (8 1/4 hours) to wake up on a peak. If you have to be up very early for training (with ice skating, swimming), then work out the peak to wake up on and work backwards for a bedtime. Shift everything by an hour when the clocks go forward or backwards.

Date	Yawn 1	Yawn 2	Yawn 3	Yawn 4

> "I find sleep really hit or miss which is really frustrating. Some nights I sleep like a rock and I wake up and I'm like I must have been out for like 40 hours and other nights I'm waking up every once in a while, with my brain thinking about one thing after another thing after another thing and it's crazy stuff too that I logically know I shouldn't be thinking about. The nights that I'm not sleeping well are hard because then I have to wake up the next morning and just try to have energy for the training session." Brooke, Footballer

Adapting the circadian rhythm

To manipulate the circadian rhythm, especially if the onset of sleep is delayed (i.e. not able to sleep until the early hours of in the morning) some use Melatonin supplements (in the UK this needs to be prescribed) to help bring sleep forward. Taking Melatonin at the right time can shift your circadian rhythm – but this needs to be designed and worked on with a doctor. Light therapy is also used to help those with delayed sleep onset. Light therapy usually takes place in Autumn or Winter and involves reducing light exposure as much as possible before bed and using a light box for 30 minutes every morning at same time for up to three weeks. Doing this alongside gradually shifting sleep and wake up times can help to regulate the internal clock better. You want to be gradually shifting your bedtime back by 15 minutes a day. If you can't get a light box a morning walk aimed at increasing your light exposure is also really helpful.

STRESS MANAGEMENT

Living with a neurodiverse brain in a world designed for the neurotypical is going to see you dealing with additional stressors. On top of the stressors that everyone has to deal with in modern life, you also have to deal with the stressors that come from your ADHD symptoms and the stressors that sport can give us. Unhelpful coping mechanisms (avoidance, emotional ranting, drinking, hyperfocus) will often make issues worse so, instead of advising blanket coping mechanisms, it can be more effective to get to the route of the problem and identify the specific stressors (using the stressors list), connecting them with the emotion (using the emotional list) and then figure out a much more specific coping mechanism (using the coping wheel).

Stressors identification

It is not the number of stressors in our lives that causes us to have poor wellbeing – it is feeling like we don't have the capacity or capability to handle them. As a result we often fear trying to delve too deep into what is causing us stress. It is much easier to ignore it or focus on something else. The problem is that ignoring doesn't make any of the stressors go away – the only thing that does is tackling them. And we can only tackle them when we know exactly what they are.

Here is a list of 75 common stressors that we might be having to handle at any one time.

- Look through the list and tick off anything which is irritating you at the moment.
- Circle those you that you don't feel you have the capability or capacity to handle.

Some of the stressors might be ADHD related (losing things), some might be regular life (like tricky neighbours) and some might be totally irrelevant (menstrual problems if you are a man) but giving you this range to pick from should highlight enough areas to actively consider.

Misplacing or losing things	☐
Fear of confrontation	☐
Troublesome neighbours	☐
Not enough money for daily needs	☐
Not enough money to enjoy self	☐
Not enough money for future needs	☐
Social obligations	☐
Feeling lonely	☐
Concerns about accidents or injuries	☐
Troubling thoughts about the future	☐
Thoughts about death	☐
Health of a family member	☐
Too much time on your hands	☐
Unhelpful expectations from others	☐
Too many interruptions	☐
Concerns about owing money	☐
Being owed money	☐
Dislike those who work with or for	☐

- Financial responsibility for others ☐
- Caring responsibilities for children or partner ☐
- Caring responsibilities for other family members ☐
- Dislike work duties ☐
- Not having a job ☐
- Needing to reduce costs and bills ☐
- Concerns about retirement ☐
- Unhealthy habits (smoking, drinking, drugs) ☐
- Caring responsibilities for pets ☐
- Concerns about job security ☐
- Housekeeping responsibilities ☐
- Too many responsibilities ☐
- Trouble making decisions ☐
- Decisions about having children ☐
- Physical appearance (weight, height or looks) ☐
- Meal planning or preparation ☐
- Difficulties getting pregnant ☐
- Concerns about health or medical issues ☐
- Trouble relaxing ☐
- Worries around car, traffic or travel options ☐
- Fear of rejection ☐
- Worries around neighbourhood ☐
- Sexual problems or worries ☐
- Declining physical abilities ☐
- Not getting enough rest ☐
- Procrastinating or wasting time ☐
- Too much life admin ☐

Difficulties with romantic partner	☐
Difficulties with ex-partners	☐
Difficulties with sight or hearing	☐
Inequality or unfairness at work	☐
Inequality, unfairness or discrimination in life	☐
Feeling exploited	☐
Lack of sleep	☐
Too many meetings / calls on your time	☐
Problems with children / parents	☐
Worries about gossip	☐
Unchallenging work	☐
Concerns about meeting high standards	☐
Feeling conflicted about choices or decisions	☐
Trouble with reading, writing or maths	☐
Regrets over past decisions	☐
Menstrual problems	☐
Legal problems	☐
The weather	☐
Lacking energy	☐
Difficulties with friends	☐
Feeling unable to express yourself clearly	☐
Overload of family responsibilities	☐
Lack of financial security	☐
Not enough time for family	☐
Crime	☐
Pollution and environmental worries	☐
Not enough time for recreation	☐
Unable to maintain living accommodation	☐
Noise	☐

Sport-specific stressors

There are a number of additional stressors that you might be subject to if you are aiming to perform at a high level in sport:

- Selection (into a team or role) ☐
- Poor communication around role requirements ☐
- Issues around sponsorship or funding ☐
- Rivalries with others ☐
- Other behaviours or fears creating difficult atmosphere ☐
- Lack of support from leaders ☐
- Feeling expectation or pressure from others ☐
- Poor time management (self or others) ☐
- Missing equipment needed ☐
- Poor organiation (self or others) ☐
- Poor or unsafe training or event facilities ☐
- Outsiders interfering or disrupting ☐
- Disruptive weather / economic conditions ☐
- Officials behaving unfairly ☐
- Unexpected changes in format / structure ☐
- Needing to compete / perform too often ☐
- Performance equipment different to practice equipment ☐
- Unable to fuel performances effectively (self or others) ☐
- Difficult relationship with team ☐
- Difficult relationship with bosses / leadership / funders ☐
- Unhelpful coaching/leadership style ☐
- Organizational tactics / approach feeling outdated ☐
- Lack of technical information supplied ☐

- Not feeling like belonging in the team ☐
- Difficulty connecting or getting on with team-mates ☐
- Lack of technical or mental preparation ☐
- Confusion / poor communication around rules ☐
- Dealing with an illness or injury ☐
- Fear of illness or injury ☐
- Wanting to live up to previous standards ☐
- Feeling 'should' be able to do well ☐
- High expectations of self and abilities ☐
- High expectations from others ☐
- Feeling you need to win ☐
- Others wanting to beat me or my team ☐
- Worried about being dropped from team or sponsors ☐
- Worries around ranking / status / reputation ☐
- Media coverage ☐
- Media interviews ☐
- Others discussing you or your performance ☐
- Social media trolling ☐
- Worrying about letting leader down ☐
- Worrying about letting team-mates down ☐
- Worry about letting friends or family down ☐
- Competing against those who are considered better ☐
- Competing against those who are considered worse ☐
- Poor behaviours from competitors ☐
- Poor preparation to challenge ☐
- Overtrained / Burnt out ☐
- Over ambitious goals ☐

Emotions list

When you are clear on the stressors you are facing your next job is to identify the emotions they are triggering within you. Here are 100 of the most common 'uncomfortable' emotions which can trigger our threat system. Use the list to match an emotion to each stressor.

Afraid	Frustrated	Rejected
Aggravated	Furious	Reluctant
Agitated	Gloomy	Remorseful
Angry	Grumpy	Resentful
Annoyed	Guilty	Resigned
Anxious	Heartbroken	Resistant
Apprehensive	Helpless	Restless
Ashamed	Hesitant	Sad
Bitter	Hopeless	Scared
Bored	Hostile	Self-conscious
Burned out	Humiliated	Sensitive
Concerned	Impatient	Shaken
Confused	Impotent	Shocked
Cynical	Incapable	Sceptical
Depleted	Indifferent	Stressed
Depressed	Irate	Teary
Despair	Irritated	Tense
Despondent	Isolated	Terrified
Disappointed	Listless	Trapped
Disconnected	Lonely	Uneasy
Discouraged	Melancholy	Ungrounded
Disdain	Mortified	Unhappy
Disgruntled	Nervous	Unsettled
Dissatisfied	Numb	Unsure
Distant	On edge	Upset
Embarrassed	Outraged	Useless
Empty	Overwhelmed	Vulnerable
Exasperated	Panicked	Weak
Exhausted	Paralysed	Weary
Fearful	Perplexed	Withdrawn
Forlorn	Powerless	Worried
Fragile	Questioning	Worthless
Frazzled	Rattled	
Frightened	Regretful	

Coping wheel

Now you are clear on the stressor and the emotion it is triggering, have a look at the coping wheel and pick out the tool you want to try:

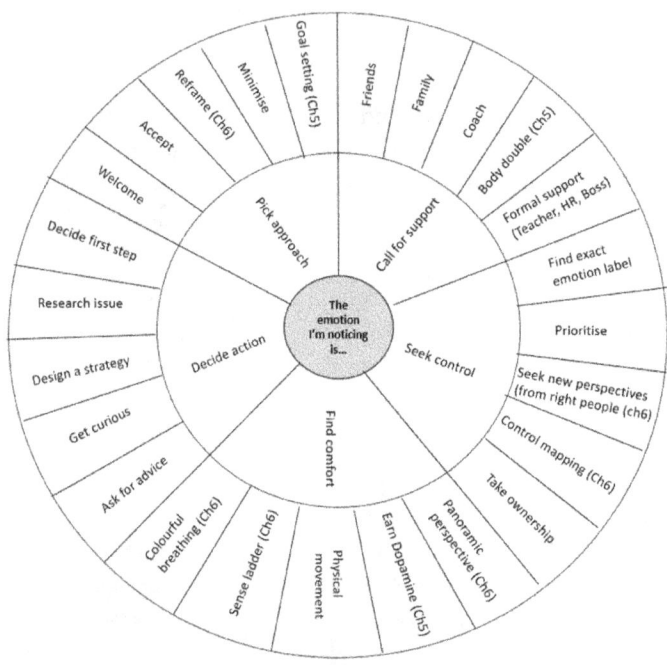

Stressor:	
Emotion:	
Coping mechanism:	

RACHEL'S STORY

Rachel is a Scottish cricketer who plays for the Northern Diamonds. She has combined type ADHD.

'I always struggled really badly with anxiety growing up and when I was 14 I got diagnosed with General Anxiety Disorder and Panic Disorder. I was taking a break from cricket [due to the anxiety] and Yorkshire cricket club sent me to see a psychiatrist. In my first session he recommended I get tested for ADHD. Before my diagnosis I assumed it was for the young boy in school who is bouncing off the walls and always causing trouble. I probably did have a few behavioural issues in school. I wasn't very well behaved, I used to get detentions and stuff like that, but academically I never struggled and I found school easy.'

'The way the psychiatrist explained it to me and spoke about it made a lot of sense and I thought it was probably a good route to take. When I got the diagnosis there was maybe a little bit of relief; I could start to see a path for things to get better and get back into cricket.'

'Now I take medication I don't know how I ever functioned without it. There were a few days when we were away on tour where I couldn't take it because you can only take a certain amount of the medication into the country [you can only take 28 days worth into Dubai] so I had to miss a few days. And the days that I didn't take it I was just wiped out. I'd go down and sit at breakfast for an hour and have a coffee and chat to people, and then I'd just end up sitting in my hotel room in bed all day because I was too tired to do anything.'

'When I was growing up I'd come home from school and nap for two hours because I was exhausted. I used to think that I'm just a tired person, but now I come home from training and I don't need to nap, so medication helps my energy levels, definitely. It also helps my concentration. I feel like I can choose what I want to apply myself to and actually do it. Before, if I went to the gym and I had the rest of the day with nothing to do, I'd go to the gym and I'd get halfway through and be like "I need to finish, I need to get home." So I'd rush through it a million miles an hour to get home quickly, and then get home and I'm like "I don't know why I've done that?" It's kind of as if you are always ticking, but for no reason. On medication I don't really get that as much. I feel a lot more calm and collected.'

'I'm a bowler and I bat low down the order. If we bat first I'd just be sat in a changing rooms or watching the game, chatting with my mates for three hours before I'm up to do anything and by the time I go out to bowl, I've got no energy to do anything. I feel so deflated. I have always been aware of that, but I just thought everyone else felt like that, I didn't realize that was not a normal thing, I just thought everyone's going to be a bit tired after chatting for a few hours. Now my social battery is better taking medication and I know how to boost it. If it's a long game, I'll try and take sugary sweets and snacks to try and give me a bit of energy, or have a coffee, or I'll take myself away for half an hour and do something else.'

'Looking back, it was so obvious. How much I used to sleep and nap. And being really bad for fidgeting. I had like a little blanket from when I was a baby and every night on the sofa I rub the label between my fingers, so much that the label doesn't exist anymore because I've worn it away. When I was about 10 or 11, I picked one of my eyebrows off just from fidgeting. I don't think it affects my life negatively but it is an obvious sign that was missed.'

'I don't think it's a coincidence that I'm having the best season of my life so far. This season I have done a lot of work in training that contributes to that but a big part of that is the fact that I'm taking medication now. Just to be able to not have to think about the distractions and just focus on my cricket is a big factor.'

'I'm not embarrassed about having ADHD. I don't think anyone ever should be. It is what it is and it's what makes some people different to others. But I think it is very misunderstood. I want people to understand it and to help me with it and be a good friend about it. The more people understand and actually know the ins and outs of it and the little details, the easier it is for everyone to deal with it.'

'I'm never going to sit here and say to people it makes you a superhero or it's a superpower because it's not. Overall, it's 100% affected me way, way more negatively than it has positively. But I think if you can get it under control and you can get help for it and you understand it then there's no reason why the positive sides of it can't still be there. If you take the positives and the negatives of my ADHD in cricket overall it was a massive negative effect. I wouldn't ever sugarcoat that and try and pretend that it wasn't, because it was.'

'The positive though would be the hyperfocus. When I was 15, I tore my ACL playing football and throughout my rehab process I would get up at 6am before school to do part of my rehab, I'd come home from school and do the rest of my rehab. Every single day for seven months. I was just like obsessed with it and I don't think I would be like that if I didn't have ADHD. A similar thing with my training is if I become obsessed with, "I wanna work on this," or if I'm in a training session and I'm really involved in it, I can just keep going, and physical tiredness just gets overridden. If I am obsessed with it and I just want to carry on with it that will have a positive effect because I can do more training.'

'It is important to have a really deep understanding of what your ADHD means for you and what you need in different situations. For me the biggest thing I have learnt is that I need space and time to myself to recharge and de-stress and get away from any other stimulus. If you're not having that space and time for yourself, it does get quite a lot, and it does get quite intense. So that is the biggest thing for me, understanding what I need, and not being afraid of doing that.'

CHAPTER **5**

Training strategies

Having great strategies in place to help you train effectively and efficiently for your sport doesn't change your ADHD symptoms but they will help you manage and lessen their impact. Here are lots of tools and techniques that might help you manage your time more effectively, be more organized, focus on things which need to be prioritized, build in routines and habits, and handle some of the self-sabotaging that can show up in sport.

COINS

Coming from Spoon Theory, a concept used within the chronic illness community, the idea focuses on how the energy we have to spend each day is limited. We can take on caffeine and good nutrition and boost our energy, but we will all run out at some point. Thinking about our energy as coins (virtual modules of energy, effort and attention) that we get to spend can help us think about how and when we use energy so that we manage it more effectively.

The concept directs us to think about how, if we wake up well rested, we have 100 coins to spend that day. The way we allocate our coins will change each day depending on our requirements, the environment around us and the other people we interact with. Sometimes the amount of coins required for an activity changes too: a difficult match against your biggest local rivals will use up far more coins than a friendly against the B team and a 90 minute easy relaxed run listening to your favourite podcast will use fewer coins that a 30 minute track session.

With ADHD how we spend our coins is really important because you can get hyperfocused very easily and use up all your energy on something you enjoy but wasn't strictly necessary today and have no coins left over for the things that should be prioritized for your wellbeing, health or work. You might also have a really difficult or stressful or boring activity to do and you need to ensure you have enough coins for it or you are unlikely to start it.

This means it is essential you figure out what in your sporting and day to day life uses up significant amounts of coins so you can plan in when you spend them and don't have too many coin heavy things on the same day. The good news is you can earn back coins to put into your mental wallet through activities which give you Dopamine, purposefully building them into your day ensure you don't go into coin debt.

If you can sketch out an average week and consider all the elements of each day that require coins. How may would you allocate to each activity?

Activities for athletes that might well cost lots of coins include:

- Competitions
- Team or club socializing
- Big, heavy effort workouts
- Travel
- Having to sleep away from home
- Sharing rooms
- Sponsorship activities or media events

Then what earns you back coins? What will make you feel reinvigorated (often this will be your Dopamine list (next strategy) plus some self-care activities like a walk with a friend, a dance class, really good sleep, a couple of episodes of your current Netflix craving, stroking your dog) and how many coins might that earn you back. You might want to put some coins put aside for the unexpected things; an urgent work request, a child that is poorly, a sporting injury that needs medical or physio treatment. These annoyances all use up coins and, if we are depleted, tend to push us into emotional exhaustion and meltdown territory.

When you are about to log off for the day look at what you have coming up tomorrow; work, school, sporting practice, gym work or caring for others and allocate coins. How many do you have left? Do you need some self-care or Dopamine fixes to balance out what you are spending? Then, ideally plan in the harder (and most coin draining) things early (to reduce anticipatory anxiety) and if they are too big and too scary chunk them down into 25 minute chunks and get that Dopamine buzz from doing the hardest thing which makes you feel good for the rest of the day and allows you to match trickier tasks to your brainpower at that moment and, if you are on medication, allow you to get the most out of being on the medication before it wears off in the afternoon. This also reduces your risk of ruminating at night when you try to sleep because you have a plan in place for the next day.

How you spend your coins becomes extra important with ADHD because focus and attention on a task (especially one you don't intrinsically enjoy) can use up a lot of coins and you need to give yourself regular recovery breaks and rewards to replenish them. Rewards, positive self-talk, exercise, meditation, glucose, thinking about future events have all been found to top up your wallet so you can get going again. Thinking about what drains and what tops up your coin wallet will help you plan your day so that you have fewer moments of feeling overwhelmed and under fuelled.

Reflect on these four questions…

What in my life uses lots of coins?	
What in my sport uses lots of coins?	
What self-care activities will earn me coins?	
How could I spread out coin usage so I don't go into debt?	

EARN DOPAMINE

When a task is too challenging or too boring we tend to get task inertia and find an opportunity to shy away from it through procrastination, procrastivity, excuse making or avoidance. The solution to getting that task done is to increase the energy you have available to give to it. Scaffolding (the next strategy) can help us to see if we can add any novelty or interest into the task and then, if not, promising to reward ourselves afterwards with a Dopamine hit. Our brain will be tempted in go for the Dopamine hit first but this leaves us little incentive to do the task. We need to see the Dopamine as something to earn. So firstly, set a timer to give the task a sense of urgency. Secondly, track what you are doing – seeing these figures as achievements can help give you that Dopamine buzz and then have a list of things which earn you Dopamine.

Some common Dopamine earners:

- [ ] Exercise
- [ ] Dancing
- [ ] Baking
- [ ] Cooking
- [ ] Games
- [ ] Jigsaws
- [ ] Lego
- [ ] Laundry
- [ ] Studying a language
- [ ] Chatting with a close friend
- [ ] Hanging out with pets
- [ ] Crafting
- [ ] Gaming
- [ ] Woodwork or DIY project

> "If I'm doing uni work, I know that in half an hour, I can go and put the laundry in the washing machine, and that's such a short task, but I get quite a lot of Dopamine from that because I feel like I've achieved something. I call them Dopamine breaks." Isla, Cyclist

DAILY SCAFFOLDING

With ADHD you usually know exactly what you need to do but sometimes don't do it. This is down to deficits in your executive functions (organization, timing, planning, working memory) reducing motivation and action. One way to take the load away from your executive functions is to outsource the action elements through putting up the equivalent of mental scaffolding.

> *"There's a lot executive functioning needed around sport. Not just the actual doing of it, but the scaffolding around it."* Jen, Runner

- Timings: Have visual timers around you for each activity, practice or conditioning or stretching routines. The digital clock and alarm on your phone can be used but sometimes an analogue clock can help you notice the passing of time more effectively.

- Reduce the need for willpower: In ADHD immediate consequences are craved so using willpower to wait for something is unlikely to happen. If you can, block notifications on your phones, install internet blockers or put your phone elsewhere when you need to be able to focus.

- Kit box: Having a kit box for each sport you do, that everything goes in once back from practice or once it is washed means you'll save hours hunting around for things you need. For other items that you need in day-to-day life as well (like keys or wallet) then Airtags and trackers can help you find them.

- Automatic payments or regular purchases: Having sporting or club memberships on direct debit means you won't have to be chased to pay. Having regular orders of nutrition or hydration requirements mean they show up automatically and you don't go without them.

- Externalize to-dos: You may well have lots of lists or goals running round in your head but you need these externalized so you don't have to internally manage lots of information. You can use post-it notes, voice notes, whiteboards, phone alarms, texts or smart speakers to help you 'see' that information at the point you need to use it.

- Amplify consequences: ADHD brains will think of 'now' and 'the future'. Most consequences sit in 'the future' so they don't give us the fear that they should in order to work towards achieving or avoiding them. When we are more aware of the consequences we will feel more motivation to get it done. This might mean asking your coach for weekly rather than monthly catch ups or for them to request video footage of gym work so that you respond to that artificial consequence and do what is required.

Remove training distractions: A 2019 study of college students with ADHD reported that staying focused is their number one challenge living with ADHD. For this reason, creating as few distractions as possible in any environment you are in can be crucial for goal completion. If you find yourself getting easily distracted remove the temptation. If you lose 15 minutes of gym time to playing on your phone, then lock your phone into your locker. If you know that every time your phone pings you will look at it, then place it in another room or silence your alerts. If you know that a messy environment will distract your post training routine find a tidier space to stretch and cool down.

Build in buffer time: Buffer time is planning for the unexpected and being honest that your ADHD often makes you misjudge how long things will genuinely take. To build in buffer time double the time you think a task will take so you have much less chance of being late.

Set up accountability partners: Ideally this will be with another team member or same sport athlete with ADHD. Having someone to check in with and be accountable to feels like a deadline and you can benefit from hard deadlines. If your ADHD is also mixed with perfectionism then these deadlines and the keenness to people please will also push you to complete the task set.

Visual aids: As you will have read in chapter 1, if we are feeling under threat (which might be more often than others will if we have ADHD) then we struggle to access our logical decision making function where we have stored the knowledge of what we should be doing and instead emotion takes over. Having visual aids that physically remind us of what we should be doing keeps that knowledge front of mind.

> "I have a calendar on my phone and it sends me a notification. Because if I have a calendar on the wall, and it's written down, I'll just walk past that every day and blank it, because it blends into your surroundings and becomes a normal thing to walk past." Olivia, Cricketer

GOAL SETTING

When we struggle to connect potential consequences in the future with what we need to do now we can make some amazing plans, feel super motivated to achieve them, and then they drop into the back of our mind and we panic last minute when we realize the day is upon us and all the things we meant to do didn't happen. Goal setting helps it become clearer as to what you need to do (the processes) to achieve the results (performances) you want to achieve your overall (outcome) goal.

There are numerous studies which show that setting clear, specific, realistic and timely goals (especially those within an athlete's control) can increase their motivation, commitment, concentration and confidence. In particular goal setting can help you to focus on processes over outcome, reduce the need for comparisons with other athletes (which can cause you to freeze) and can give you reassuring confidence that you have prepared to the best of your abilities.

Goal setting helps you do what you struggle with the most; turning intentions into actions. You will need to consider every element required for your success; planning physical training, practising mental strategies, understanding the logistics, strength and conditioning and nutrition. You need to be strict about having only one outcome goal (otherwise you get distracted and have some inbuilt excuses for not focusing on the hardest one) and then you can break that down into performance goals (these might be times or distances or scores – usually something measurable) that an athlete can see will help them hit their outcome goal and then broken down again into the process goals that will be required to make it happen. The process goals are most important as these are the elements of your practice (the behaviours, actions, strategies and tactics) you will want to turn into routines and habits.

You will mess up and miss sessions here and there but this is not a reason to beat yourself up. It is an opportunity to keep assessing whether you are working on the right things at the right time.

When you have worked out what these processes will be then putting them into sporting diaries, give them to your coach and build in scaffolding activities to ensure the processes are actioned.

> "How I schedule my days now has got a lot easier for me and has helped me be productive with my energy, I'm not punishing myself all the time for not being able to do things." Isla, Cyclist

TRAINING STRATEGIES 97

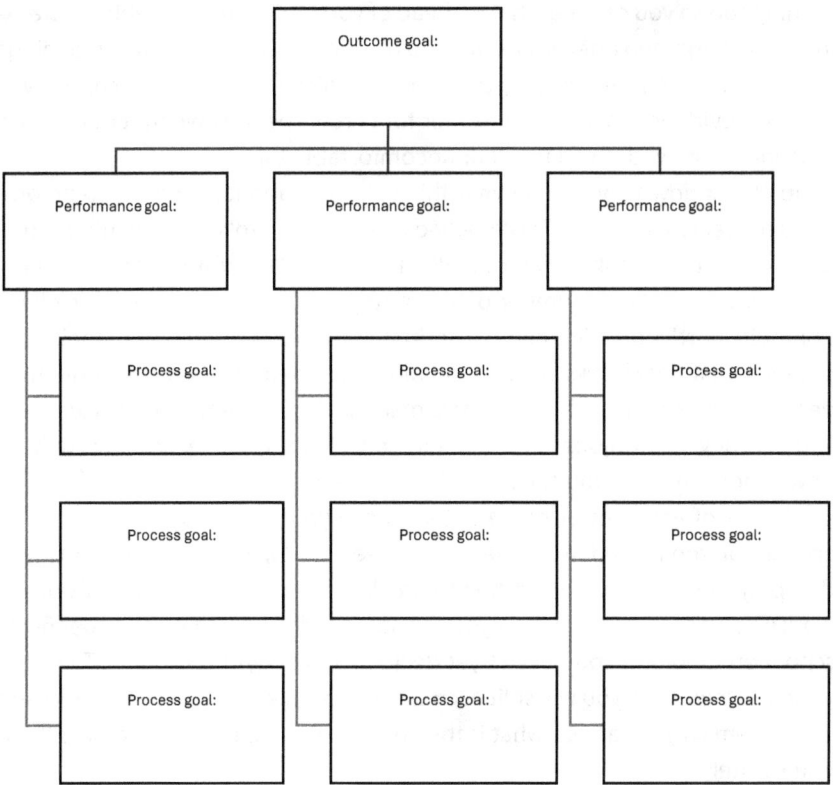

CHUNKING DOWN

When you have too much on your plate, have things on your to do list that are really dull or know that you need to do boring but essential tasks like stretching or sports admin then it can feel overwhelming. Breaking things into chunks can make them feel more manageable and may even help you preserve your attention. It is thought it may work due to the way that when we anticipate a reward, Dopamine is released. So breaking things down into smaller sections will help us get mini-surges of pleasure each time we achieve one of them. The more achievements we have, the more often we get our Dopamine shot.

    This is a great approach to use in competition to make it feel less intimidating and pressured – and in fact many sports do this automatically with quarters, halves, rounds and sets. It means you can be more strategic or tactical with the processes you follow at each specific point, increasing your chances of achieving your ultimate competition goal. Chunking can be used day to day in training too so you can see what is ahead of you is more manageable by breaking down large, and often scary, training plans or sessions into bite sized things that are easier to face. Not only this, having achieved lots of these 'chunks' will give you evidence that you can suffer for certain periods when required and that you coped with the difficult or uncomfortable thing.

To chunk down your next event think about it about a week or so beforehand to create a timeline. This timeline can then be broken down into natural breaks; quarters or halves (for football, rugby or cricket), distances (for running, swimming or cycling), number of attempts (for jumps or throws), disciplines (for multisport), bouts (for combat sports) or rounds or games (for tennis, golf or fencing). If the chunks still feel too big break them down further until they get to a level where each chunk feels manageable. Once the chunks are clear you can devise a physical and mental strategy for each section and write it down somewhere so you can refer to it between chunks.

The list of activities or process goals from your chunking won't take into account all the individual elements you need to do, in order, in order to tick that project off so you need a 'first things' list. 'Sign up to gym classes' doesn't work if you don't know whether you can sort childcare for that day or get finish school on time or if you haven't yet decided which gym you prefer. To create your first things list, you will split each task into smaller and smaller chunks and order them so you can see what is the first thing to do. Then do that first thing immediately.

CREATING A COMMUNICATION PASSPORT

The difficulties with staying on task, poor organization and only seeing 'now' or 'the future' mean that time management can be really difficult. The brain areas associated with time perception are those impacted by the ADHD which can cause time blindness, a lack of perception of time so you have difficulty estimating how long a task will take or how long you have spent on a task. This can mean a difficult relationship with a coach who doesn't understand that you might be late, why you don't always have the kit you need, why you are more anxious than they think you need to be and how to stop you getting fixated on specific elements of your sport. A communication passport can help explain that.

Communication passports for athletes can provide a short cut to the hours of rapport building that can be required for a coach and athlete to get to know each other. It helps you pull together your views, the ways you work best and distils them together into a clear, positive and accessible format so you can both make better sense of events. Your communication passport should be a simple, clear, direct, honest, specific and detailed summary of key information to help others know how to get the best from you. It can be really helpful if you have a number of different people you work with in your sport or if you change coach.

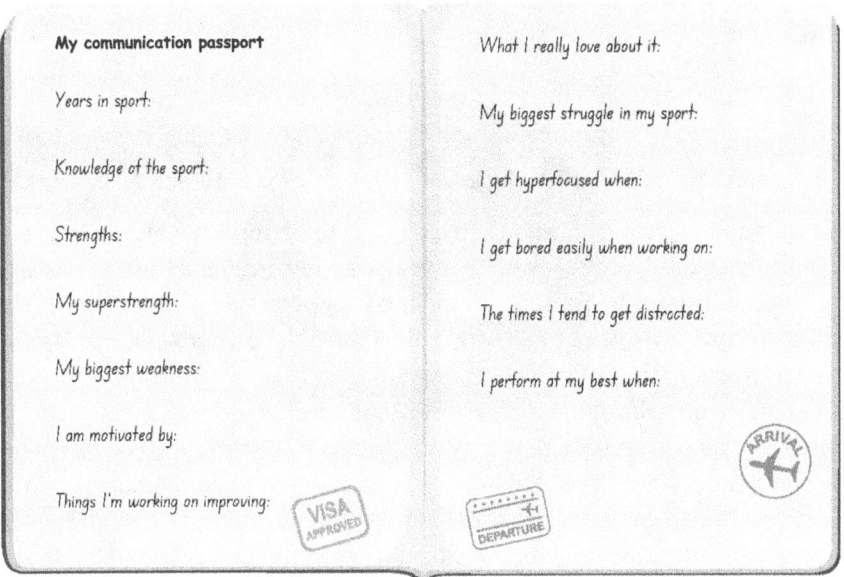

> "I need calm around me, probably an antidote to the internal chaos, in order to regulate my nervous system enough to execute what I'm trying to do." Jen, Runner

PRIORITIZING PREPARATION

One of our biggest and most robust sources of confidence in sport is feeling well prepared. When we don't, and also throw in issues around anxiety, organization and time management we are prone to feeling overwhelmed. The better you can prepare for your sporting training and events (usually by turning the actions you need to do into habits) then the better you will feel heading into them. For competition you might want to create a packing list of everything you will require and design a pre-event routines so nothing vital gets forgotten. Day to day, prioritizing tasks, having a kit box and having easy to grab snacks / breakfast in the fridge will keep you going and create less chaos when trying to get out the door.

When we struggle with preparation we tend to do two things; procrastination (where we put off tasks till later – often leaving ourselves no time at all to do it properly) and procrastivity (where you do easier but less important tasks first to make us feel good – even though we have still ignored the important thing). Being aware of this can help us question more… why am I doing this task?

BUILDING HABITS AND ROUTINES

As we learnt in chapter 1, when you are trying to perform at a high level there will be three parts of your brain that you need to consider so you can reflect on which elements might sometimes limit your potential. When we can build up all the things we need to do within our habit function our ADHD gets fewer opportunities to throw us off track.

Research on habits from University College London suggests (on average) it takes 66 days to develop a new habit so this should be built into your preparation and expectation. If you have only just started learning something new you won't yet have it embedded so shouldn't get frustrated about why it still needs energy and effort to remember and put into practice. Doing something every day for two months will really help to embed it, especially if it is a totally new skill you are learning.

This is where the concept of a 'non-zero day' can come in. It's point is to keep up momentum towards building a new habit and so you do one activity (however small) towards each performance goal every day so you build the habit quicker.

Another way to try to speed up developing new habits is 'habit stacking'. This is where you add an action you would like to develop into a habit after something you already automatically do. Think about when you brush your teeth, right afterwards you might also floss or rinse out with mouthwash. Then you might wash your face and apply moisturiser. Each of these individual habits 'stacks' up until you have a routine that you don't need to proactively think about and it means you become more likely to follow helpful and healthy behaviours. Morning routines like this can be particularly helpful when you are taking ADHD medication so that you don't forget to take it. In being able to embed actions into habits and finding order where you can through routines and habits you free up brain capacity for more cognitively demanding tasks that would otherwise significantly fatigue you.

BECOME AN EXPERT IN YOU

There are (hopefully) lots of techniques in this book that might be able to help you with the way ADHD manifests but most important is that you understand how your ADHD impacts you. A wide range of research has found that teaching those with ADHD (and those they live with) about their symptoms can be really effective in improving core symptoms, reducing behavioural issues and conflicts and increasing adherence to medication. Looking through chapter 3 and ticking off all the symptoms you notice in yourself can help you to build this awareness and understanding.

Wider elements will concern your sex. These might be centred around whether your behaviours are externalizing or internalizing and how hormonal surges influence your symptoms. Whilst very reductive, in general we tend to see that males will externalize many of the ADHD behaviours (so the hyperactivity and impulsivity may present as aggression or risky behaviours) and females tend to have more internalizing behaviours (like struggling with emotional and relationship issues). This might mean as a male athlete with ADHD you need to focus more on your behavioural control or as a female building up emotional and mood focused support. Both genders should also consider how their ADHD symptoms can be influenced by hormone surges at different times of life like puberty. Females specifically need to consider how their menstrual cycle, pregnancy and menopause might impact their symptoms.

It is also really important as an athlete though that you understand how you function in your sport because as you develop in your sport it is not just your ADHD and your sport you become an expert in but how you personally behave within your sport. Becoming an authority on yourself helps you to become far more self-aware of your likes, dislikes, preferences and fears so you can design or adapt your competition environment to maximize your performance preferences and avoid those elements which reduce your enjoyment and potential success.

One of the biggest areas to understand is your own personality and the way your traits may impact on your sporting preferences and performances. If you are high in extroversion you might benefit from the external stimulation of working with a team or training for a race and you are more likely to stick to plans if there is a social element to it. High in introversion (where you recharge your batteries by being alone) then you can feel overwhelmed by too much external stimulation and will benefit from exercising alone at times. Your ADHD focus on novelty might mean you have high levels of openness; making you keen to try new exercises or ideas (we sometimes call this Magpie Syndrome when attracted to all the new shiny things) and it can make you an early adopter of new technologies or gadgets. If you are high in perfectionism then you may work very hard in their training but struggle with the pressure of competition. Those with an external locus of control may believe that things will happen to them and that others control outcomes – this may reduce the amount of impact they feel they have on the outcome of a competition, feeling any success is down to luck rather than their efforts.

Identify your sporting preferences:

Safety	Who do you feel safe with?	
	Who do you like to have around you?	
	What do you like them to say?	
Time management	How early do you like to show up for competitions or training?	
	What strategies and tools can you put in place to ensure this happens?	
Food and drink	What food or drinks do you like before or after training or during competition?	
	If your medication means you lose appetite what can you put in place to fuel training and recovery?	
	What plans do you need in place for competition day?	
	Do you have a stash of your favourite snacks for competition day?	
Injury management	Do you like to hide away or spend time with sporting peers?	
	Do you have specific coping mechanisms for injury?	
	Do you have 'go to' experts for when you are injured?	
	How do you return from injury; throw yourself back in, step in cautiously or get lots of help?	
	How do you take steps to prevent getting injured again?	

(Continued)

Knowing your 'why'	List three reasons you do your sport	
	Which of these reasons helps you when you feel overwhelmed?	
Training preferences	Do you prefer to train alone or in groups?	
	Do you prefer to train in short bursts of concentration or in a steady manner?	
	Do you like to have training partners or find them frustrating?	
	Does teamwork give you helpful responsibility or stressful expectations?	
Getting to the right **arousal level**.	How do you get to the right level of arousal before competition?	
	Do you like to chat to manage nerves or to have your own space and quietness.	
Which **coping mechanisms** work best for you	Do you have a 'go to' breathing technique for when you feel under threat?	
	Do you have a 'go to' grounding tool for when you feel under threat?	
	Do you have process goals to follow in training?	
	Do you have process goals to follow in competition?	
	Do you have a 'team' of people you know have your back?	

> "In the FA cup, before kick-off, I focused on looking for my parents in the stand, it gave me a task to focus on instead of feeling other things around me." Brooke, Footballer

BODY DOUBLING

The presence of others can help you to focus, allowing you to procrastinate less and not feel so overwhelmed. We can use this knowledge when we have something important to do by 'body doubling'. 'Body doubling' is the practice of having another person present while you try to complete a task so that you are in the company of others (using accountability) but working towards your own individual goal (so you don't procrastinate). Studies find that body doubling can be particularly effective in physical activity. The sense of community – even from just one person people alongside you – boosts enjoyment levels and increases participation. To body double someone you complete a task of similar nature to the one that they are doing. You might not have to be working on the same cricket skills or doing the same number of reps or distance at the track but being there, completing tasks at the same time, in the presence of each other helps you focus on what you need to achieve.

Someone who might be a good body double for me is:	

BEHAVIOURAL SKILLS TRAINING

There is an increasing amount of evidence for using psychosocial interventions like behavioural skills training in ADHD. These techniques have been seen as effective in improving specific sports skills, game knowledge, sportsmanship, and gross motor proficiency.

A specific area of behavioural skills training are social skills training where you practise to improve 'small c' communication skills (like voice volume, tone and body positioning) and 'big c' communication skills (like offering compliments, providing constructive feedback, turn-taking, listening skills, conflict resolution or being assertive). These can all make day to day interactions easier and help you 'play the games' that feel like they shouldn't be necessary but often are if you are to progress to where you want to get to in high level sport. One of the best ways to facilitate learning all these skills is through role playing. This can be done ahead of a specific interaction that you might find intimidating like an interview, selection trial day or meeting with sponsors.

Another area of behavioural skills training will be to learn specific problem-solving strategies – tools you can use to think constructively about a problem so you can come up with flexible and effective ways to deal with it. In fact, many with ADHD cite one of their strengths as being able to problem solve in a way that is unlikely to have been considered by others, and when you have been functioning in a neurotypical world with a neurodiverse mind you may well have already developed an array of unique strategies to problem solve. The goal then is to have confidence in using them so positive self-talk can be used here to 'think out loud' when engaged in a task and talk yourself through it and use self-monitoring to assess how well it works for you.

REDUCING PROCRASTINATION

Procrastination is a really common side effect of ADHD as you will have a number of reasons to hold off on what you know you should be doing. Identifying the causes can give you clear elements to focus on to reduce it.

Cause	Solutions
The task is boring	Turn it into a game Make it competitive in some way Add in rewards Listen to great music or a podcast while doing it.
Feeling hyperactive	Move! Use up some energy with sport or exercise. This is why some athletes like to train earlier in the day so they make the most of the hyperactive feeling.
Can't motivate myself to start	Keep things that you will react to (emails staring at you in an inbox, voice notes asking you to do it, post it notes) Body double with someone else so you have an incentive Get someone else to set you a deadline
The task is overwhelming	Chunk it down into much smaller sections Give yourself a reward after ticking off each section Do some Colourful Breathing or the Senses Ladder until you feel calmer and better able to tackle one of the tasks. Touch the task – find something within the task that is simple and easy and do just that element of it – often the rest will follow,
I'm too disorganized	Think about where you might start the task and physically go there. Write down what you will need (equipment or others' input) in order to complete. Estimate how much time it will take to complete – double that! Chunk down the task into 15 minute blocks Put the blocks into a realistic timeline – and set calendar reminders for each Agree just to do the first block.
Using procrastivity instead	Sometimes known as 'productive procrastination' this is where we stay busy by doing less important tasks – but still feel unproductive and stressed because the big, real tasks is still hanging over you.

JAMES' STORY

James is an amateur equestrian showjumper.

'I'm not yet fully diagnosed. I'm on the really long waiting list, about a year and a half in, but I found once I started to look at my struggles as ADHD it immediately changed something; explained things. It might be a reason why I seemed intelligent in school but pretty much failed my exams at GCSE. Why I struggle with reading, why I am easily distractable, why I get obsessed with things, why I let myself get in certain situations.'

'However, that overlying label tells you nothing. I think one of the reasons why I never explored an ADHD diagnosis until I started looking at it differently was because the archetypal view of what ADHD was didn't identify with how I was. I wasn't an obvious ADHD child. I was fairly well-behaved. I just didn't apply myself particularly well in the teachers' eyes.'

'If I was interested in something, I'd work really hard on it. if I wasn't interested in something, it was hard for me to engage. When it came to writing an essay, I just couldn't do it and exams didn't work very well. My dad was very intelligent, and my sisters got into private schools and they did very well and got good GCSEs and then I came out of my GCSEs with two Cs in double science. And nothing else. I was also really bad at timekeeping and was nicknamed "Late again Lovatt" by my teachers.'

'At school I played a lot of rugby and basketball. What I used to find with sport, is that I'd either be useless at it, or really, really good, and rarely exist in between. With horses though I didn't even have to be really good at it.'

'When you ride a horse you want a horse to shape itself in a certain way. A common way is to bring it into that shape is through manipulation whereas I understood that the reason why that happens if because of what this leg is doing, so if the horse steps under itself more, then it will have to lift the neck up and bring the nose in in order to balance against that force coming from behind the hind leg. And so that flow of energy made sense to me.'

'I think I've got synaesthesia so I see how things interact. So when I look at a horse, I can see how the hind leg interacts with this, interacts with this, interacts with this, so I kind of see a flow and a rhythm and all those things make sense to me. That allowed me to become quite good at solving problems with horses and that sort of built the obsession.'

'Once I got into riding I ended up working in the riding school for free that summer and then I applied for agricultural college to do equine studies and just became completely obsessed. Now I've got two horses. One's retired, one's in work and I do some showjumping and dressage.'

'It is hard to know if my strengths are coming from the ADHD or are they coming from my cognitive individuality. I think certainly having that focus is beneficial. I also think the difficulties help you develop different problem-solving approaches, because you don't generally succeed in normal environmental approaches to things, you look for alternative ways of doing things. I think in the sporting environment, where that's nurtured, that slightly different way of solving a standard problem can give you the competitive edge.'

'In showjumping the mistake I am most likely to make is to forget the course. A common situation is that I go into a flow state and I end up making up my own course because I'm just going to the next logical fence rather than what's specified on the course. One time my horse was jumping really well and I come off a fence, see a combination over there which was a logical fence for me to go to. And I was like "yeah, we're in our flow and he jumped in beautifully." But then the buzzer went, and I was like "oh, I've been eliminated." So I could feel me and the horse were in deep connection, in total harmony, total balance, but I'd lost track of the world around me.'

'It's my responsibility to fix that problem and to do that I visualize and imagine myself riding the course and I am pre-imagining how I'm going to cut corners or make approaches. If I change my mind mid-course, I'm more likely to make a mistake. Therefore, I need to be much more focused on my planning as to how I'm going to do it. It forces me to ask questions that probably a lot of other people don't need to answer. But in those answers you get certain benefits.'

'Ultimately, if you consistently experience issues with executive functioning, you've got a fairly good track record of making mistakes and doing things wrong. And there's only so much pointing out of that that you can take. I know I find things a bit more difficult, I just need the freedom to solve this problem for myself, and then if you give me that space, I'll do a better job than I will if you force that solution upon me, because the way you make me change is not going to be the way that's going to work best for me. I think that desire for autonomy and freedom to solve problems for yourself mainly comes from the fact that whenever people try to solve problems for you, they've never done a very good job. As they've not understood you properly.'

'If you have those difficulties in executive functioning, you've got that determination perhaps through the hyperfocus to really go for it anyway, then you will develop strategies that probably a lot of other people won't use. And that will give you a bit of an edge. I think that strategy has come from me understanding myself better and knowing why I have, make them things I do.'

CHAPTER **6**

Competition strategies for ADHD athletes

The last two chapters have hopefully given you some tool and strategies for day-to-day wellbeing and training as an athlete with ADHD. This chapter focuses on strategies for the competition phase. All three areas are required if we are to perform well but it is the moment at which you need to step up and complete a difficult task (like competing in a race or using skills in a football match) that we most often consider 'performance'. When an athlete has ADHD we want to look at these moments to see which executive functions are not being employed to get the job done and consider what can be done to instead increase the pool of self-regulation tools to be able to achieve the goal.

Many of the strategies and tools in this chapter are ones that will be beneficial for any athlete to perform better. They are included in this chapter though as they will specifically help to balance out some of the ADHD traits that can be unhelpful for sport; in particular around impulsivity, emotional dysregulation and executive function which is it valuable to be able to manage when you are in a competitive environment.

CONTROL MAPPING

Competition outcomes are rarely controllable – well certainly not in a way that is legal! Even the world's best athletes will have a bad day, an injury or unexpected conditions every now and again. It is very easy to worry about the uncontrollables but it is entirely wasted energy which could be much better used on something you can actually control and would positively impact your performance.

Control mapping can help you identify which areas impact your performance and, within that, what you can and can't influence. When you notice your brain fixating on something you can't control a control map gives you a list of where to switch your mind to instead; allowing you to take more responsibility for the things you can control and influence and stop wasting effort and attention on elements you can't.

Here are some areas to consider when you list out what you can control, may be able to influence, and what you cannot control. Tick where each may sit for you and your sport.

Area	Can control	Possibly influence	No control
Performance environment (surface, venue facilities)			
Personal worries			
Nutrition / hydration			
Weather			
Kit			
Equipment			
Logistics of travel			
Warm up times and facilities			
General supporters			
Family or friends supporting			
Own attitude, skills, effort levels, thoughts, feelings & behaviours.			
Competitors (their attitude, effort levels & behaviours)			
Officials (their attitude, effort levels & behaviours)			
Managers or coaches (their attitude, effort levels & behaviours)			
Team-mates (their attitude, effort levels & behaviours)			
Results or outcomes			
Costs			

STRENGTHS AUDIT

If you have spent much of your life feeling like you need to 'mask' or behave a specific way in order to 'fit in' then your strengths can get a little lost. When we add to this the fact you may also have had years of being told 'you can't' or you are too slow to respond or you got things wrong because you weren't listening properly, your head chatter can start to mirror that negativity. Instead of assessing the competition in front of us and seeing opportunities to score or shine we see opportunities to fail. If we head back to chapter 1 we can remember that our brain's most central, vital job, is our safety – so our brain gets very good at remembering the negatives because they will remind us not to try doing them again and risk our physical, psychological or physiological safety. To balance out this negativity bias we need to actively focus on our strengths, in fact neuroscientists have found that for every negative thought we have, we require five positive ones to stay in a good place.

Focusing on our own strengths can remind us of our skills and of what we should do more of. It helps us develop what we can do, rather than consuming the head chatter that tells us what we can't. Capturing these thoughts in one place as evidence can be like a shopkeeper conducting a stocktake to know what they have to sell. If you can conduct a strengths audit you can better recognize and value your powers so you can use them more to boost your performance.

A strengths audit is a list of all those elements which make you feel confident you can achieve your goals. If you have proactively identified your strengths ahead of a competition and have them somewhere you can visually see them, then you have them front of mind when you need them. This can help you boost your confidence and focus on doing what you do best. Without this, when you are under pressure and your threat system has triggered then those positive memories (and the strengths they highlight) become inaccessible. Let's do yours.

You will be looking to identify 12 strengths (two in each area). You can get these through looking back through your training diary, reflecting on your best performances or by asking a coach or peer who has observed you regularly in your sport.

Area	Strength 1	Strength 2
Fitness		
Sporting strategies		
Physical strength		
Sport specific skills		
Mindset		
Support		

When your strengths audit is complete keep a copy of it in your kit bag or wallet so whenever you feel nervous and your brain is telling what you cannot do, you have something to look through and remember all the areas you are strongest and all the things you can do.

SURROUND YOURSELF WITH THE RIGHT PEOPLE

You will see above that we asked you to consider strengths that might come from having good support in place. This is because many people with ADHD can struggle with relationships (either under or over-investing) and may also struggle with social anxiety so regulating social effort becomes important. Consider who in your life has an impact on your social battery; either draining it or charging it.

Those who charge your social battery will be those you can relax with and not worry about how they may interpret your traits so you don't feel the need to mask. Those draining you will make you want to hide away and will make heading into any type of competition tricky. Who are your people?

- A person I like to speak to getting ready for competition:

- A person who makes me feel calmer in competition:

- A person who helps me feel better about any mistakes I make:

- A person who can make me laugh:

- A person who I find helpful to analyse competition with:

- The people I should avoid on competition days because they distract me are:

- The people I should avoid on competition days because they irritate me are:

When you are clear on who the positive people are try to build in a regular time to check in with them. This might be while waiting for transport, during your cool down, stretching routine at the gym or when waiting for the kettle to boil – but making it habitual will ensure you keep those people in your life.

Try to collect any positive messages you get from this group of people. Maybe an email file you put them in or a list on a board. Good people telling us good things about ourselves helps to boost our confidence significantly.

POT OF POWER

If the negative head chatter pops up before a competition it can soothed a little by reminding ourselves what we can do well. The strengths audit helps this but so does a Pot of Power. OK – so a super cheesy name but collecting together all the difficult, brilliant or scary things we have do so far in our life can remind ourselves that we can do hard things, even when we are feeling daunted by them. The goal is to be able to think back on times when you persevered despite the discomfort you felt.

To create your Pot of Power find a small box or jar, clean it out and get fifteen small (matchbox sized) pieces of paper. Write down:

- Five times you achieved something of which you are really proud.

- Four times you achieved something that you had thought would be too difficult.

- Three times you had a big setback and coped.

- Two times you were really scared, and how you overcame that.

- One thing you like about yourself that makes you a great person.

Now you have fifteen pieces of evidence that you can do hard things. Reading through your pot before a competition can help soothe noisy, negative head chatter so it doesn't trigger your threat system.

Name your common sporting emotions

We often hear in sport that big emotions pull down our performance and must be hidden with commentators dissing athletes for being 'too emotional' or 'too sensitive'. I dislike this judgement and prefer to remember that the word 'emotion' actually stands for 'energy in motion,' suggesting we can use these feeling to help us move better and with more intent. If we are to use our emotions though we need to be able to regulate them.

Competitions can induce big emotions. If you have invested lots of time and energy in your event or have a strong identity around your sport then feeling like you are about to be judged for it may mean you take even small losses personally so focusing on increasing emotional control will be beneficial. One specific tactic to increase emotional control is thought labelling. Some athletes worry that putting negative feelings into words will intensify them but research has found that writing down what you are feeling, a process known as 'affect labelling' can reduce the level of emotion. Think of the idea: 'name it to tame it.'

Neuroimaging studies using MRIs found the process of thought labelling diminished the response of the amygdala (the area we learnt about in chapter 1 which sets off our threat system). This suggests that consciously recognizing emotions reduces their impact on us. Ideally then, when you name or label your thoughts, the emotion attached to them reduces so you are better able to talk about, and handle them. A feelings map is a really good way to practise naming your emotions.

COMPETITION STRATEGIES FOR ADHD ATHLETES

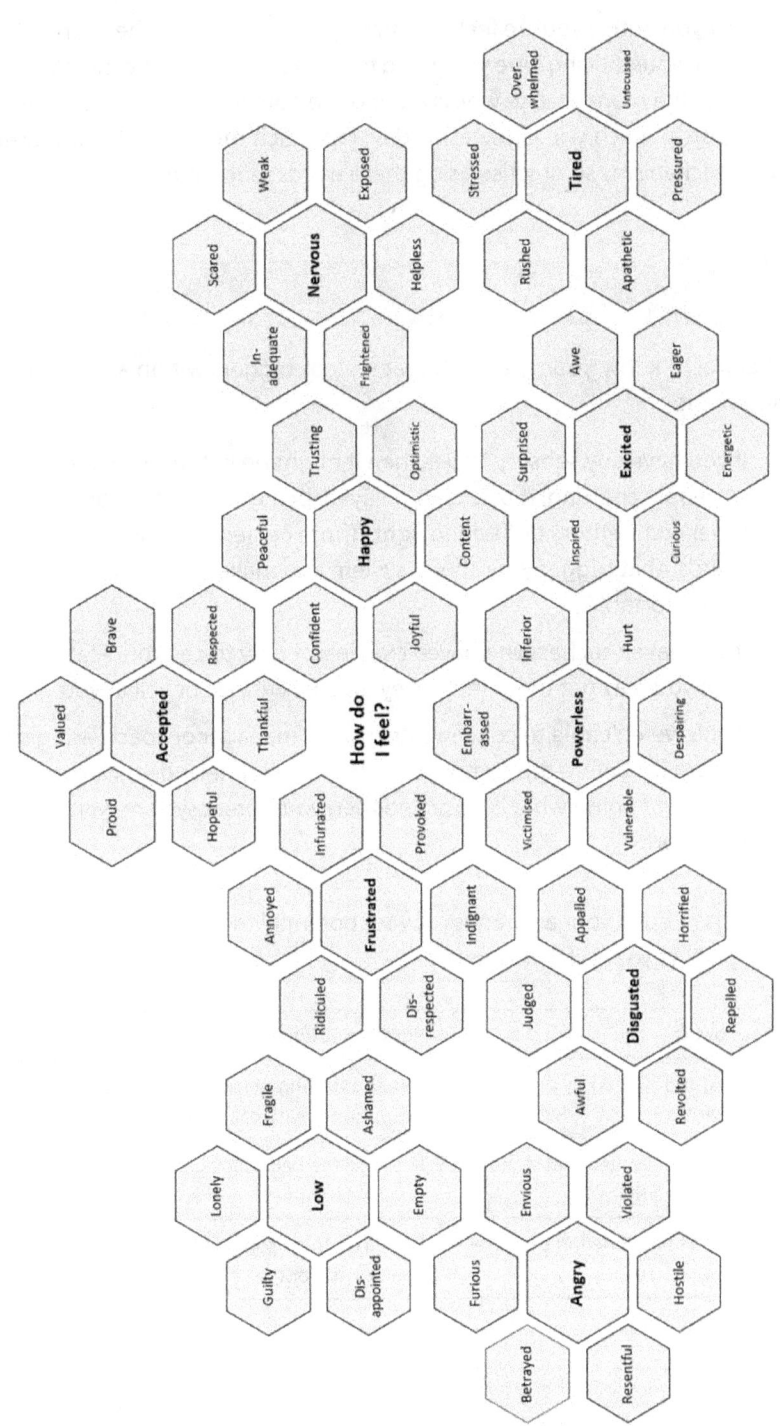

Whenever you notice you are feeling a strong emotion look at the chart. Which emotion are you noticing? Are you going to the bold words in the middle (most of us do) or the more precise words around the outside of each block? It is the precise words which will allow us to develop much more specific and useful coping mechanisms so practise using these words more often.

KNOW YOUR TRIGGERS

It is helpful to know your specific threat system triggers within a competition environment:

- If you have any sensory issues then it might be ill-fitting kit, lots of people chatting, music being played, being incredibly close to other competitors or flashing lights (from cameras or advertising stands) that trigger your threat system and make you feel really uncomfortable.
- If you have coaches who haven't yet learnt how to communicate well than you may get triggered if they unfairly criticize or yell at you.
- If you weren't able to concentrate when a manager or coach was giving out advice before the competition or in a half time and you are worried about not doing what is expected then your threat system will be on high alert.

The goal is to build your awareness of your potential triggers so you can have a plan to protect yourself. For example:

Trigger point	Possible solution
Hate being surrounded by people before a race	Join the starting pen as late as possible. Wear headphones with calming music.
Coach gets over excited and stands at the side yelling 'advice'	Focus on the ball – block out 'playstation coach'
Missing a half time briefing because you were distracted	Have a go to person on the team you trust who you can ask for the key points.

Your version

Trigger point	Solution

> "If I am frustrated with myself or with a run, it is almost certainly because I was too overwhelmed by things out of my control to execute it how I wanted. I am not an idiot; I know the difference between underperforming and ADHD preventing me from doing what I know I can do." Jen, Runner

DEALING WITH WAITING MODE

Waiting mode is when you feel stuck in limbo because you have an important thing happening later that day. It can feel a bit like time has stood still and you are just counting down to that event. If you tend to have early morning events this is fine but many team sports have kick off times much later in the day and waiting mode can mean that you waste a day waiting for the event, are unable to do any of your other tasks that day and you feel anxious.

It is a coping mechanism, but not a very helpful one. As we saw in chapter 1, when we have some type of anxiety inducing event (just like a competitive sporting activity) the brain can go into a state of hyperarousal. It is trying to prepare you for the unknown, except it isn't done in a helpful way as it gives you a heightened state of alertness, focusing you solely on the upcoming event and shuts out everything else you need to do that day.

If you struggle with waiting mode there are seven steps to try:

1. Get ready everything you will need for the competition first. Put it by the front door.
2. Write a list of anything else you might need that isn't ready yet: drinks, charged up headphones or watch, kit in the washing machine.
3. Set an alarm for the time you need to start getting ready

4. Set another alarm for 10 minutes before you need to leave
5. Time block your day – organizing it into task-focused time blocks with specific goals for each one.
6. Make as many of the other activities as 'minimal effort' as possible as you want to balance out getting stuff done, but also saving as much mental energy as possible for the competition ahead.
7. Make one of these time blocks a brain drain. A brain drain is where we reflect and write down what we are afraid of in our forthcoming event; essentially trying to drain our brain of all our worries and fears. If we write down as many things as we can that are worrying us on a piece of paper, when they are in front of us, they feel less scary and it frees up head space to focus on more helpful things. The University of Chicago ran a study to test the brain-drain strategy. Before a maths exam, half the students were asked to spend ten minutes writing down their anxieties about the exam, the other students just sat and waited. The second group scored 12 per cent lower than expected; those who completed the brain-drain improved their anticipated score by five per cent.

Brain drain:

☐	Injury	☐	Losing motivation
☐	Unfairness in judging / refereeing	☐	Shoelace coming undone and tripping over
☐	Not living up to own expectations	☐	Letting down the coach / teammates
☐	Being too slow to respond to a move	☐	Being yelled at by teammates
☐	Seeing negative comments on social media	☐	Getting disqualified
☐	Getting distracted	☐	Losing against someone lower ranked
☐	Losing my temper if I start doing badly	☐	Equipment failure
☐	Feeling ill	☐	Toilet issues
☐	Not being able to listen to instructions fully	☐	Feeling overwhelmed
☐	Missing an important shot or move	☐	Doing an impulsive but unhelpful movement
☐	Getting hurt mid event	☐	Getting yelled at by the coach

TASK-FOCUSED GOAL SETTING

We looked at goal setting for training in chapter 5 but we should also be goal setting in competition because with slower processing and working memory issues it can be beneficial to cut down the number of things you need to focus on in an event. Your habit function will hold a huge amount of things you need to do but any extra work you have been focused on recently will need to be held closer to the front of your mind and clarity of this will help. Remember, ADHD is not a knowledge problem, it is a performance problem, so you know full well how to do it – but don't believe you can. Task focused goal setting allows you to accept what is ahead and do it even if it might be boring.

To get to this action you start at your outcome goal for your competition, work backwards down your performance goal and then you will find the task you will need to focus on. For example:

Sport: Football
Outcome: Help my team win the match
Performance: Prevent at least two goals going in
Task: Stay within 3 metres of the player I am marking whenever I can.

Sport: Swimming
Outcome: Qualify for National Championships
Performance: Complete the distance in under 60 seconds
Task: Pull hard through the water

Sport: Tennis
Outcome: Get selected for the county squad by impressing selectors
Performance: Show my key skills at least five times in the 20 minute slot
Task: Scan the court for opportunities.

IF...THEN PLANNING

Going into a competition that matters to us there will inevitably some worries. If you did the brain drain as part of dealing with waiting mode then you will already have listed all your worries. We are looking for every single worry you have about the competition ahead; both big and small worries, even if they seem really irrational or silly.

Look though each issue you have put down and work on your 'If…Then' plan for what you would do if it did happen. Your goal here is to create cues that prompt pre-planned behaviours, rather than feeling a need to make decisions as you go. This means if the worst happens you don't have to think what you do – you already have a plan so you will be much less flustered and can move away from immediate (and usually emotionally driven) reactions and towards more logical, thoughtful and goal-driven responsiveness.

Worry (from the Brain drain)	If it happens then I will…

A great example of this is from the swimmer Michael Phelps, another athlete who has talked about his ADHD diagnosis. In his book, *No Limits* he tells us how his coach Bob would arrange practices and drills around the idea of being uncomfortable to see how he responded under pressure. Bob's intention was that if Phelps could deal with anything when tired and in training, he could deal with anything that came his way in competition. One of Phelp's worries was his goggles filling up mid race so he and Bob prepared for what he would do if it happened. In the 200 Individual Medley in the Olympic final his fear came true and his goggles leaked. His vision under water got more and more blurry. With 75 metres to go they were completely full and he couldn't see a thing. He carried on, focused on just counting the strokes, won the race, and set a new World Record in the process.

> "If I'm feeling okay, I can run really well. I can race really well. But at any point I can be struck down by a sniper and that really throws me off." Jen, Runner

Emotional regulation tools

When your threat system is triggered one of the physiological effects of the cortisol and adrenaline flooding your body is that your focus narrows and senses tend to switch off. You don't need to be able to hear or taste when you are running away from something scary. Your brain, quite sensibly, only uses the senses it needs in that moment. By proactively switching these senses back on we tell our threat system there is no need to be fearful.

PANORAMIC PERSPECTIVE

When the threat function kicks in and you lose your peripheral vision you can quickly switch it back on by zooming out; proactively broadening your perspective. You can do this visually by trying to have a panoramic view. Don't focus on the thing in front of you, instead, slowly turn around as if you are taking a panoramic picture on your phone.

SENSES LADDER

This helps you use all five senses to get away from worries about the future, and bring you back to the present moment. Look around you and list to yourself:

- Five things you can see
- Four things you can touch
- Three things you can hear
- Two things you can smell
- One thing you can taste.

A lovely cheat for this is keeping a tin of mints in your kit bag so any time you need to switch back on your senses you can see, touch, shake to hear, smell and taste them!

As we learnt in chapter 1, when our heart and respiratory rates rise under threat it doesn't just make us feel uncomfortable, it also causes another problem, activating a threat surveillance system feedback loop triggering yet more adrenaline and cortisol to be released. Intentionally slowing down your breathing can start to break this frustrating cycle and calm the whole system.

COLOURFUL BREATHING

A great tool to break the threat cycle and get the right amount of oxygen into our blood is colourful breathing. It doesn't just slow down your respiratory rate but when you are focused on colours there is no space in your head for rumination, so you stop worrying about what might happen in the future or what you have messed up in the past.

Pick your two favourite colours.

- Draw air in through your nose for a count of four – as you do this think of the air going in as that first colour.
- Hold for a count of two
- Breathe out the second colour through your mouth for a count of six.

It slows your breathing down to about six breaths a minute and stops your brain going over and over all the unhelpful thoughts.

ALIEN BREATHING

A fun breathing tool is alien breathing. Imagining you are an alien and have just stepped onto a new planet where people breathe differently. On this planet the beings breathe in through their feet and breathe out through their hands. Try it for a few minutes; imagining breathing in through your feet, holding and breathing out through your hands. The silliness of the idea can be relaxing, the process slows a racing heart and you'll get lost in the concentration of where your breath is coming and going so you forget to worry about the future and this slows the threat system.

GIVE VISUAL REMINDERS

> It is important to remember from chapter 1 that when our threat system has been triggered we are unable to use our logical decision-making function. The problem then comes in that we will have the threat system emotional regulation techniques lodged in our logical decision-making function and can't access them. This means it is essential that the soothing tools you choose to use are written down somewhere easy to see; on your hand, a sticker stuck to your water bottle or wrist band or a note stuck to your sports bag.

FUEL UP

One of the biggest triggers of our threat system is low blood sugar levels. As we read in chapter 4, your brain makes up about 3-5% of your body weight (depending on your body size) but however it actually burns about 20% of your metabolic budget. Any time you lose your appetite (which is common on ADHD medication), forget to eat or don't get time to eat properly this can mean your threat system is far more likely to trigger as you have cut off its fuelling system. This is really important to remember because when we are under-fuelled it is our amygdala that starts to run the show and, as we know, the amygdala is emotional and dramatic and doesn't make great decisions. Planning your food on days when you will have tricky, threat inducing activities is essential to your success as it is one of the key ways to ensure you don't overthink.

COACH ON A SHOULDER

To prevent distraction and direct attention effectively we want to be able to focus on just the most important thing (this may well be the task focused goal you came up with above). We do this by giving ourselves a specific instruction, just like you have a (tiny little) coach sitting on your shoulder.

The phrase you say should be short and sharp and something that could be repeated rhythmically to sustain attention on the right task. It might be tactical, technical or behavioural. It works particularly well when you use the phrase to work on your strength, accuracy or fine motor skills. Before you go out to compete, write it on your hand or, if you wear gloves, write it on tape stuck on your wrist, or stick it onto a water bottle. This gives you regular reminders to focus on that task. And make sure you tell yourself what to do, not what to avoid. 'Focus on space where you want the ball to go' is much more effective than 'ignore the spectators'.

Here is some space to practise a couple of instructions you could give yourself for different situations mid competition.

Situation	Purpose of instruction	Instruction

REFRAMING

Sporting competitions can vary enormously from the 100 metre sprints taking less than 10 seconds for the elite men through to 90 minute football matches, hours of golf or tennis through to endurance stage racing in running or cycling lasting many days. Each event needs a different approach and understanding yours will be helpful to focus positively in competition.

If we find we have similar thoughts over and over again in competition we can learn to reframe those thoughts into much more helpful versions which help us perform better. Often the unhelpful thoughts are those which set off our threat system; fear of failure, judgement from others, losing to athletes we think we should beat or disappointing others, so finding a way to turn the fear into a facilitator helps our performance immensely.

Three types of thoughts to consider are those which are shaming, those which are negative and those which are unhelpful.

> Shaming thoughts: These will be the words you notice your threat system giving you mid competition designed to shame you into doing something differently next time: 'I should have', 'I could have', 'I would have' done better if.... We often call them: 'shoulda woulda coulda' thoughts. The goal is, when we notice one of those thoughts popping up, to reframe it.
>
> Unhelpful thoughts: When we notice negative thoughts we are not trying to make them into something that is untrue or toxically positive but we are trying to give a different, and more helpful, meaning to those thoughts. We need to practise it continually though so we are able to do it in the heat of the moment, particularly if our threat system is likely to be triggered mid competition.
>
> Negative thoughts: Negative thoughts tend to tell us we really dislike what we are doing – usually if we have pushed ourselves really hard physically and got to the point of discomfort so we would like to stop. A way to reframe these types of thoughts is to consider Type 1 and Type 2 fun. Type 1 fun covers enjoyment in the moment; actively enjoying the thing you are doing. We might get this feeling in easy training but less so in tough competition when pushing hard. This means in competition we will often have to have type 2 fun; difficult, hard and uncomfortable in the moment but makes us feel good afterward. Reminders might be: 'I don't have to enjoy this – I just have to get it done. The quicker I

go the sooner I finish. I know I'll feel great afterwards.' This helps you challenge some of the beliefs we have about sport like 'it is supposed to be fun' or 'I am supposed to be motivated'. The more we can label these beliefs, the easier it becomes to identify them and start to roll our eyes at our own thoughts. Freeing ourselves of the idea that we have to be motivated or discomfort free to get started.

Some example reframes could be:

Type of thought	Thought	Reframe
Negative	I will never be able to do this skill	I'll master this skill if I keep practising like I am right now'
Shaming	I should have hit that better	Next time I'll hit the ball with less spin
Shaming	I could have scored – but didn't	The ball was a little to the left: next time I'll slow down and straighten up before shooting.
Unhelpful	I'm out of my depth in this competition.	This competition is tough but it's a good chance to see what I need to do to prepare for the next one.
Negative	This hurts too much	It is supposed to hurt. If it was easy everyone would be doing it.
Negative	I hate going up hills	Hills suck – but they make me stronger.
Unhelpful	I can't do this.	I can't do this yet – but if I keep practising I will get it eventually.

Now, when you know your most likely reframes get practising. It might feel silly and awkward to begin but once you get the hang of it, it starts to feel more natural and you will have a brilliant tool in your toolkit forever more.

STOP APPROACH

If the competition didn't go the way you wanted and you feel frozen with overwhelm or are told by others that you are acting overly emotionally then you can use the STOP approach to get back on track. It stands for Stop, Take a breath, Observe and Proceed.

Stop: To stop you would use 'thought stopping'. Here, as soon as you notice the negative or unhelpful thought you purposely do a sound or action to stop. You might click your fingers, ping a hairband on your wrist or gently pinch your hand.

Take a breath: Here you would do a breathing technique called: 'The Sip'. You breathe in through your nose as deeply as you can until you can't breathe in any more (imagining you have totally filled your lungs), then you add in one extra 'sip' of in breath before slowly breathing it all out through your mouth.

Observe: Here you do a body check. You mentally skim up and down your body to notice what sensations you notice. You then might be able to notice aches and pains following the sporting exertion but also elements of your threat system like a fast heart rate, too much muscle tension, high breathing rate, niggles niggling and the tight or nauseous stomach. It helps you figure out if you are feeling physically or mentally under pressure and it pulls you back into the moment rather than ruminating about the competition.

Proceed: Now your threat system has started to calm what step would you like to take next? Would you like to jot down your analysis? Would you like to debrief the competition with your coach or a team-mate? Would you like to do something totally different for a while until you have the headspace to do the analysis?

ANALYSIS

To reduce the impact of the threat system on performance we want to focus our sporting work on developing mastery and continually improving rather than thinking purely in terms of whether we won or lost. To ensure we are continually focused on improvement and self-critique (in a positive, helpful way) we can do an analysis after every competition or event. You will be thinking about five areas.

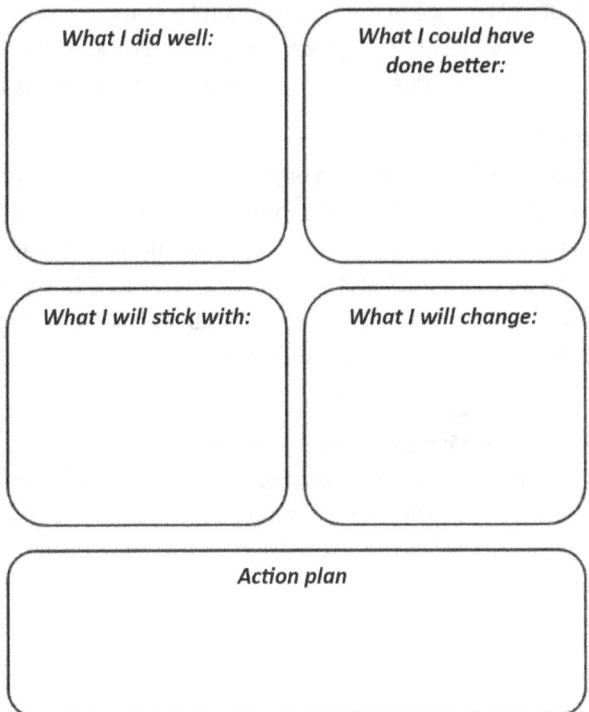

CURIOUS QUESTIONS

If something didn't go to plan in the competition and you don't think you handled it well the goal is not to beat yourself up but instead to get curious about what happened and why. Some 'curious questions' to ask yourself post competition:

What happened that triggered me or made me feel on edge?
Sometimes this could be receiving negative feedback, being yelled at, being blamed for a mistake, being blamed unfairly, feeling ashamed or seeing injustice.

What did I notice in my body when my threat system was triggered?
Think back to chapter 1 where we tend to notice a tummy ache, racing heart or faster breathing rate, tight muscles, a loss of peripheral vision or senses switching off.

What behaviour did I notice myself doing when I was triggered?
These tend to involve lashing out, freezing, having black and white thinking, attacking others, catastrophizing, blaming or getting very defensive.

What helped me calm down?
Sometimes these might be breathing techniques, grounding tools, speaking to someone, expelling the anger, leaving the environment.

What would I like to be able to do in the same situation in future?
Is it something you could get better practiced at ignoring? Is it something that you could acknowledge but learn to keep in perspective, could mantras help you stay task focused, could you visualize moving on quickly?

> *"I hate having processes forced upon me. I like to see the pattern and work the pattern. Being told like, you do this, this and then this, I don't do very well in. The key thing is that I really need to know why, rather than just what. If I really don't understand the why, then I really, really struggle to engage with it."* James, Equestrian

JEN'S STORY

Jen has a professional career and is a long-distance runner who has represented England at Masters level. She has combined type ADHD so some traits that would fall into hyperactivity and other traits that would fall into inattentive.

'I didn't seek out a diagnosis, it came to me. I was 40 before I was diagnosed. I first sought help from a psychiatrist as I felt I wasn't dealing very well with life and it was in that context that neurodiversity was first suggested. At that time his diagnosis was ASD with OCD. Of course, we now know the OCD is actually the internal hyperactivity, the obsessive rumination not coming from an OCD place but coming from an ADHD place. The suggestion that I might have ADHD came from my psychologist as a sort of an explanation for why I experience certain things in certain ways. And she was right. Some of the traits that I think led to ASD initial diagnosis can very clearly be explained by ADHD.'

'Having the label helped a lot. It helped with understanding why some things are difficult for me, why I react in certain ways, and understanding why I behave in certain ways, and why I feel different and I always have.'

'I am academically gifted, it came very easily to me. I was always viewed as too capable to struggle. When I did struggle with things, I felt shame in myself for it, but also, I experienced lack of understanding from others because they'd say "you're so clever and talented and able and capable, why can't you do that?" I didn't know why either, but all I knew was that I'm not doing it on purpose. Because I have never been disruptive I didn't get any help with anything. When I went to university it was really the first time that on reflection, I needed help and it just wasn't in anyone's sphere of consciousness that I might be a person that needs help.'

'I got into a cycle of seeing that the only way that I can be acceptable to other people, and by association, acceptable to myself, is by continuing to achieve. I became such a cliché, stereotypical straight A* student, grade 8 distinctions in two different instruments, county level sport, but all the time feeling there's something not quite right. Feeling wrong, inside. And also feeling huge pressure to continue to achieve because that's the only thing I have, it's the only thing that's mine. But that's really, really hard to do for 40 odd years.'

'It is very frustrating and upsetting that, even though I try to describe my situation, and why things are difficult for me, and that I have different support needs, people can (usually) only see how "capable" and "intelligent" and "able" I am, and they seem to think that this means I don't need help and support – as if my supposed "talent" somehow compensates for everything else. But really what is happening is that I'm "performing well" despite my challenges, not because they don't exist. I describe it as trying to run a marathon on a bouncy castle, with a brass band being blasted into your ears at full volume, the lights being switched on and off randomly, and a giant foam comedy hand being waved in front of your face. All whilst being told to "relax" and "be positive," and "just enjoy it" … I'm fairly sure that most people would find that a challenge (to say the least), but that is my reality.'

'No one sees the things that I was and am struggling with because they're just not things that are necessarily visible to other people in day-to-day life. I'm never late but at what cost? They don't see the stress, and the panic when it took me three hours to get out of the house. It is exhausting.'

'ADHD can be benefit in sport, but it's a fragile benefit, because the snipers are always there. So, for me, specifically with running, the hyperfocus is really useful in that the intensity, if it can be channelled in the right conditions, can be a big gift. But it is a fragile strength because the flip side is all these snipers that can shatter that very easily.'

'The other benefit is when there's no time at all to think, and you just have to react on instinct, that is when my brain comes into its own. If there is sudden chaos, or something unexpected that just happens and you don't need a thinking response but a doing response, then I'm really good at that. My ADHD brain loves that. I just see a solution. I see what needs to be done. And can do it. It happened on a training run actually. We planned a lovely new route along a new section of the canal and we got to a bit that was completely flooded. Straight away, I saw what we needed to do, which was to climb a fence and shimmy round it because I could see where it would dip down and where the drain might be.'

'The running is the easy bit though. If I could be fed and watered by osmosis and dressed and then teleported to the running track and have the session put on my watch or have someone in real time tell me what to do I'd be a champion! The portion of time when I'm actually running is the most successful bit but there are a lot of what I call snipers in my head that can shoot me down either before, during, after or all three! Which then feeds into a quite a negative spiral.'

'Even though I know why, I often struggle to not fall foul of these snipers. Forgetting to eat is a sniper, so is forgetting to drink, and I need calm around me, probably an antidote to the internal chaos, in order to regulate my nervous system enough to execute what I'm trying to do. Day to day, it can be things like lots of people doing something in the park, because people do unpredictable things. Or in a group session with lots of music playing. A race is complete sensory overload. These snippers aggregate and that feeds into the emotional dysregulation and I don't seem to have any ability to experience any emotion moderately. Sometimes I will get so dysregulated by something that I am just not able to access my strategies. If I'm feeling okay, I can run really well. I can race really well. I train beautifully. But at any point I can be struck down by a sniper, and it really throws me off, and I feel huge shame and embarrassment that these things can short-circuit my brain so much.'

'If we're meeting at 9 o'clock, I will be there at 9 o'clock ready to run. And if other people take a long time to get started I am like "what is it, what are you doing, what's the difficulty? Why can't we just go now?" I've found that really hard. Especially juxtaposed with the fact that I've broken heaven and earth to get myself there ready to run on time. That brings in the emotional dysregulation because it annoys me more than it should. And then of course the shame pops its little head in, because I know I shouldn't be pissed off about this.'

'I don't start crying and shouting. It's internal, it's losing my shit internally. Because of a sniper. Because of that sort of internal circuit-breaker, I lose my ability to regulate my thoughts and my emotions and therefore to implement the things that any athlete needs to implement. It's like something happens and it short-circuits my nervous system in a way that is almost impossible for me to control. In a way that is really disabling because no one can see it and it's perceived as a weakness.'

'The ADHD nervous system is interest-based and things need to feel good, and be interesting and exciting. If a coach sets me boring training, or training that is too easy or not challenging enough, I will still do it (because I am a good girl) but you won't get the best out of me. Set me something challenging, and give me the right conditions to settle my nervous system, and I can and will run faster and better than you would have believed possible.'

'It is the conditions that need to be adapted, not the training itself. A coach shouldn't expect me to be able to run well on a busy track after being hemmed in a noisy tube train. But it is the track and the journey that need to be adapted, not the training session; don't make the training less challenging to "account for" this. Otherwise, I just get no real training stimulus and have a shit experience in an overwhelming setting – which is utterly pointless in every way (and is distressing for me).'

'Add to this, with distance running you're going to go right to the edge of that really perilous red line and hang out there for a couple of hours. Its incongruent with a place of comfort and safety. You have to apply a stress in order to get any adaptation. Applying any stress is of itself inherently 'unsafe' because it's a stress. It is such a double-edged sword. Because if you remain in a place of safety then you don't get the adaptation, the stimulus to improve and to excel.'

CHAPTER **7**

Common ADHD co-occurring conditions

When you have ADHD there is a higher chance of you also having another condition alongside it. In one study among primary school children, 62.5% of those with ADHD had other conditions too. In adults the figure has been suggested to be as high as 80%.

Managing symptoms of ADHD alongside day-to-day functioning can be stressful and frustrating, and present many practical barriers to everyday life. Experienced in conjunction with one another, the physical, psychological and physiological load of two or more disorders can be intense.

The more co-occurring conditions you have, the greater the burden of symptoms you need to navigate. Not only is this rather unfair but often the symptoms can feel entangled, making it hard to know how to manage each element. It is one of the reasons many psychologists prefer to support athletes with their symptoms rather than requiring lots of individual diagnoses.

It is important to understand if there are other issues or elements going on for you though because these additional challenges can interfere with the way you learn, move and impact the approaches you might take to managing your ADHD symptoms. As a result, this chapter looks at some of the most common co-occurring conditions which have a significant impact on you as an athlete, either on your wellbeing, health or performance.

There are lots of statistics and prevalence rates mentioned throughout the chapter. These will obviously vary from country to country depending on when and where the research is conducted, the diagnosis approach used, the culture around mental health and the awareness of those issues – so nothing is definite or exact but they are included to give you some idea of how common these co-occurring conditions are.

Other neurodiversities

Neurodiversities often share predisposing environmental and genetic factors and can also share symptoms and so it is quite common to find that someone (like Olivia whose story comes next) who has one neurodiversity also has another.

AUTISM SPECTRUM DISORDER (ASD)

What is it: Autism is on a spectrum (meaning everyone with it will experience their symptoms differently) and tends to be known as Autism Spectrum Disorder. With autism you might find it harder to communicate and interact with other people, understand how others might think or feel, find bright lights, loud noises or lots of people overwhelming or stressful, get very anxious when things are unfamiliar or unpredictable and like to have routines in order to feel safe and secure. Just like ADHD, Autism is something you will have been born with. Unlike ADHD, medication will not be able to support your struggles but there will be approaches and tools you can use to be able to function more comfortably in life.

How prevalent is it in those with ADHD: In a 2019 Swedish study of 27,176 patients who were newly diagnosed with ADHD the most common co-occurring condition found was autism. The latest version of the DSM (the Diagnostic and Statistical Manual used to define medical conditions) allows for a joint ASD and ADHD diagnosis which becomes known as AuDHD. The co-occuring rates of ADHD and ASD have been found at a high level; with various studies suggesting that between 30% and 65% of children with ADHD also have clinically significant symptoms of ASD. When scientists have looked to find reasons why they see that at least half of the contributing genetic factors of ADHD and ASD overlap. They also see there are very similar deficits in attention related areas such as executive function, social cognition and motor speed in both disorders suggesting it is the biological pathways in the brain that have similar developmental processes.

How can it impact you as an ADHD athlete: As autism sits on a spectrum the severity of ways it can impact you as an athlete is far too wide to cover here. If you have also been diagnosed with ASD this will often be the area to consider first when working out to how handle your symptoms in sport – but overall it will be incredibly important to do the work on getting to know you and the difficulties you experience really well so you can make an overarching plan to develop your comfort in sporting environments and situations.

DYSPRAXIA/DEVELOPMENTAL CO-ORDINATION DISORDER

What is it: Dyspraxia is also known as Developmental Co-ordination Disorder (DCD) and is a fairly common condition that impacts your movement and co-ordination so you might find it harder to carry out tasks that need balance, struggle with some sports and you may have difficulties with physical skills like writing neatly or using small objects. It will start in childhood and has been found to persist into adulthood in between 30% and 70% of those who have it. Things that might be impacted by dyspraxia…
- co-ordination, balance and movement
- the way you deal with emotions
- time management, planning and organization skills
- the way you learn new skills, think, and remember information
- regular living skills
- how you function in social situations

How prevalent is it in those with ADHD: Many of the symptoms of Dyspraxia are also very prevalent in ADHD. They are distinct conditions but they are related and frequently occur alongside each other with estimated 50% of those with ADHD also having dyspraxia.

How can it impact you as an ADHD athlete: Dyspraxia can have an impact on the motor skills and coordination you will want to use in your sport and on your likelihood of injury. This can be a significant issue for children – especially if they are learning new skills in a sport. Many adults do learn to manage the motor skill difficulties as they develop (and sport can definitely help this) but the cognitive elements of dyspraxia can remain and these can make it trickier to excel in sport as elements like time keeping and organizational skills are required to thrive in sport.

DYSLEXIA

What is it: Dyslexia is a learning difficulty that causes issues with reading, writing and spelling. Someone with dyslexia may read and write slowly, get certain letters mixed up (d and b is common), have poor spelling and struggle with organization. It is caused by a weaknesses in phonology, working memory and visual processing skills. It is usually diagnosed at school and will remain throughout life but you can learn tools and skills to improve reading and writing skills.

How prevalent is it in those with ADHD: It is through about 10% of people have some degree of dyslexia. In those with ADHD it is thought 25-40% also have dyslexia.

How can it impact you as an ADHD athlete: Those with dyslexia often had to develop stronger skills in areas outside of reading and writing such as creative thinking and problem solving and these can prove incredibly valuable in sport. Additionally they tend to develop strong verbal reasoning skills which can be helpful to communicate well within teams.

ALEXITHYMIA

What is it: Alexithymia is best described as emotional blindness where someone with it struggles to recognize and express their emotions. In Greek the word means 'without words for emotion.' Alexithymia is on spectrum, and a person can have mild to severe alexithymic traits covering difficulty in identifying emotions, describing their feelings and actively avoiding thinking about their own inner state. Alexithymia and ADHD will both cause someone to struggle to regulate emotions but with ADHD, this will be an executive functioning issue which impacts the brain's ability to regulate emotions. With Alexithymia the issue is a difficulty in registering emotions until they have become too intense to manage.

How prevalent is it in those with ADHD: Studies suggest between 22% and 40% of those with ADHD also have Alexithymia. It is thought to be around 10% in the general population.

How can it impact you as an ADHD athlete: Identifying our emotions plays a crucial role in our ability to regulate our emotions so if we cannot identify them we will struggle to distinguish between emotions and bodily sensations. If we can't identify our feelings then we also struggle to describe them to ourselves or others and this means we cannot express ourselves coherently which can be really tricky when we need to work with coaches, managers and other players or athletes in a team and makes open, compassionate relationships difficult. Additionally, if you have both ADHD and Alexithymia you may struggle more with handling emotionally difficult environments particularly if impulsivity is part of your diagnosis. Those with alexithymia and high levels of impulsivity are more likely to seek out novel situations, exciting sensations, and are prone to riskier behaviours. In athletes this can increase the risk of injury or substance abuse.

HYPERMOBILITY

What is it: Hypermobility is a connective tissue disorder where joints overextend beyond typical ranges, may dislocate easily, and may regularly move into awkward positions which fall short of full dislocations. Connective tissues support a large number of elements in the body: skin, tendons, ligaments, blood vessels, organs and bones. Those with hypermobility then often experience a wide range of issues connected to connective tissues including chronic pain and heart, gynaecological, migraine and autoimmune issues. Overly flexible tissues can also cause proprioceptive issues. Proprioception is your body's ability to sense movement, action, and location. This is essential in athletes; imagine a gymnast trying to perform a move, jumping up high on the beam and landing back on it without proprioception.

How prevalent is it in those with ADHD: A 2022 study run through the University of Sussex looked at 109 adults with neurodiversity (diagnosed autism, ADHD or Tourettes and found 51% had signs of hypermobility, compared to 20% of those who are neurotypical. Females are more likely to hypermobile than males.

How can it impact you as an ADHD athlete: In a 2012 study of those with hypermobility it was found the volume of the amygdala (the part of our brain which scans for threats) was significantly larger in the hypermobile group than in the control group. This has a few potential implications:

- A larger amygdala could make someone more sensitive to the threat of pain – which of cause may make them more fearful in sports where acute injury is a possibility.
- A larger amygdala may also make us more sensitive to interoception (the way our brain senses how different organs are functioning and feeling – i.e. heart beating, breathing speed or skin itches) so makes them physically very self-aware of risks or efforts – which may interfere in their performance when they need to be able to push through discomfort or limitations.

BEHAVIOURAL DISORDERS

What are they: Behavioural disorders that can have a significant impact in sport include substance use disorders, Conduct Disorder and Oppositional Defiance Disorder (ODD). ODD is where someone has regular and continuing patterns of anger, irritability, arguing and defiance towards anyone in authority. Someone with ODD may well lose their temper quickly, is easily annoyed by others, can be openly hostile and comes across as refusing to follow others requests or rules. These behaviours can cause issues in family, school and work making relationships difficult as others walk on egg shells around you and you live with constant anxiety and fearing rejection. Symptoms of ODD are common within childhood; they can show up as a child goes through specific stages of development, but diagnosable ODD will continue. Often these behaviours may be more harmful to performance than the ADHD symptoms alone.

How prevalent are they in those with ADHD: The average prevalence of ODD is around 3% – however half of children with ODD also fulfill the diagnostic criteria for ADHD. Some studies have found around 50% of children with ADHD also have ODD. Numbers of adults with substance use disorder have been found to as high as 58%. These figures will be much higher in those who have untreated ADHD. Behavioural disorders in those with ADHD have been found to be more common in males than females.

How they can impact you as an ADHD athlete: A big concern for those hoping to succeed in sports is that any addiction to substance use can be a big barrier to success; either in terms of harming performance (i.e. if you smoke) or if you take substances that are illegal (in terms of reputation or expulsion) if the substance is banned under WADA. Both substance misuse and ODD alongside the impulsiveness and novelty seeking in ADHD can mean that involvement in the criminal justice system is more common. Treatment for ODD primarily involves family-based interventions including talk therapy and training. It will often include parenting skills training (to learn defusing and positive behavioural strategies), and therapy to learn communication, problem solving and social skills. Medicines alone generally aren't used for ODD but when it is found alongside ADHD then the medication used for this may help a number of the ODD symptoms too. Anger control and stress inoculation help prepare for possible upsetting situations or events that may cause anger and stress.

ANXIETY-BASED DISORDERS

What is it: Anxiety based disorders will cover anxiety itself (and specific variants like social or performance anxiety), Obsessive-Compulsive Disorder (OCD) and trauma or stress related disorders.

How prevalent is it in those with ADHD: The impact of being neurodiverse in a society with structures and systems designed with neurotypicals in mind can create an environment where you feel incredibly anxious and or depressed. The symptoms coming from this can get tangled up in the symptoms from the ADHD and will also need support if you are to do well in your sport.

It is thought that up to around 10% of general population have an anxiety disorder – this rises to up to 47% of those with ADHD. Some of this may come due to the impact of their ADHD symptoms on their day-to-day life. If a child is regularly being told off, or assumed to be 'naughty' then they will live in a state of anxiety. It is also thought that the higher-than-expected number of accidents and injuries in those with ADHD can influence a higher level of anxiety. Additionally, the social and relationship issues that can come from some ADHD symptoms can impact anxiety. There is also a thought that ADHD and Anxiety

Disorders come from similar regions in the brain that are involved with the executive function control network.

How can it impact you as an ADHD athlete: Anxiety as an athlete can be debilitating as your internal head commentary will focus on all of the reasons why you won't be able to achieve the outcome you want and how that will mean you are not the person you want to be. This negative commentary triggers your threat system to flood your body with cortisol and adrenaline which can have a strong physiological impact on your body (nauseous tummy, increased heart and breathing rate, tight muscles and a loss of senses) and make it much harder to perform to your potential or execute the skills you have been mastering in training when you get to competition. Anti-anxiety medication can help, as can regular non-competitive exercise. Talking therapies can also be really effective and you can find some of the emotional regulation tools in chapter 6. For OCD you need a specialist therapist, ideally someone who can compassionately support you through exposure therapy.

DEPRESSION

What is it: Depression involves having long lasting feelings of unhappiness and hopelessness, losing interest in the things you used to enjoy, often feeling very tearful and develop anxiety. Physically, it can make you feel constantly tired, unable to sleep, see you lose your appetite, lower your sex drive and notice lots of aches and pains. It can impact people very differently and with different symptoms showing up in different ways so you may not always notice that you have depression. In mild cases you may feel persistently low. Severe depression can make you feel suicidal and believe that life is no longer worth living. Sometimes there is a very clear trigger for depression; the death of someone close to you, being in a traumatic incident, losing a job or having a baby can all trigger it, but sometimes there is no clear reason which can make it harder to recognize and get help.

How prevalent is it in those with ADHD: ADHD and symptoms of depression have been found to be linked. In the general populations, the prevalence of any depressive disorder was estimated between 1% and 12%. In those with ADHD it has been estimated at between 8%

and 55%. In fact, those with ADHD are thought to be 2.7 times more likely to have depression symptoms than someone without. At its worst, a Danish study looking at 2.9 million people aged over 10 found a five-fold higher rate of suicide attempts and three-fold higher rate of death in individuals with ADHD compared to those without. Some researchers looking at the possible mechanisms of depressive disorders and ADHD within the brain suggest that the two might share similar pathophysiologic regions of the brain; including decreased activity in the prefrontal cortex, amygdala, and hippocampus regions.

How can it impact you as an ADHD athlete: Depression can make it very hard to train. If you are having overwhelming feelings of worthlessness then your brain may well tell you it is pointless to exercise or you may struggle to remember why you enjoy your sport and going to play it will seem irrelevant. Some people with severe depression may struggle to get out of bed or shower so making it to a team practice or following a training plan might feel impossible. Treatment for depression often involves exercise so if you are susceptible to depression you may find it becomes worse if you are injured or in a period of longer term recovery. If you find you can't do your own sport due to injury any other type of fitness that is safe for you to do without slowing down your recovery then doing it can help protect you from depression. Alongside this, making healthy lifestyle choices is also helpful so ensuring you are not smoking, you are eating a balanced diet and you limit alcohol intake. As an athlete you are likely to be doing this anyway but healthy habits can definitely slip when we are depressed or injured. Additionally, talking therapies can help you work through how you are feeling and allow you to develop some coping mechanisms for difficult situations. With moderate to severe depression anti-depressants can be prescribed.

BIPOLAR

What is it: Another mood disorder that can be seen occasionally in those with ADHD is Bipolar. Bipolar disorder is a mental health condition that affects your moods where they swing from one extreme (depression) to another (mania). The swings can last several weeks or even for months. During a manic phase you might feel really happy, have a tonne of energy and ideas, feel creative, talk super quickly and overspend money on things you don't need or really want. During a depressive phase you might completely shut down from those around you.

How prevalent is it in those with ADHD: Bipolar is another area where we see higher than average levels in those with ADHD. A review of ten studies found the worldwide prevalence rate of bipolar disorder is estimated as 1–3% but the prevalence in the ADHD group was greater than 3% in every study.

How can it impact you as an ADHD athlete: Bipolar can make your moods unpredictable and hard to work around; in a manic phase you may have all the energy and enthusiasm required to perform brilliantly in training or competition but in a depressive phase you might feel unable to do anything. Bipolar episode triggers include extreme stress, life changing events and overwhelming problems so extra awareness should be taken if any of these might be going on. Treatment for bipolar will often mirror that of depression. There is medication known as mood stabilizers which help to prevent episodes of mania and depression. They are taken every day long term. It is also very helpful for you and those around you to learn to recognize the triggers and signs of a depressive or manic episode so you can treat it sooner. Talking therapy can help as can all the usual healthy lifestyle choices.

REJECTION SENSITIVE DYSPHORIA (RSD)

What is it: Rejection Sensitive Dysphoria (RSD) is when you experience extreme emotional pain when you fail at something or feel rejected by others. If you have RSD you are more likely to interpret more neutral comments or behaviours as rejection and struggle to control your reactions. RSD might lead you to overreact to feelings of rejection or anticipation of possible rejection and this might show up in behaviours connected to negative emotions like anger, rage, sadness or extreme anxiety.

How prevalent is it in those with ADHD: RSD is specifically linked to ADHD and it is thought that it occurs as a result of differences in brain structure (seen in both ADHD and RSD) which means that your brain can't regulate rejection-related emotions and behaviours. This emotional dysregulation means you feel emotions far more intensely than others, causing you physical pain.

How can it impact you as an ADHD athlete: If you have RSD you might sometimes be thought of as people pleaser, overly focused on avoiding disapproval – this can limit you in your sport if you need to be competitive or stand up for yourself again coaches or others who don't have your best interests at heart. You might also struggle to start projects, tasks or goals where there's a chance of failure – and this can be crippling in sport where there is often a high chance of failure. Often this shows up as perfectionism: aiming to be perfect to reduce the risk of failing – but often limiting opportunities as you won't take any that might be risky. Additionally, with RSD your self-esteem might be dependent on others and what they think of you – what others think of us is uncontrollable so you might struggle with confidence. You might also see neutral feedback from a coach as criticism and react negatively to it. RSD isn't an officially recognized medical condition and so there isn't much research on how to handle it. ADHD medication is typically used to treat it as both conditions affect the same part of the brain. Therapy is also helpful to help you learn strategies to handle the feelings and emotions so they are not so overwhelming and cause less pain. Working on tools to build up resilience and learning that imperfection and regular failure is essential to being successful in sport can also be helpful.

SEASONAL AFFECTIVE DISORDER (SAD)

What is it: Seasonal Affective Disorder (often known as SAD) has been found to disproportionately effect people with ADHD. It shows up as feeling low for more than two weeks starting in autumn or winter, usually resolving in spring or summer. Within this period there will often be an increased appetite, particularly craving carbohydrates, increased weight, more need for sleep (though falling asleep late and waking up even later) and low levels of energy.

How prevalent is it in those with ADHD: In a study of Dutch patients with ADHD, 27% reported symptoms of SAD and it was found to be much more common in females.

How can it impact you as an ADHD athlete: Finding life harder in winter, putting on weight, having less energy or needing additional sleep can be difficult particularly if you play a sport that competes at that time of year like Football, Rugby, Hockey, Cross Country or any snow sports. The most commonly used approach to SAD is light therapy. Studies have found that after about two weeks of starting light therapy you should have better mood, better sleep, more energy and a decreased appetite. It's thought the light may improve SAD by encouraging your brain to reduce the production of Melatonin (the hormone we read about in chapter 4 that makes you sleepy) and increase the production of Serotonin (a hormone that affects your mood). Light therapy involves sitting near a special lamp for up to an hour each morning. Alongside this you can also ensure you get as much natural sunlight as possible, make your environment as light as possible and, when indoors, sit near windows.

BURNOUT

What is burnout: Burnout is a when you are totally and utterly exhausted. Some say they feel 'empty to their bones'. It might be mentally, physically or emotionally; or all three. We usually see it when someone has lived in a state of stress or anxiety for too long without recovery breaks. Burnout is more common in those with ADHD for a number of reasons:

- You use excess mental and physical energy masking.
- Everyday tasks cause extra stress and use more energy because you are doing them with higher levels of anxiety.
- If your ADHD shows up in procrastination and time blindness then you tend to encounter more stressful situations.
- Daily overwhelm causes events and activities to feel stressful.

These means that you spend more of your life feeling stressed and so use up more mental energy than your body maybe able to cope with.

How prevalent is burnout in those with ADHD: Studies suggest that burnout is about five times higher in those with ADHD than in the general population.

How can it impact you as an ADHD athlete: When we have burnout we struggle with motivation and our energy levels feel much lower. Even simple things feel harder than they should and everything has a higher perception of effort. Instead of excitement for training or practice or competition we feel apathetic. In this state you cannot perform at your best, and when your sporting performances fall your confidence might drop too, reducing your motivation levels further. To prevent burning out the Coins method can be really valuable. You can learn about this approach at the start of chapter 5.

EATING DISORDERS AND OBESITY

Eating Disorders are more common in those with ADHD. Some of this will be explained by the medication reducing appetite so that you develop a habit of going long periods without fuelling your activity and then either not making up for the calories you need or binge eating because you are so hungry when the medication wears off. Some may be explained by anxiety from trying to mask and concentrate to fit in and 'behave' causing constant nausea making it hard to eat the right foods. As this is such an important subject for athletes we covered eating disorders and ways to be more aware of them as an ADHD athlete in chapter 4.

ACCIDENTS, INJURIES AND ILLNESS

Studies of a large Danish clinical register found an increased mortality rate in children, adolescents and adults with ADHD, even taking into account the other co-morbid disorders that have serious health risks like substance use disorder. They believe the increase in mortality is largely driven by deaths from unnatural causes such as accidents. Another study showed children under four with an ADHD diagnosis were 70% more likely to be admitted to a hospital than those without one. They found admissions for head injuries, burns, poisons, all other injuries, diseases of the tonsils and adenoids, asthma and early infections were all more common in children with ADHD. Other studies have found that once medication has been started injuries and accident and emergency visits in children with ADHD significantly reduce. There are some theories as to why; it could be dyspraxia causes more acute accidents; lower levels of internal self-awareness means pain or physiological symptoms of an illness or injury not noticed until later (and more serious), impulsivity not allowing time for consequences of actions or behaviours to be taken into account, risky behaviours causing risky outcomes, gross motor skills to be delayed or simply when doing something physical that requires focus, the ease of distraction means that the movement can go wrong very quickly.

PHYSICAL CO-OCCURRING CONDITIONS IN ADHD

Finally, studies have found that neurodivergent people experience negative physical symptoms at a rate higher than the general population:

- Cardiovascular issues have been found in 18% of general population but 43% of those with ADHD. This is important because ADHD stimulant medication can raise blood pressure and heart rate so heart checks are advised for athletes before it is prescribed.
- Gastro-intestinal issues are about twice as common in those with ADHD (33%) than the general population (19%)
- Immune system issues are also about twice as common in those with ADHD (7%) than the general population.
- A study based on data from 136 GP practices in Scotland published in 2024 found that those with ADHD are between 60% and 90% more likely to miss GP appointments which, when we already know there are a number of co-occurring conditions, leaves them more vulnerable to health complications.
- Finally, using data from the Neurodevelopmental Genomics Cohort Study, it was found that children with central nervous system conditions (this would include issues like seizures and epilepsy) were significantly more likely to have ADHD.

One final area of interest bearing in mind is that there is still so much research to be undertaken in this area we don't yet know all the links or co-occurring conditions. For example, it has been found that of children undergoing an adenotonsillectomy (the surgical procedure to remove tonsils and adenoids) 27.8% had ADHD, even though fewer than 10% of children in the general population have the condition. We don't yet know why this might be.

> "My psychiatrist also thought I had OCD, which, of course, we now know is the internal hyperactivity, the obsessive rumination, it's not coming from an OCD place, it's coming from an ADHD place." Jen, Runner

OLIVIA'S STORY

Olivia was diagnosed with ASD aged 8 and ADHD at 16. She plays Cricket for Lancashire and North West Thunder as a right-arm leg break bowler.

'I weren't the best-behaved kid in class and school sent me to CAMHS when I was about seven. They diagnosed me with autism. Then it was quite apparent that I did probably have ADHD too because my brother got diagnosed with it and my mum was questioning me too. When I was in senior school, probably about 14, I was tested. My hyperactivity and inattentive scores were both in the 90 something percent but I didn't score high enough on the impulsivity bit. I went for another test though and the impulsivity was high enough as well, so I ended up getting diagnosed at 16.'

'How I coped at school depended on which teacher I had. I didn't really have that many mates at school because of the school I went to and because I play cricket. I was fairly clever and good at cricket and the people at my school, if you were different, you'd just get ripped. So, friendship-wise I struggled to make and keep friends at school.'

'Football was my sport as a kid, but anything with a ball I love. I can entertain myself for hours on end. Even now! My mum worked in my primary school and I had to stay and wait for her to finish work until I could go home so I would just run riot in after school sports clubs, and one of the clubs in Year Six was cricket. Lancashire Cricket Foundation came in to school to run it and after six weeks, the coach pulled my mum aside and was like, "your Liv's quite good. Do you wanna bring her up to Lancashire trials?" And then it just went from there.'

'That became my main sport as I got to academy level. I dropped football at about 14 because cricket was taking up too much of my time and they'd go mad if you got injured playing football so I had to knock it on the head.'

'There is no sport with a ball that I don't love. You're outside all day in the sun, you're with your mates. But there are definitely more bad days than good days with cricket. For one good performance, you'll have ten that aren't great.'

'The ADHD means I don't really tend to get that tired in the field. So, if you need someone to run boundary to boundary, I could just field all day, I love it. I also hyperfocus on cricket, and it's just become everything. I'll bowl and bowl and bowl, and bat and bat and bat, because it's my one thing I can do. Because I can, I'm so hyper focused on it I'm almost more determined than others to get better and take it further.'

'I've definitely got a cricket brain. I've always been told that I read the game well. It's like I've got a really strange sixth sense; a sporting sense. I don't necessarily think about it, I just am where I need to be. Like, if I'm playing football, I'm in the space I need to be in. If I'm playing volleyball, I know where they're gonna hit that ball. When playing cricket in the field, I know as soon as they let go of the ball, I know where that ball's gonna end up.'

'People always say to me, and it's probably to do with my ADHD, that like I'm a little box of frogs and I'll just dive and throw myself round in the field. That's become a massive strength. Fielding is the best aspect of my game and that's because I don't really see the danger of diving, that's not a thought, so I just do it. I'll just launch myself across the floor and pick up the ball and lob it in and that's why my fielding's probably come on loads.'

'The downsides are that sometimes, if I am batting, if I switch off or zone out, and then all of a sudden you're out. And it's "shit – I'm out now." And then I kick myself because I'm like if I had just concentrated for that little bit longer I'd still be in. That lapse in concentration means you're out, or you've dropped a catch. Or sometimes with the impulsivity side of things, I'll just play a shot. And instantly be like, "I shouldn't have played that shot. And now I'm out." And it's dead frustrating.'

'Also, I'm a bit of a nightmare for the captain because I wander. She'll put me somewhere, but I'll just drift, and I'll end up 10-yards further than where I need to be. If I'm meant to be fielding on the ring, I'll creep in and all of a sudden I'm about 10-yards away from the batter and it's like "what are you doing? Go back to where you need to be."'

'I'm much better with sleep now, but up until probably sixth form I'd sleep like four hours a night max. I just could not fall asleep. And then when I did fall asleep, I'd sleep for like an hour and a half. And then I'd be up for an hour, then I'd fall asleep for half an hour, so it weren't even four hours in one solid block.'

'I was on medication but I've come off it because I didn't eat, I didn't sleep, I were like a zombie. I just didn't feel any emotion. And then because I didn't feel any emotion, it would all just hit me and I'd lose me head. The amount of times I was losing my head at cricket and fully going to like meltdown mode, it just weren't worth it.'

'I didn't tell my coaches about the ADHD for a long time, my mum made me sit down and tell them. I think the coaches are great when you speak to them and I think they understand my ADHD in theory but I don't think they understand it in real terms. Like they might understand that it'd take me a bit longer or that I will struggle because sometimes I switch off and they are like "yeah I get it." And then when I'm in the net and I get out with a silly shot, they're like "why did you miss that shot?"'

'Coaches need to remember they will get more out of me by giving me a little bit more leeway than by constantly hammering me. You'll get 10x more out of me than if you're constantly peppering me and constantly asking "why did you play that shot?" I've just not concentrated for a moment – it's not the end of the world is it?'

'Giving me leeway isn't letting me off, if I've just done something that's being a shit person, then fine. But if it's that I'm not concentrating or I'm struggling to sit still in a meeting, you don't need to hound me. I get it's a professional environment, but you don't need to hound me about that.'

'It is important to remember that no one with ADHD is doing anything annoying on purpose. I'm not trying to be an ass. I don't think people understand how frustrating it is for us. It's gonna frustrate me more than anyone that I had no concentration and got myself out. I don't need you being all frustrated at me, because I'm already kicking myself. I'm already beating myself up.'

CHAPTER **8**

Medication

Athletes diagnosed with ADHD need to make a choice as to whether or not they would like to take medication. According to the British Journal of Psychology, in 2020, 62 per cent of children in the UK with an ADHD diagnosis were receiving medication. It is thought to be similar in diagnosed adults. When tested in school aged children it was found to be effective in between 65% and 75% of cases and for these people their symptoms have been found to improve by up to 90%.

There are two types of medication: stimulants and non-stimulants. The most popular by far are stimulants – studies find that over 50% of individuals with ADHD are prescribed one. They have been found to be an effective treatment to improve executive functions in many of those with ADHD.

HOW STIMULANT MEDICATIONS WORK...

It might seem counter intuitive to give those with hyperactive ADHD stimulant medication – surely they are already over-stimulated? The Dopamine hypothesis that we learnt about in the introduction explains why they are thought to work. When they have run brain imaging studies researchers find that people with ADHD may have slight differences in their brain's structure, the way different brain regions engage to perform actions and the way neurotransmitters pass on information. Of the neurotransmitters (the chemicals that send signals in the brain) Dopamine is a really important one for a number of reasons; it helps us use our motor skills and cognitive abilities, plays an important role in our reward and motivation system, spikes when we anticipate something good or significant happening, can impact our memory and regulate attention. In fact, ADHD is sometimes described as a Dopamine deficit disorder. Stimulant medication can increase Dopamine and norepinephrine (another important neurotransmitter) levels in the pre-frontal cortex (the part of our brain that drives our cognitive and executive functions).

There are two ways stimulants can increase Dopamine and Norepinephrine: either by increasing the release of Dopamine and norepinephrine into the synapse (the tiny gaps between neurons) or by preventing the neurons from 'reuptaking' the Dopamine and norepinephrine so that more remains in the synapse, improving the way different parts of the brain connect and communicate. This means these stimulant medications don't resolve ADHD long term but while they are active in your system they can help to reduce the symptoms.

Some medications have an 'immediate-release' version which acts quickly, lasting for 2–5 hours and wears off rapidly. These might be needed to be taken a few times a day. Others are extended-release so they are taken in the morning and are released into the body over the day, lasting between 6 and 14 hours.

The optimal stimulant dose will vary but medical professionals will usually have a 'start low, go slow' approach, where the stimulant can be gradually increased until they find the most effective dose for you.

> *"It makes me feel like I have more space in my brain. I have calm and things are not as tightly woven. They have a bit more space to percolate. And that seems to feed into my nervous system. And have a very calming effect. It just kind of, just takes the edge off the extremes so I feel better able to deal with stuff. A calm focus rather than the sort of intense crazed focus."* Jen, Runner

ADHD stimulant medications are known as 'controlled drugs' because they can be tempting to those who don't 'need' to take them but would like to because, for those without ADHD, they can cause euphoria and an improved feeling of wellbeing. Most people taking them also notice some weight loss which might be seen as a positive for those unable to lose weight in other ways.

Stimulants tend to be the first approach a psychiatrist would take. However up to around 30% of those with ADHD either do not have a beneficial response to stimulant medication or find they are unable to tolerate the side effects and these people may take non-stimulant medication which tends to focus on drugs which stop the brain reuptaking certain neurotransmitters (like Norephedrine) or act as anti-depressants.

Taking medication is a very personal choice and so in deciding whether to take it, in particular as an athlete, there are a number of elements to consider.

BENEFITS OF MEDICATION FOR GENERAL FUNCTIONING

The benefits of stimulant medication in day-to-day life for those with ADHD can be found in both behavioural and cognitive areas.

Enhances...
- Productivity
- Task focus
- Attention
- Alertness
- Peer interactions
- Persistence
- Response inhibition
- Cognitive functioning
- Reaction times
- Working memory
- Self-regulation

Reduces...
- Impulsivity
- Aggression
- Stressful interactions
- Hyperactivity
- Disruptive behaviours

Emotionally, improving both cognitive and behavioural elements means someone with ADHD is less likely to have a low quality of life, reduced academic achievement and poor self-esteem as they stop feeling like they are constantly failing. It is often suggested too that the earlier someone gets their diagnosis, the earlier they can start treatment which means they have fewer long-term issues or outcomes from the behavioural elements of ADHD.

BENEFITS OF MEDICATION FOR ATHLETES

Putting these benefits into the sporting environment we can see how it may be help an athlete with ADHD to take medication.

Overall, it is suggested that, in taking stimulant medication, a balancing takes place where the athlete's cognitive and behavioural activities become closer to the abilities of a non-ADHD athlete. A large meta-analysis (a study pulling together lots of other studies) says that the benefits of the medication can be that it improves cognitive functioning including memory, reaction time, reaction time variability, and response inhibition, all of which can get an ADHD athlete closer to the level of cognitive function of someone without it.

Behaviourally though is where, for some, we can see a big difference. ADHD athletes on stimulant medication have been found to improve their sportsmanship and peer relationships and have fewer rule violations and to cause less disruption during practice. It has also been found to improve effort levels and sporting knowledge in juniors, perhaps because they are able to focus and absorb more of the sporting information. If an athlete receives fewer yellow and red cards, and they don't develop an unhelpful and negative reputation which can squash their self-esteem, then they will do better long term in their sport.

When looking at the impact on skills, the research suggests that the medication doesn't improve gross motor skills (skills using the whole body and large movement) – but enhances conditions for better performance so if you have the skills you are less likely to mess them up by losing your temper or patience, being impulsive, getting sent off for poor behaviour or not following instructions. Some studies have found stimulant medication does improve fine motor skills (skills requiring co-ordination to do activities with our hands) and visual motor speed (how quickly we can integrate the information in front of us to take action) in sport.

Injury is the biggest cause of upset and distress I see within athletes as a psychologist and the improvements in attention, impulsivity, and risk-taking behaviours that can come from ADHD medication could explain why those using medication have a lower risk of injuries, as they are less likely to be putting themselves in as many risky situations.

> "Since I had the diagnosis I'm really learning to embrace who I am I and be less bothered that I don't fit in in as many places as others. The medication has really helped my energy levels throughout the day, so I don't find things as tiring, and that has helped my mental health hugely." Isla, Cyclist

RISKS OF STIMULANT MEDICATION IN DAILY LIFE

The common adverse side effects of stimulant medication (most were found the be moderate and short lasting):

- Neurological effects (headache, dizziness, insomnia, seizures, tics, irritability, agitation)
- Gastro issues (nausea, constipation, abdominal pain, loss of appetite, dry mouth, excessive thirst)
- Cardiovascular issues (increase in heart rate, Jitteriness, palpitations, body temperature)
- Gynaecological issues (menstrual problems, reduced libido)
- Sleep disturbances (insomnia, fatigue)

SPECIFIC SIDE EFFECTS TO BE AWARE OF AS AN ATHLETE OR A COACH...

Some of the adverse side effects can be amplified when someone with ADHD is playing sport and most sport governing bodies state that athletes with ADHD approved to use stimulant medication should be monitored by health care professionals and regularly physically evaluated. Three of these adverse side effects can have specific negative impacts on athletes health, wellbeing and performance; the loss of appetite, the rise in body temperature and risks for those with cardiovascular issues. We will consider each here...

Underfuelling

As we saw in chapter 4, it is important athletes fuel their exercise effectively if they are to thrive and maintain high levels of performance. However, ADHD stimulant medication is an appetite suppressant and many athletes on it report finding it very difficult to eat as much as they need to. Research has found those taking the most common stimulant for ADHD (methylphenidate) were around 15 times more likely to have a decreased appetite than those not taking it.

In one study on an ADHD stimulant medication, 91% of those taking it lost weight and the average weight loss was 3.6kg. This weight loss in adults can show up as reduced growth rates in children. Studies that use longitudinal data suggest that children using stimulant medication generally have a reduction in both height and weight gain of, on average, a reduction in height of approximately 1cm a year during the first one to three years of treatment and a reduction in weight gain of 3kg lower than predicted over a three year period.

As well as possibly unwanted weight loss and growth limitations underfuelling has implications for sporting performance too. At a basic level athletes need energy to physically perform the movements required. At a psychological level we now our brains need lots of fuel; mainly glucose. When an athlete is underfuelled they struggle to make good decisions, can think irrationally and their threat system triggers very easily causing emotional dysregulation (often known in sport as getting the red mist).

Overheating in competition or training environments

Studies have found that many stimulants that are used to treat ADHD symptoms can increase the body's core temperature. This can cause the athlete to overheat in hot environments and increase risk of heart injury, mask signs and symptoms of fatigue and cause collapse. This suggests that athletes training or competing in hot environments and pushing themselves really hard will need to consider use of stimulants and if they do take them be very mindful of the potential risks.

Pressure of medication on the heart

A number of studies have found that stimulant medication can cause an elevation in blood pressure. Additionally, both stimulant and non-stimulant medications have been found to cause a small increase in heart rate averaging 1–4.8 beats per minute (at both rest and active) but the way data is averaged in trials may hide some much larger increases; in rare cases it has been found to rise by up to 50 beats a minute. This increase may be significant for those with an underlying heart condition. No risk has been found between the use of stimulant medication and cardic events in those without underlying cardiac conditions, but there is thought to be an increased risk of complications when an athlete already has a cardiac condition. The rise in rest and exercising heart rate may also have implications for the RPE (rate of perceived exertion) making an athlete's effort level feel harder.

MITIGATING THE RISKS

Pre-prescription heart check: A number of sporting bodies state that an athlete must have a cardiac check before being prescribed stimulants to protect from this risk. They will often run a syncope on exercise and discuss any family history of sudden death below the age of 40 years or death associated with exercise, ask about pre-existing arrhythmias and channelopathies and any elevated blood pressure before ADHD stimulant medication could be offered.

Timing of food and medication: If a stimulant does cause appetite suppression it can be helpful to have a big breakfast before taking the medication, have lots of easy to access healthy snacks within grabbing distance and then plan for a big dinner so that it matters less if you don't eat so much at lunch. To do this, spend some time really working out what snacks feel acceptable, are high energy and you feel able to eat even if you don't feel hungry and have lots of those stored at home.

Heat awareness: Being incredibly mindful of the higher body temperature than ADHD medication can cause so having plans in place to manage the heat in competitions or hard training taking place in warmer climates.

Monitoring: Monitor height, weight, appetite, heart, blood pressure and common symptoms such as headache, insomnia, anorexia, nausea and emotional upsets. WADA requirements say this type of monitoring should take place at least every 12 months and the athlete should be reevaluated for ADHD every 4 years.

Medication holidays: If growth is found to become limited or the medication is harming some element of performance then some athletes take a medication holiday. This is where they stop taking the medication for anything from a few days to a few months. Some will take medication specifically on certain days when they have tests or competitions. Some might take them regularly as they find they help with studying and training but stop ahead of a big match or event where they want to have the impulsiveness and additional energy. These drug holidays are not unusual in ADHD medication but can be contentious so worth looking at the pros and cons of taking one:

Pros of taking ADHD medication holiday	Cons of taking ADHD medication holiday
• If the medication has caused any restrictions on growth (such as reducing appetite then research suggests that a drug holiday will see children return to their regular growth percentiles and adults better able to fuel their activities. • Can allow you to control some of the adverse effects like long-term increases in blood pressure. • Can counteract waning effectiveness after a long period of continuous use (because they interrupt the development of drug tolerance) so upping the dosage is less likely to be needed. • They can be used to see how effective the medication is being. The break will show what life is like without the side effects so you can make a more considered decision as to whether to carry on with medication. • A drug holiday might allow an athlete to compete using the elements of ADHD which give them an advantage – like impulsivity.	• ADHD symptoms can emerge during the break or worsen when the medication is withheld. • Accidents and Injuries can become more likely when someone used to being able to focus on ADHD medication stops it. One study found that a high number of children who had to attend a burns unit had not had their usual dose of ADHD on the day they burnt themselves. • WADA specifically advises against using stimulant medication inconsistently as this can cause an increase in risky or in conflictual type behaviours like altercations with referees.

THE ETHICS OF MEDICATION IN SPORT

Athletes taking stimulant medication need a Therapeutic Use Exemption (TUE) as the medication is on the WADA banned list. This can prompt some stigma as judgement can follow the need for a TUE, even self-judgement as some athletes say they feel they are cheating. To help you consider the ethics of taking stimulant medication let's go back to chapter 1 where we looked at the five key factors on which optimal performance in sport is said to be based upon…

Area	Impact	Outcome on performance
Physiology	Medication does not impact this positively – in fact there are elements where it may cause risk; weight loss, heart issues, raised blood pressure, overheating will all need additional monitoring. These elements can negative impact performance through lower body composition, fuelling training poorly, an inability to meet training demands, finding it harder to get the right levels of intensity and increased recovery time.	Potentially negative impact on performance Additional monitoring required
Biomechanics	Medication will not impact this but in allowing an athlete to focus more it may reduce the number of acute injuries they receive.	Potentially positive impact on performance putting the athlete on a par with non ADHD athletes
Psychology	Quality of life and wellbeing can be impacted by a history of failure, underachievement, poor social functioning and low self-esteem. An ADHD athlete trying to compete in sport may well have spent years struggling with these elements and medication may be able to level the playing field a little.	Potentially positive impact on performance putting the athlete on a par with non ADHD athletes
Tactics	Medication may be able to help an athlete focus on a single strategy and analyse the game around them better which can help with tactics. Impulse control can also be improved on medication – for some this is helpful and for others this might cause slower reaction times.	Can be a positive or negative impact on performance depending on the sport
Health/lifestyle	ADHD is associated with a lower quality of life. Taking medication can improve their quality of life which for many will be essential to access elite sporting performance.	Potentially positive impact on performance putting the athlete on a par with non-ADHD athletes

There are issues with stimulants being coveted by athletes and students who do not have ADHD. They are classified as controlled drugs which provide positive medicinal effects but can be abused by those who do not have ADHD. In the USA, ADHD medications are the second most common form of illicit drug use in university students (after marijuana) as they have the ability to prompt weight loss and help students focus for exams or assignments. This means they can be abused. In fact, one study found that 54% of students legitimately prescribed ADHD stimulants were approached by peers to share their medication and in one study 29% admitted they had given or sold their medication to others.

Those taking stimulants with an ADHD diagnosis will be having regular mental and physical check-ups to ensure the medication is not putting their health at risk. Those without a diagnosis or that system in place put themselves at significant risk of heart disease, over heating during exercise and mental health issues.

WADA GUIDELINE SUMMARY

If you choose to take stimulant medication it is worth reflecting on the latest WADA (World Anti-Doping Agency) Guidelines (from October 2023) which state that:

- There must be a comprehensive assessment (by a psychiatrist or clinic psychologist) meeting the DSM-5 or ICD-11) criteria along with a description or summary of how the criteria were assessed and which criteria were met, referencing which diagnostic instruments and scales were used to assess the symptoms and impairment.
- For those diagnosed over the age of 18 there should be evidence of symptoms during childhood but if this is too difficult to get, a second opinion from another independent specialist medical practitioner (usually a psychiatrist) confirming the diagnosis may be required.
- Optimal doses vary greatly so are best decided on an individual basis.
- There is no need to cease treatment during competition periods. It is now generally considered that cessation of treatment can have a number of negative effects including an adverse effect on symptom control, which can take time to re-establish.
- In newly diagnosed ADHD patients there will be dosage changes until optimal management is achieved. Given this, a range of doses may

be appropriate on the approval certificate with a maximal 12-month approval allowing for the next approval to be granted for a stable dose. This prevents the need for repeat TUE applications in the first year for changes of doses whilst stabilizing the symptoms.

- Due to the chronic nature of ADHD, a TUE, in the case of a well-documented diagnosis of ADHD on a stable dose of medication, can be granted for up to four years at a time. A recent diagnosis with ongoing dose titration could initially be approved for 12 months and at the next application, if the dose is stable, a 4-year approval could be granted.

- A TUE reapplication should include current and appropriate notes from the treating physician. Any change of medication or significant adjustment of the dosage during the approval period should result in a re-submission or advisement to the ADO (Anti-Doping Organization) granting the TUE.

Guidelines will change regularly though so make sure you check the latest WADA guidelines and those specifically from your sporting governing body.

Medication and more

Research looking for the most effective treatments tend to identify a gold standard of using stimulant medication alongside psycho-social and behavioural interventions. Many of the suggested psycho-social and behavioural interventions that are advised will be found in chapters 5 and 6. The research suggests that by combining both medication and behavioural tools, those with ADHD can perform equally as well on low doses of both as they would on high doses of either one individually.

ISLA'S STORY

Isla is a professional cross-country mountain biker based in Scotland.

'Riding was very much a central part of my childhood and my dad and I would race as a pair in the long distance events where he would do most of it, and I would do a tiny bit, and then we'd win! I was not one of those kids who was pushed really hard in sport, I was actually at a specialist music school in Edinburgh. It was like a really intense environment and I wasn't very happy there in the end, and realized that music wasn't really my calling. Then, with my mountain biking, over the next three to four years, I quite rapidly reached the top of the national level for age group. I didn't see myself being a professional, I liked doing it because it was fun. I liked being outside. I really liked exercising. So, I've been full time racing since I was eighteen with the occasional part-time study in there. It happened by accident, and now it's my full-time job and I can make a living.'

'I grew up in a family who didn't understand neurodivergence. So, I grew up not understanding what it actually was and how it can impact every part of somebody's life. And then I, on the flip side, have struggled my whole life since I was in nursery, with social relationships, with the structure of schools. It misinterpreted as me not being challenged enough in school but actually it was because I had ADHD and nobody realized. Looking back now, it's very, very clear.'

'As somebody being diagnosed late you have to reshape your entire narrative of your past. Since I was a mid-teenager, I've gone through periods of depression, was on anti-depressants for a period, diagnosed with generalized anxiety disorder. They felt like isolated kind of struggles but two years ago my partner [who is a nursery teacher with lots of experience with neurodivergence] joked this is something somebody with ADHD would do and I started to connect all these things I had been struggling with; feeling like an outsider in so many parts of my life.'

'I have tried to do a degree. I'm on attempt number four at the moment, but obviously it's clear now why I've always struggled. I started a degree in French, and then changed to global cinema. Then my second attempt was a German degree. And then I started a degree in Human Biology and Nutrition. And I'm now genuinely doing the degree I was supposed to be doing which is Criminology and Sociology. I'm doing that with Open University, which is way more ADHD friendly than others.'

'The trigger moment was when I was visiting my sister in New Zealand. I had booked my ticket, and googled do I need a visa. I read no, but I only read the first line and you do need a form to say you don't need a visa. I turned up at the airport for my flight and they wouldn't let me on the plane because I didn't have this form. Instead of waiting 10 extra days to get my flight rearranged for a small fee, I impulsively booked a next day ticket, still requiring this form that can take 40 hours to come. I ended up having to get the train to London because it was the only way to get a flight the next day, and I almost missed my train after spending £3,000 extra pounds for this flight. I phoned my partner and I was like, why is this happening? Why do I keep doing this? Why am I not learning from mistakes? I did lots of reading and it became increasingly obvious I have ADHD.'

'I have combined type but my inattentive traits are through the roof, whereas my hyperactive ones are, somewhere in the middle. There's lots of ways in which the diagnosis helpful but one was the more I read, the more I realized that there was this whole community of people that had a brain like me, it was really validating and really empowering.'

'I was constantly taught that I was less good than others in school, incidents with teachers where I have been told where I am not good enough, and if you are told this repeatedly throughout your childhood, and constantly shut down and crushed you learn to believe it. The biggest thing about the diagnosis is that I have the ability to change that narrative now, and learn to love myself and forgive myself, and actually embrace who I am. Before, I was trying to function in ways that didn't work, in areas of life that didn't work and now I can be proud of who I am now instead of wondering why I'm not like other people and thinking that I'm less rather than just different.'

'I ride for an all-women's team. Everyone's super nice, everyone's super neurotypical, so it can sometimes be challenging for me to articulate struggles and its a lot of work, living in that space every day and sharing a room with people. They know I have ADHD and they try to get it but they don't get it.'

'I am very against the superpower rhetoric with ADHD because it's just not been my experience and I think that narrative is actually quite harmful because it just totally dismisses my entire existence.'

'Being neurodivergent and being a sportsperson is really beneficial in training. In training I have super hyperfocus and you can see it in my numbers but then I take it to a race and it is so hard.'

'Racing in my sport lasts around one and a half hours, it's mass start, there's 80 riders on the start line. 6 laps on the same track including technical sections, A-lines, different line choice. It's obviously very noisy because of the spectators and it's quite intense. You have to be able to process things very quickly. Something I have struggled with always with is multi-stage processing.'

'If we've got a technical descent, and I've like practised my line the days before the race, because my brain is already like loaded up from like this sensory stuff from the start line and the processing, it's exhausted already, so by the time I get to a section which in practice, when my brain is like fresh, I've been able to ride fine and ride fast, I'm not able to process it quick enough, so I have to ride slower because my body is like waiting for my brain.'

'My world ranking is not good enough to be starting right at the front so normally I'm starting 4th or 5th row with another 4 or 5 rows behind me. I have always been, totally unable to go in the space when a space opens up in front of me, I just get swallowed all the time. And likewise when it's really chaotic on the first lap because everyone is trying to go onto these narrow trails, I can't make quick decisions, so I lose a lot of positions. It's always been so frustrating for me. In so many races I have started way further back than my actual level and then I ride through the field, and then my last couple of laps are like top 15, top 10, but I finish 25th because of all the stuff happening at the start. The medication has completely solved all of these problems. A space would open and I would just be able to respond and go into it and make quick decisions. It's opened up this whole new headroom.'

'Because I have grown up with this narrative where I have been taught that I am inferior I have grown really comfortable with that. When I am successful or do a really good race, I don't know how to deal with it emotionally and I have this subconscious self-sabotage routine going on in my head because it's almost easier. I'm like 'that's not me, I'm not successful'. I don't know how to be that person so then I go back to the space where despite being really horrible and shitty and actually emotionally quite dark, it is at least space that I'm used to.'

'The broad problem I've always struggled with is training would always go really well, recovery would go really well and I would do the textbook taper and be 'fresh' for a big race and I would be exhausted. Now I understand why, I'd done everything right but was still exhausted, and now I see it is the time management, the social relationships, the sensory problem and the anxiety, and understanding that has been huge for me.'

'I've struggled with a lot of aspects with racing that I now understand are because of my ADHD. I have been racing professionally for ten years and during that time, I have continued to deliver occasional performances that have shown my potential but they happen like once in a blue moon. And I can't make it happen consistently. I have never been able to get the timing right. Now I'm on the medication and it's been life changing.'

'The first day of medication two things happened. I have massive problems with object invisibility. I had taken a tag off something and chucked it on the desk and then my head was like "I should put that in the bin when I leave the room" knowing full well I'm not going to remember to do that. Then, 10 minutes later I went to leave the room, and my brain reminded me that I had left this thing on the desk. The other thing I noticed was that I was able to move from task to task without this feeling of resistance or lethargy in my head.'

'I now understand that I have ended up being a professional athlete because exercise has been subconsciously medicating me because I get a lot of Dopamine and endorphins from that and it helps to calm my brain.'

CHAPTER **9**

Coaching an athlete with ADHD

If you are a coach, or you are working in a professional capacity with athletes (perhaps as a PE teacher, sport psychologist, nutritionist, physiotherapist or team manager) and are noticing some traits that might indicate ADHD, this chapter is for you. You may (hopefully) notice that many of the tools suggested here to help you support an athlete with ADHD would also constitute best practice for neurotypical athletes too and so hopefully you are already using a number of them. The more you can incorporate the better able you will be to offer a neurodiverse inclusive coaching environment.

Firstly, one of the best ways to get the best out of an athlete is to openly ask them what already works well for them – they will be the biggest expert in themselves. If working with under 16s you can additionally ask the athlete's parents for advice on how they get the best from their child and adopt a similar approach if possible. If you can show a real interest in what the athlete or their parent says has worked so far for them, you have already done half the work.

> *"Being able to come in and say how you feel, whether it's good or bad, and not feel like it is a thing that you should be judged on, or a negative thing, will make a difference."*
> Rachel, Cricketer

Then, try to understand the ADHD brain. Read chapter 1 to understand the high performance brain and chapter 3 to see where the elements of ADHD can disrupt high performance creating a highly sensitive threat system. Even with the best possible preparation and physical and mental strategies for a competition, if something happens that causes the nervous system to feel 'unsafe' then it will be impossible for the athlete to perform to their potential, or even to perform to their current training level. Their nervous system will not allow them to push beyond threshold effort because it thinks it is already threatened enough – it cannot risk the additional threat of not being able to breathe well, regulate the heart rate or get into physical discomfort. When you work with an athlete to create tools and environments where they feel 'safe', then they can push themselves harder and perform better.

Finally, consider your communication style. This can benefit all athletes.

Ten tips for communicating effectively with ADHD athletes

1. Ask closed answer questions
2. Be specific in your language
3. Check the athlete has the right message from a briefing
4. Be clear in briefings on what information applies to who
5. Slow down your communication
6. Give as much certainty as you can
7. Set a communication goal: Know what you trying to communicate, what you want to gain from the communication, what are you trying to avoid and why?
8. Offer clarity: Asking an athlete with ADHD 'for a chat' without giving any context may see them catastrophize. Explain up front why you want to talk and what you will cover.
9. Deliver information simply: Long streams of instructions with lots of distractions around won't give an athlete the clarity they need to do the task being set.
10. Give clear instructions and follow through with appropriate consequences when needed.

Beyond communication style we must remember that there are so many elements and features of ADHD that individual athletes are likely to experience their version differently to others. This means it is essential to ask, learn and adapt. The goal is to help those with ADHD better navigate a world that has not been designed with their needs in mind. This means you won't develop a blanket approach to supporting an ADHD athlete but as you get to know them you can consider the way their specific version of ADHD (and any co-occurring conditions) shows up and support them in a way that specifically works for them.

It is also important to note what will work for an ADHD athlete will fade in power over time and a new approach might be needed. This means you need to evaluate your approaches and tactics regularly to modify when required and to increase your ability to get the best from your athletes.

To help here we cover some of issues you may notice in some of your athletes with ADHD and some ideas you can try to help support them effectively and allow them to thrive in their sport.

DISORGANIZATION

What you might notice: Disorganization will come from poor planning and time management. In an athlete you might notice they arrive at practice without key pieces of kit and equipment, they show up late to practices and competitions, they may not respond to team messages about availability for competitions, they miss appointments, seem unable to prioritize, dawdle and don't seem to have a sense of urgency. Some of this will be because, with ADHD, decisions are assessed by whether they have an effect now (this very moment) or in the future (which is usually ignored as out of sight means out of mind). This means all decisions will be made with what is best in this very moment, regardless of long-term consequences. If an athlete is not taking 'the future' into mind their decisions will all be based on immediate rewards and excitement, not potential long-term hardships or sporting or fitness requirements.

How to help:

- Avoid public criticism and do not openly highlight any of these issues in the wider group.

- Do some goal setting with the athlete which focuses on getting the basics in place.

- Communicate clear timelines of any deadlines.

- Keep requests simple and ask only one question at a time.

- Help athletes create checklists of kit and equipment required.

- See if you can set up automatic text reminders of training sessions or competitions.

- Make a session relevant in the moment. A regular strength and conditioning session that will reduce injury risk will not resonate but the same S&C session sold as an opportunity to hang out with friends will see them show up.

- Externalize information into charts, images, lists, reminders, noises.

- Highlight consequences, not punishments. Punishments are unfair when the athlete does not have a brain that is naturally tuned for organization. Any consequences of performance limiting behaviour should be highlighted as this might motivate to put more tools in place to improve organization. For example being late (on average 15 minutes late) to all four sessions over a week would allow you to highlight they are now an hour behind their competitors in training, fitness or skills development.

> "I really like a loop to run round, or a track, because there's enough things to think about. You want me to do three lots of this, plus this, plus this, plus that, with that, break in between. That can quite easily get jumbled up in my head and then I become frustrated." Jen, Runner

EMOTIONAL DYSREGULATION

What you might notice: An athlete with ADHD is likely to struggle with regulating their emotions, particularly when they are feeling unsafe or threatened in some way. You might notice that they seem unable to sit with uncomfortable emotions, they lose their temper quickly if something is not going well, they regularly receive yellow or red cards and have fall outs with their peers and the coaches. To feel in control of your emotions as an athlete they need to aim to respond (slower, rational and thoughtful based on an assessment of longer term consequences) to anything that happens rather than react (immediate, emotional, over dramatic and driven by threat) as it is reacting too fast that can sometimes get us into trouble.

How to help:

- Get to know the signs of ADHD dysregulation so you can spot quickly when an athlete might need additional support.

- Be very clear in feedback using specific examples of where their behaviour impacted performance. In this you can focus on the harm the dysregulation does to their performance to open up a discussion on ways to make them feel safer and less under threat in each environment.

- Have a code word they can use to highlight that they are struggling.

- Anticipate the moments that will be hardest for your athletes with ADHD like transitions (such as from free play to organised activity) or changes in rules (maybe from one element of the sport to another).

- Help to create an environment where all athletes have a more stable, less fragile threat system. The athletes still need high level training stimulus but they also need to do it in conditions that feel safe in order to feel emotionally regulated.

- While sports can help an athlete to self-regulate, to do well they will need to learn their own tools to self-regulate. When an athlete is under stress, tired, ill or struggling with low blood sugar levels they will find this harder, and of course many of these elements show up in sport as a competition or training session goes on. To help them top up their self-regulation energy you can offer: short breaks during activities requiring lots of self-regulation, opportunities to relax, meditation, visualization, self reward, positive self-talk reminders and snack breaks.

- Offer positive reinforcement of any effective and restrained behaviours and offer praise immediately you spot it – this can reduce the need for athlete reaction and allow them the space to respond.

- The weaknesses in executive functioning associated with ADHD means behaviour is less regulated by internal information. Asking your ADHD athletes about how they physically feel and where they might be noticing discomfort showing up in their bodies can help that self-awareness. All athletes should be doing this anyway (only those with ADHD will be less likely to) so having a regular noise (like a Beep) that sounds when you want athletes to self-reflect and notice how they are feeling can be a fun tool to try occasionally.

FORGETFULNESS

What you might notice: If an ADHD athlete seems to be forgetful it will be coming from their poor working memory. This means they can feel like they are failing if they are struggling to do as asked, even if they are incredibly physically gifted. You might notice that they might forget instructions quickly, make the same mistakes over and over despite being corrected, struggle to process multiple pieces of information at the same time and don't seem to take your feedback on board.

How to help:

- Break down instructions and feedback into smaller chunks and just give one at a time.
- Ask the athlete to repeat the instruction back to you to ensure it has been understood at the start of each activity.
- Streamline feedback and just give the most important piece.
- Write feedback down so it can be reflected upon after the session.
- Offer visual cues. Instead of continually reminding the athlete to do something (which is annoying for both of you) physical, visual cues can help athletes remember what they should be working on. Instead of a rowing coach in the boat beside the crew yelling 'look forward' at the ADHD athlete in bow you could put a sticker on the back of the rower in front with a direction 'stare here'. This reduces stigma, frustration and keeps the athlete reminded and away from distractions.
- Rather than single out any athlete who is seen to 'misbehave' by not connecting the rules of the club with their own behaviours in the moment, rules could be posted on the wall and turned into a team chant before each session.
- Reducing the gaps between asking for something to be done and when it should be done is helpful. Instead of a list of instructions with advice like 'leave all the equipment outside of the storage unit after you have finished' it is better to do one instruction at a time, only requiring the equipment to be outside of the hut at the actual time it needs putting away.

COACHING AN ATHLETE WITH ADHD   171

> *"Set the training for me, not for my ADHD. Don't patronise me by giving me baby sessions or reduced volume. Set training and expectations for the person you see when I'm not overwhelmed or dysregulated."* Jen, Runner.

HYPERACTIVITY

<u>What you might notice:</u> If one of your athletes is hyperactive you will know it. They will be unable to sit still, need to be constantly moving, unable to engage with tasks they find boring and will really struggle when sessions are unstructured or you offer 'free play'. They will not know what to do with themselves (and so may get into trouble).

<u>How to help:</u>

- Create a consistent schedule and structure with clear expectations of conduct.
- Consider how changes may cause stress and forewarn them in advance.
- Give them responsibility for any logistical tasks that require additional movement: putting equipment out and away, setting up sessions, running to an office to pick up something.
- Don't leave 'empty space', instead offer suggestions of movements or activities to do when others might be asking for downtime.
- Give them a fidget toy to play with during any sit down thinking type sessions.

HYPERFOCUS

<u>What you might notice:</u> Hyperfocus, as you will have read in many of the athlete's stories in this book, can be an incredible benefit in sport as, if the athlete's sport is the thing that they love, they will put all their time and energy into it. If they are obsessed by the sport and spend a significant amount of their time (and money as adults) on it they may well have this hyperfocus.

How to help:

- Teach them how to use imagery and how to practise skills this way. This will allow them time to do additional skills development away from the sporting environment and without risk of an overtraining injury.

- Help them see their value and identity in other areas of life too so they don't struggle so much if their form dips or they become injured.

- Talk to them about how their focus can be their super-strength.

- Emphasize the importance of rest and recovery to become a better athlete.

IMPULSIVITY

What you might notice: You might notice impulsivity if an athlete is struggling to wait their turn, reacts instantly to others rather than responding with consideration and takes more risks than are good for their performance in their sport. If they seem to underestimate the consequences of any risky actions they may get into difficulties more often than other athletes, particularly in terms of getting a poor reputation for unsportsmanlike behaviour if they 'kick' off and getting too many yellow and red cards. If you get to know the athlete outside of the sport you might discover they are using unhealthy coping mechanisms for sport or life stresses like substance abuse or gambling.

How to help:

- Positive behavioural reinforcements for good attitudes and efforts to 'wait'.

- Intentionally creating opportunities for impulsivity in training sessions so their need is met.

- While medication has not been found to be particularly effective on sportsmanlike behaviour: praise, tokens and delayed rewards were able to improve this behaviour.

INATTENTION

What you might notice: When inattention shows up in an athlete you might notice they have a short attention span, are easily distracted, unable to focus for long, have difficulties concentrating, pay little attention to detail or may seem as if they are daydreaming.

How to help: Remember that an ADHD brain finds it difficult to screen out stimulants and prioritize information so giving an athlete lots of different pieces of information in a busy room is never going to be effective. If you want an athlete to focus on something away from doing their actual sport, give them a pencil and a sheet of paper (not a pencil case full of pens), seat them somewhere quiet and limit the work to 20 minutes so they can have a movement break afterwards.

- Reduce opportunities for distraction during a session. Plan your transitions, have equipment ready, move quickly between activities.

- Break down tasks into smaller chunks.

- Keep messages and feedback short and clear.

- Be very precise with language: instead of 'focus' say 'keep looking at the ball and follow where it goes with your eyes'.

- Create individual and small group activities as well as large group ones. This will keep engagement and activity levels high.

- Occasionally you could offer a task focused sporting session where you have a regular noise (like a beep) which can go off unexpectedly. When this happens each athlete is to evaluate whether they are on task (i.e. following the process goal they had set). If they are they reward themselves a point and the athletes with the highest amount of points at the end of the session get to pick the activities for free play time.

- Offer clear reward systems. Studies have found that achievements and improvement can be rewarded using both short- and longer-term reward systems and that in doing so it improve the athlete's ability to focus and reduces their inattention which improves performance.

- If you have the space, give ADHD athletes a low stimulus environment for recovery or meetings.

> "If you create an environment where conversations can happen and if someone can come in and say, "actually, I feel like I've got no energy to socialise, and I've got a million things going on in my brain, but still can't seem to focus on my training", then that's obviously going to help." Rachel, Cricketer

LACK OF PERSEVERANCE

<u>What you might notice:</u> A lack of perseverance might show up as someone who gets easily frustrated if something isn't going well or a skill takes lots of time to develop. They may show frustration at themselves or others.

<u>How to help:</u>

- Offer positive reinforcement when perseverance occurs, openly and intentionally rewarding the effort.
- Focus your goal setting with the athlete on process goals.
- Offer reward charts (for younger athletes) or reward activities for seeing an activity through to the end. This helps the athlete celebrate the small wins and clearly see their progress which clarifies the importance of perseverance.

> "I suspect that the coach I worked with for a decade also has ADHD, so we subconsciously had strategies in place that enabled me to thrive in many areas. An in-depth understanding of neurodivergence is essential to coach an ADHD athlete effectively." Isla, Cyclist

LOW SELF-ESTEEM

<u>What you might notice:</u> Athletes who are neurodiverse may struggle with low levels of confidence and self-esteem when trying to perform at a high level in an environment designed for those who are neurotypical. As a coach you might notice they need lots of reassurance, they become deeply ashamed or overly focused on any perceived failures. As their coach you are in a great place to help them build up their confidence.

How to help:

- Helping them identify and playing to their strengths.
- Offering positive reinforcement of activities completed well.
- Offering constructive feedback rather than critique.
- Helping them identify their super strength and find their niche role in the team or event.
- Find easy confidence boosting wins. Perhaps assign a chore that's needed and that won't get done unless this athlete does it. Start off with tasks that are fairly easy to do well and don't require many instructions and then gradually blend in more-important or challenging jobs. This becomes a really good opportunity to reinforce positive behaviour.
- Reward effort and praise process rather than outcomes.
- Don't try to control them. Give them autonomy in competitions to thrive.
- When other athletes have maxed out their motivation through potential reward, research suggests that those with ADHD might still profit from additional reward. As a coach trying to get the best from your ADHD athlete you are countering possibly years of that athlete being told they are not good enough or not listening properly. Using praise effectively will help you build that confidence which will improve their sporting skills and outcomes.

> "I think the good coaches are able to allow their players to make decisions by themselves, regardless of what they see. They're able to teach before the games and in training so that the player can make an informed decision during the game."
> Brooke, Footballer

MOTOR SKILL DEVELOPMENT DELAYS

What you might notice: Some athletes with ADHD may take longer to develop some of their motor skills. This means you might notice they become injured more than others, have poor balance, struggle with some coordination and can take longer to progress at learning new skills.

How to help:

- Develop with the athlete a sheet of all the skills they need to practise and get them to write down the date next to each one every time they achieve it so they 'see' their competencies develop.

- Use lots of visual feedback when working on new skills; video footage, watching others and physically (with permission) placing them into the correct position so they can 'feel' the movement.

- Offer regular progress updates.

PROCESSING DIFFICULTIES

What you might notice: If an ADHD athlete seems to be taking much longer to pick up instructions than others it could be their poor working memory (above) but it could also be that they have a slower cognitive processing speed.

How to help:

- Avoid criticizing their speed of action and instead praise their ability to reflect.

- Reduce external interference when giving instructions or feedback.

- Offer really tangible feedback.

- Offer regular updates on their progress.

- Explain the equipment or new movements (both sporting skills and rehab requirements) step by step. Perhaps have instructions up on the wall so that the athlete feels confident on how to use it safely. If there are a lot of instructions given all in one go they will won't be followed and then the activity won't be done effectively.

- Offer rewards for action – studies have found that the reaction time and accuracy of responding in people with ADHD have been found to be enhanced when they are provided with rewards.

> "Coaches are never mean about the ADHD but I also don't think they think enough. If they were to give me practice time beforehand to see what the pattern's supposed to be or walk me through it real quick before training then I could actually understand it." Brooke, Footballer

PROCRASTINATION

What you might notice: Procrastination is an avoidance tool we all use to protect ourselves from the potential physical (pain), psychological (boredom, risk of failure) or physiological (internal discomfort) threats that we perceive could be caused by the potential outcome of the action we should be doing. As a coach you won't see the amount of time it has taken an athlete to get to the gym or to do their training away from the club but you might see them doing things at the last minute and in a massive rush.

How to help:

- Positive reinforcement when things are done in time.
- Regular reminders of what is required by when.
- Breaking down any 'big' activities into more manageable chunks.

REJECTING ROUTINE AND STRUCTURE

What you might notice: An element of ADHD can be a craving for novelty. With this an athlete might push back against any forced routines or structure or they may be happier with routines they have developed themselves. They may seem excited in a crisis or when things are mixed up and done differently and they may be the athlete that is constantly asking you about new equipment or training, recovery or improvement methods they have heard about. We sometimes jokingly call this Magpie Syndrome when someone is constantly having their head turned by new shiny things!

How to help:

- Bring in something novel or exciting to the end of each practice session (something to look forward to). This can often be athlete led or co-created.
- Ask the athlete if they would like to design the structure or routine they require.

- Rather than rejecting their new 'shiny' ideas out of hand suggest they research them. Their hyperfocus might mean they really drill down and help you understand if it is a tool worth testing.

- Challenge yourself to set interesting sessions – The ADHD nervous system is interest-based so things need to feel good and they need to be interesting and exciting. It will keep all your athletes engaged longer and you will get more from them.

SENSATION SEEKING

What you might notice: Some athletes will be sensation seeking in training and you might see them constantly picking things up or being unable to leave equipment alone.

How to help:

- Offer fidget toys in sit down sessions – but use toys that won't disrupt others.

- Move them away from any dangerous equipment in training sessions.

- Ask them to take on a chore during any information giving that will fulfil their sensation seeking and ask a peer to give them the highlights of the information afterwards.

- Consider sensation soothing tools they can use in matches or competitions: velvet sown into the inside of a glove, fabric tape on the inside of the wrist, elastic band or hairband around the wrist.

UNHELPFUL TRAINING BEHAVIOURS

What you might notice: Some with ADHD might struggle to inhibit behaviours which can make it harder to coach them. You might feel they often do the opposite of what is asked, act defiantly if a decision is made against them, argue with both yourself and their peers, interrupt, talk over others and can become loud and disruptive in training sessions. It is important here to pick your battles. There are elements of behaviour that an ADHD athlete may do through boredom, distraction or impulsivity that will be frustrating to you in your role as a coach and make coaching harder. It can feel like the athlete is wilfully ignoring or disrespecting you and it would be easy to get into a power struggle but, expecting an athlete with ADHD to follow a long list of instructions, in a noisy environment and then punishing them when they can't do it, is the equivalent of telling someone in a wheelchair to go upstairs, not offering an elevator or ramp and then shouting at them when they inevitably fail. You would be punishing something beyond the athlete's choice.

You can use this knowledge in two ways: to build acceptance so it doesn't frustrate you in the same way and to take it on as a challenge – how can you present information in a more engaging, simplified and inclusive way? When you are able to do this all athletes benefit.

How to help:

- Establishing a predictable practice schedule and structure which has clear conduct expectations. Make these rules obvious and visual so they are regularly within line of sight.

- Agree a private code word or action with them for poor behaviour that won't embarrass them in front of others but will remind them of behavioural expectations.

- Have a very biased focus on 'positives before negatives' offering lots of positive, specific feedback to help them self-reflect (for example 'excellent pass to Freddie – where was your focus when doing that? Or 'you nailed the first part of that skill, where did you place your hands? Would you be able to do that again?').

- Any consequences for poor behaviour should match the issue (i.e. be a natural consequence) and be delivered quickly as delays in consequences reduce their impact. Ideally there should be a reward-to-punishment ratio 2:1 or greater so their sport remains a positive influence and not another area where they get told off.

- Offer 'noisy time' breaks for talking, playing/off task and clowning around.

- Unless there is a safety aspect, do not cancel free time or movement time as punishment. Those showing unhelpful behaviours are likely to be those most in need of the Dopamine that will come from being active and this will help their behaviours improve.

- To create more ownership and engagement ask the athlete with ADHD to demonstrate exercises.

- Rewards and punishments need to be rotated regularly if you are to use them to maintain motivation.

> "Some coaches sort of innately tap into a sort of cognitive diversity within their teams, and some don't. Rather than being a sort of paternal relationship where they're the coach and I'm the person learning, it needs to be like a conversation and working together. Good instructors for me, they'll ask a question like 'that was much better, what did you do that time and can you explain it.' That tends to work." James, Equestrian

Five tips from a parent of an athlete with ADHD who has observed helpful and unhelpful coaching...

1. If someone in your cohort has got ADHD use them to do the 'show and tells' – it will keep them active. If training is stop and start the ADHD brain disengages.
2. Keep challenging your athletes with ADHD – don't let them coast because they will never show you their best unless you push them out of their comfort zone.
3. Understand that coping behaviours might look bizarre but don't assume that if somebody isn't looking at you that they're not paying attention.
4. If you want an ADHD athlete's attention, use their name to bring them back to the room.
5. There is an impact on maturity of ADHD – they can be three or four years behind in terms of commitment and timekeeping, and the elements that lead to excellence. Try and think whether your expectation of them would be the same if they were three years younger.

JESS' STORY

Jess is Head Coach of a heavily neurodiverse grassroots women's Rugby team.

'If you are super player centric then your sessions will be inclusive, because you care about the people that you coach. Sometimes new people will rock up to a session, bringing some beautiful energy with them and I think "you might be neurodiverse" but we just focus on building a relationship with them and making sure they know that they are safe to be themselves. Not everybody needs to come to you presenting their formal diagnosis but we want them to feel comfortable if they do.'

'I don't really do anything different with a player who's neurodivergent but it is encompassed within our whole approach; coaching the player as a person. To support athletes with ADHD there is no checklist that I go through but I think it's being aware of different wants and needs of how neurodiversity might present itself. If you do this then you're going to tailor to their needs, which is automatically going to make your sessions more inclusive. I don't set out and go "right today I will coach in a neurodiverse friendly way," it's more a case of just thinking: "who are the players that I've got coming to the session? How do they like to receive information? What type of stuff do they need in a session?" and then just tailoring that accordingly. If you are really player specific and you're coaching the person in front of you, whether they're neurotypical, neurodiverse, they've been playing for 10 years or this is their first month playing then it's gonna be the best session for them. With this approach the players who are neurodiverse have then felt more able to say that they are neurodiverse so we can support them better.'

'We do a lot of priming around what will be within our sessions so players will know what to expect when they rock up. On the Whatsapp chat before training I put little clues in gif form about what the session might be. Everybody has guessing games and it acts as like a primer to generate some excitement. Whoever gets it right obviously is buzzing because they've got it right. But for everyone else there's also just a bit of stability so that when they rock up to a session, they know what the theme is before they arrive.'

'We think about Rejection Sensitivity Disorder (RSD) and how we all perceive feedback. We've just tried flipping some of our language into "What is your superpower" and "What is your Even Better?" So it's not a "weakness," it is a "I would be even better than I am now if I could execute X skill" so it's that you are already awesome but you could be even better if … This has helped me in my coaching but also flipped a narrative for players not to be so instantly negative on themselves.'

'Players that have come to me and said that they're neurodiverse will say they sometimes need a break for 5 minutes. We'll say "take whatever time you need" and model that for everyone – "If you've got period pain, take a minute." "If you've had a hard day at work, take a minute." It is a rule that is applied for everybody which means those who need it can really take it without shame, without guilt.'

'We've become really conscious of noise recently so we've changed how we end the session. We used to end it with a hands in and a cheer which was quite loud. So now I'll give each player a chance at the end of training to come up with a clap sequence. That seems to be a much better noise to end things on. We sometimes have music at our sessions but I'll tend to space it away from players that will find that noise a bit oppressive. I'm constantly moving the speaker so that the sound is with us but it's never on top of us. It means players can enjoy it more.'

'I don't blow a whistle, cause that can be really grating sometimes too, and it feels very authoritative, like coach with capital C, which I don't really like. So I'll tend to just use my voice and that way I can alter the volume a bit more and I can better control the level and intensity of the session.'

'I'll ask for hot feedback from the players right after training – from whoever I'm walking down to the car park with after packing up. It'll be different people each week so I'll ask "how was the session? What did you like? What were your best bits?" And I might also ask that in formalized stuff at the end of a session where we go around the circle, and I get a bit of feedback and also players share what worked for them so that everybody gets a better understanding of what everybody else likes.'

'From the ADHD athletes I see a lot of what might be perceived as excitable energy. I also see what might be perceived as unruliness. If we bring players together in a huddle, they'll be the ones that are stood next to me, taking the mic, engaging everybody in a bit of a banter, or distracting the person opposite them with some cheekiness. This can actually bring real value. Just because I've brought them into a huddle doesn't mean I expect them to instantly be able to swap from a very energetic game to now paying attention and being quiet. The value that those players bring is just helping everybody transition from what was a physically high energy moment to a mentally high energy one.'

'It is Rugby so we've got to do some serious stuff and we gotta be safe but there is never a session without a laugh and a giggle where we have shared some banter and somebody has absolutely ripped into me, and it's been hilarious. Nine times out of 10 that might be kick started by someone who we think might have ADHD.'

'The other week there was a beautiful moment where, following our captain's idea, we went around and we shared our own kryptonite; what we struggle with and then they shared their superpower as well. That created a space for chats. We are social creatures, and we know that not talking to each other can lead to mental health issues so it's very deliberate that we create social spaces at training; little pauses where you'll have a chat about how you played and connect with each other. What it's done, I think, is allow people who are neurodiverse, to get together and chat, and do little check ins with each other, which is really important.'

'We now also think about "brain stretch" so if we've been doing something really challenging then I'll make sure to include something in a session that dials the brain stretch right down; like a comfortable game at base level that will not require as much intensity. We want people to be learning, but we also don't want them to come away feeling that they've stretched the whole way through and therefore they must be rubbish.'

'We don't play with bibs. We play with headbands. Mostly it came out of body image issues, because bibs are typically one size only, and we're expecting players of any size to fit into this one size bib and you're going to feel uncomfortable and self-conscious if you're wearing a bib that's either too tight or too loose and not able to focus on the Rugby so we just use headbands, because chances are you can either wear it around your wrist or you can wrap it round your head.'

'This year we are theming our "ways of playing" – We've got constellations as our theme with laminated sheets printed off: for example, one is Gemini, which is twins, so it shows pairs moving into place for support. We'll bring these to match days and lay them out so it'll help frame some conversations and reduce the amount of information we need to give.'

'Now I realize it's normal for a coach to go through a journey of discovering their own authentic way of coaching but when I first started coaching I was very shouty. I was even shouting on sidelines on a match day. Then I became really aware of how to speak to players and find out what they wanted and what they needed. And then from that the neurodiverse needs came out. I think just being more open as a coach has helped. I'll chat about my vulnerabilities like "this is a new game today. It might not work. It might be bonkers. We'll give it a go. If it doesn't work, give me some feedback." When I started I felt I had to know everything but when that started to strip away, I became egoless at training sessions and better able to enjoy some banter and make the session much more enjoyable for everybody. The more vulnerability I show, the more open the players are.'

'In Rugby it feels like there is a perception that the coach must know everything, must control all controllables and uncontrollables, and that the team executes the coach's plan. This frustrates me. A player who's neurodiverse spoke up and said: "We hear other coaches shouting on the sidelines on match days, and you just allow us to be ourselves." And I said, "because I'm not coaching robots – I'm coaching human beings. I'm not sitting there with my Xbox or my Ps5 Controller on a match day. When you step onto the pitch it's your game." I said to them, "if I shout on the sidelines on a Saturday or a Sunday then I've failed in the week to prepare you. That's a 'me failure'." If I feel the need to control then then that's a me failure too as I have failed to prepare you.'

'There has to be give and take and mutual respect. For me, the way I've garnered that mutual respect is through banter. It makes me approachable and accessible because they can absolutely take the mic out of me, and they do so on a weekly basis. I'm also not afraid to show when I am myself frazzled, or I've forgotten something or been a bit scatterbrained; it is all about being authentically me.'

'When I started being this player centred was probably mentally taxing and used a lot of extra mental energy but now, I've just added on the layers over time and it feels comfortable.'

CHAPTER **10**

Supporting an athlete with ADHD

Whether you are a parent or a partner of an athlete with ADHD, living with someone who has both the traits of ADHD and the mindset required to be excellent in sport can be challenging. Learning what you can do to make their lives easier, how to scaffold around some of the deficits and put in place strategies to make them feel safer so their emotional dysregulation reduces can improve the lives of everyone in the household.

The athlete stories in this book all show people who are highly creative, able to think outside the box and work exceptionally hard when inspired. These are all skills and characteristics that bring joy and fun and adventure into family life. Other elements of ADHD can also be embraced into family life when they are used at the right time; impulsivity and hyperfocus to start a new project ten minutes before leaving for a holiday would not be welcomed but impulsivity and hyperfocus to do that same job when there is time to do it and no other pressures will give an excellent outcome and use skills well. Therefore, as a supporter of an ADHD athlete the most important element you can offer is in the shape of scaffolding. Scaffolding is about engineering the environment around an athlete with ADHD so that they have the best possible chance of success. Much of this will be done by giving them external tools that others would have done automatically by their executive function.

For any family where there is a member with ADHD, there are three fundamental elements that can help create a little more harmony: a weekly meeting covering the six Cs can help put everyone in the best place to start the week, communicating clearly and effectively reduces tensions and misunderstandings and practising patience allows you to set realistic expectations creating fewer tensions.

The six Cs...

A weekly meeting (ideally on a Sunday) where everybody runs through the six Cs (celebrations, communications, cash, care, calendars and concerns) so you are all aligned and cognisant of what others will be dealing with can be really effective.

Celebrations	Everyone to share something good or positive that occurred in the last week. This helps build strength awareness, gratitude and confidence.
Communication	Any communication issues over the past week can be raised now, when threat systems are soothed so you can discuss calmly and rationally. Here ask questions, be direct but kind, honest and open. Explain how you are feeling. Consider the communication conventions below for this.
Cash	Financial issues to be caught up on. We joke about the ADHD tax (the extra amount that life costs you due to forgetting to pay bills or fines, late night Instagram scrolling purchases, sporting equipment that got you excited about but abandoned or booking tickets for dates when you already have plans) but it can have implications and addressing these together can limit some of the costs.
Care	How is everyone looking after themselves at the moment? Any medical issues, friendship worries, self-care to be prioritized.
Calendars	Run through the week ahead; work, school, training, competitive events, social events, caring responsibilities. Everything goes onto a whiteboard in one place giving visual reminders of everything and pre-warning about stressful days.
Concerns	Being pre-prepared for difficult situations when there will be some pressure is vital to reduce the amount of stress. Are there stressful events coming up that might be tricky? Does someone have a big game, selection trials, exams, scary work meetings? How can they be handled? How can everyone support them?

Communication conventions

Dynamics in any family can be tricky to manage but can be harder when neurodiversity is present. Communication conventions can help the dynamics be easier to manage. There are four conventions to consider:

- Non-confrontational language – Changing our language so it is not confrontational will allow you to show how you feel (rather than what someone has done or not done) and moves you all forward…

Instead of	You could try…
You forgot yet again	Is there anything we could put in place to help you remember?
I'll do it – you never do it properly	Which part of this would you like to do?
You always talk over me and drown me out	I feel unimportant you when you talk over me

- Honesty – With less confrontational language in place then you can more openly talk about the frustrations. Not in the heat of an argument when RSD might trigger but when calm and in a good place to be reflective. The insights from all sides can be quite enlightening and give more patience and compassion. The goal for everyone is to be as nonjudgmental as possible so you all have a safe space to explain how you are feeling.

- Actively listen – Give full attention to show active listening; use eye contact, nod to show you're engaged and try to avoid interrupting. Afterwards, offer words of encouragement.

- Be solution focused – Focus on solutions rather than finding fault or allocating blame. This can be hard to do at times but will create more harmony. You don't want to let things fester so bring up the issue the week it has happened and look for a solution together to reduce the chance of it happening again.

Practising patience and setting realistic expectations

While some ADHD symptoms will be frustrating to live with as a parent or partner, the athlete experiencing them will be far more frustrated. In remembering it is a condition they have and they haven't chosen to behave in the way they do, it can help you illicit more acceptance, sympathy and patience from yourself.

With this acceptance, we can start to accept that our athlete might well be mentally exhausted. Sport, school, work and day-to-day living can be exhausting for all of us but if you are trying to do that with a neurodiverse brain in a neurotypically designed world everything can use up more energy. Even if they have a hyperactive version of ADHD, which means they seem to have endless physical energy, they might struggle with mental or cognitive fatigue. Additionally, if they have spent years being reprimanded for not being good enough, not being fast enough, being too much, too noisy or too daydreamy, then motivation might be limited; so it can be helpful to adjust your expectations for what you expect from them.

These expectation reductions should bring patience. It is only human to want to explode occasionally with frustration but it is incredibly hard to roll back from this and you can cause long-term damage to your relationships. Before speaking think…

- Why is this behaviour creating a specific problem?
- What is the problem?
- Can we deal with the problem another way?
- Will saying something cause longer-term harm than this specific problem?

Thinking through these questions in your head and using curiosity (you can read about it in chapter 6) can help you decide when saying nothing might be a better longer-term option for you.

An important element to remember is that the functions we need to fulfil in different times of our lifespan, alongside coping mechanisms and maturity, can mean that some symptoms get expressed differently as you age, reducing its impact on your abilities to perform well. A child who feels a sense of restlessness, struggles to relax and is constantly distracted will really struggle with the requirement to sit in a classroom and focus and it is likely they will be continually reprimanded for disrupting others and not following instructions. When that child grows into an adult however they will be able to choose a job where they have more autonomy to move about, have learnt skills or strategies to follow managerial instructions and have joined a sports team to exercise off stresses after work. They still have the ADHD symptoms but they are older so have learnt some strategies and are not restricted by school rules. This means externalizing behaviours (running away, drinking, smoking, damaging things, taking drugs) might reduce in adulthood but internalizing ones (like anxiety, low mood and self-harm) increase and if you live with someone with ADHD you will need to adapt the way you support them. For this reason, the rest of this chapter looks at how you might support those around you with ADHD differently at different times of their life.

SUPPORTING CHILDREN

Research from back in 1992 found that how children with ADHD do as adults is not predicted by the levels of their symptoms but by the quality of their relationships with their parents, their ability to do well at school and their social skills. This means that as a parent or carer of a child with ADHD you may well feel a lot of responsibility on your shoulders. This is especially difficult as studies have found that parenting a child with ADHD increases your risk of depression, self-blame and isolation. When we are struggling with these it can become harder to parent our child and may end up using counterproductive parenting strategies which can exacerbate the issues. Training yourself to be able to effectively parent an ADHD child is thought to be one of the best ways to influence a long term positive outcome for them. When parents have been taught how to help their children enhance their levels of attention and to better self-regulate their children did significantly better than those who hadn't had this training. In the UK the NICE guidelines recommend parent training for the families of children with ADHD before they become teenagers.

Evaluations of this type of training have found that when the parents are neurotypical the children have a reduction in ADHD symptoms, parents have a wider range of skills and strategies to draw upon and overall there are decreased levels of family distress. There interventions are less effective when the parents have ADHD symptoms so if you do have it too then it is important you prioritize finding your own effective treatments first so then your heightened attention and impulse control can support your parenting.

Set routines

Research finds getting children into organized sporting activities and systems as young as possible is an excellent way to keep them active, establishes a framework for how to build a routine and establishes exercise as a tool to manage ADHD symptoms.

Get them goal-focused

One of the reasons sport works so well for those with ADHD is that it automatically activates goal driven behaviours; achieving a new skill, making the team, winning a match, getting faster or higher. Goals help develop the knowledge of consequences and working towards something and can be set in academic, sporting and social environments. Younger children need fewer goals and more regular feedback. They also need lots of reinforcement. As they age you can add in more goals and reduce feedback.

Offer safe responsibility with consequences

Assign a household chore that's needed (but not critical) and that won't get done unless your child does it. Tasks that are fairly easy to do well and actively contribute towards family life will set your child up for success and then you can gradually blend in more important and challenging jobs. Give clear, easy-to-follow instructions and use this as an opportunity to reinforce positive behaviour.

Behavioural diaries

Use systems like behavioural diaries to target and monitor any difficult behaviours so you can identify and manipulate the triggers and outcomes of your child's behaviour. Behavioural diaries between school and home should help you focus on the positives; rewarding great and social behaviours through praise, positive attention and tangible rewards – charts with tokens that can be exchanged for desired rewards can work well for some children.

Catch up with coaches

Regular chats with coaches on what you find is working for you with handling your child's ADHD behaviours can not only be helpful for them but good for you to get feedback and work on any other interventions. Feedback any praise that coaches have mentioned to your child as this will be confidence boosting and help them understand their strengths. It can also be helpful to share what you both see as the triggers of difficult behaviours to manage (often transitions, highly competitive moments, time given over to learning or watching rather than moving and playing) and share tools that either of you are finding effective.

Minimize punishments

Many of the day-to-day behaviours you might have to manage as a parent to a young athlete with ADHD will be coming from their ADHD; not from negative intent so you need to think strategically about how you support behavioural change rather than relying upon conventional discipline. Punishing these behaviours would be punishing your child for being themselves and this can cause low self-esteem. Ignoring behaviours when it is safe to do so and praising the good can subtly train the athlete as to what they will be able to receive attention for. Where a behaviour is unsafe (usually because it is impulsive and done without consequences considered); like ignoring safety instructions, running into roads, jumping off sporting or playground equipment then some kind of time out might be needed but make it clear it is not a punishment but to keep them safe.

SUPPORTING A TEENAGER

ADHD can often be masked well in primary school as young children are more likely to be regularly moving around, not asked to sit still for too long, be given simple sets of instructions and will often be doing organized sports in and out of school. On top of this, when under 11 they will usually have parents/carers and teachers (and coaches) on hand to organize, remind and keep them on task. As they transition to senior school then parent/carer and teacher support may be reduced which can leave those with ADHD struggling and feeling exposed.

One of the toughest elements with teens is that their brains are trying to develop into adult brains and in doing so can become much keener on learning from and fitting in with peers than their parents or carers. This makes life hard as a parent when you are trying to help but your advice is rejected. While it will feel personal it isn't; it is a teenage brain trying to figure out its place in the world. This is difficult enough in a neurotypical brain but harder still in an ADHD one where some of the skills required to navigate an adult world; like time keeping, organization, focus and emotional regulation are harder to access. This puts you as a parent in a really difficult place; needing to support if they are to thrive but often having your teen pushing back, not wanting it. There is no tool or strategy to fix this – but solidarity that you are not alone. I once taught a workshop for a school team and one of the students told me how much he hates his dad giving him advice and how he will automatically reject it. I asked if his dad knew anything about his sport. 'Suppose so', he replied. 'He has an Olympic gold medal in it.' So, if his dad isn't going to be listened to, don't feel down if your advice isn't wanted either!

A few things you can try though that the athletes interviewed for this book said helped them when their parents did them when they were in their teens...

Brain education

Lots of the teens I work with who have ADHD enjoy learning about their brain, how it works in a sporting environment and how their specific ADHD brain might interact with that. It can help them understand why they behave in the way that they do so that they can reflect more and make decisions differently in future. Get them reading chapter 1 to understand themselves better and chat about what resonates for them and what triggers kick off their threat system. Most importantly, ask them how they would like you to support when their threat system does kick off.

Praise over punish

Just as suggested for the younger children, the process of ignoring bad behaviour unless it causes safety issues and instead praising the positives, creates less tension. Additionally, using the sport they do as a way to keep them from harmful behaviours can be valuable; knowing that they are unlikely to be picked for the school team if they are suspended or they won't be able to qualify for a competition without having shown up for training, helps.

Tools for time and organizational management

To ensure they make it to training, practices and school on time then countdowns can help them know when to leave. Timetables on walls, phone reminders and questions from you can be good too.

> "I used to get really overwhelmed when it was time to pay bills and stuff so my mom bought me this organiser where you write down all the bills you have and what dates they are due, how much money you have to send to each place and I have that on my calendar. I feel like once I have all my admin stuff done, or organised at least, it helps me to focus on the football stuff." Brooke, Footballer

Keep instructions simple

The more complex the sentences the more your teen has to keep in their working memory and, as we know, their working memory can struggle. So the simpler the instructions and only focusing on one concept at a time the easier it becomes to get them to do what is necessary.

Rewards

Rewarding the things that have to be done (like homework or physio) with things that might be on their Dopamine list (chapter 5) can keep them and you happier.

Goal setting

Again, just as for younger children, teens who are focused on sport should also be supported with goal setting. Look at chapter 5 to see how they might do this.

Keep an eye on the three Ss

When behaviours seem to be challenging reflect on the use of the three Ss: Sleep, screens, sugar. Sleep can be either particularly difficult or too easy with ADHD (as seen in chapter 4) but when they are tired, have rollercoastering blood sugar levels and are too focused on a screen (often to the detriment of movement) then their threat system will be on hyper alert and much more likely to trigger emotional dysregulation.

Lower organizational expectations

Louise (the story you will read next) offers helpful advice that we should try to think of ADHD children as being around three years younger in developmental terms than they are. This can help you lower expectations so you get less frustrated if they are not 'stepping up' in terms of organizational management as to where you would like them to be. It does mean though when you thought you could step away from so much planning when they reach teenagerhood you will actually need to keep on doing it if they are to pass exams and get to training or competitions on time.

> "When I was younger my mum made sure I had everything. She was like, 'have you got this, have you got that, have you got this?' She still does it now – makes sure I've got everything." Olivia, Cricketer

SUPPORTING AN ADULT

The difficulties with ADHD might mean the adult athlete you live with can come across as a poor listener, insensitive, easily distracted or forgetful. Or they may have been successful in learning strategies not to do these things but in doing so will be utterly fatigued and not able to give you the focus you would like from them. Alongside this, if you feel you have to be in control and 'manage' your partner to get everything done, then they will most likely feel ashamed and their threat system will trigger (prompting a fight, flight, freeze or fawn response – see chapter 1) and you will feel frustrated that all the extra you are having to do is not valued.

The most important thing to remind yourself when you live with an adult with ADHD is not to try to parent them. Even if you are technically their parent (if it is an adult child living at home) they need the autonomy to direct their own life or else you resent doing more than your fair share and they resent feeling controlled.

With this in mind a number of tactics and approaches can be taken so you can support your adult athlete with ADHD (partner or adult child) so you can both thrive without resentment.

Educate yourself

Read chapter 1 in this book to understand the way the brain works in both high performance and ADHD. Then read through chapter 3 so you can see which of the ADHD traits you recognize in your partner. This knowledge can help you identify potential challenges, the strengths they may have and give you more tolerance and empathy for what your partner might be dealing with on a day-to-day basis. One of the hardest areas to handle as a partner can be if your ADHD partner has moments of emotional dysregulation that you may witness. Learn and talk about it what is coming from the ADHD and make it part of the conversation so you can have a strategy to cope when they are emotionally dysregulated.

Focus on strengths

A strengths-based approach helps you to each focus on the positive things you bring to the relationship so you can recognize each other's individual areas of expertise and share out tasks more effectively, enabling you both to focus on what you do well. Focusing on strengths means instead of focusing on what goes wrong or where you might annoy each other you make more of an effort to notice the things you value and appreciate in each other, reducing resentment. It also means you can see how you work as a team and both input equally. For example, if your ADHD athlete is poor on planning and organization but great at active roles could your household role be around bills, direct debits and utilities and theirs be on garden, house and bike maintenance. If you have to organize everything for children at school could they physically take them to their extra-curricular classes? Instead of seeing the impulsivity as a risky irritant try to remember what you used to find fun about their impulsivity, before it caused issues. Can any of that be bought back into the relationship safely by focusing on how they are spontaneous, fun and creative.

Additionally, a focus on the strengths also helps you to celebrate successes – for both of you. This is really helpful when someone has spent much of their life feeling like they are failing. The praise and validation of the work they do and the efforts they make helps boost their self-esteem and confidence so they are happier and you have someone who is more able to relax and enjoyable to spend time with.

Clarity of roles

A relationship between someone who is neurodiverse and someone who is neurotypical can be amazing when their strengths and weaknesses balance out – but it can also cause some frustrations when they have different approaches towards decision making, organization, timeliness or consequences. If there is a lack of balance then slicing up responsibilities to those which suit the diversities within the relationship can help you to thrive without nagging or resentment. If they (or you) struggle to articulate your strengths then a strengths audit (chapter 5) is super helpful – this gives you both an ego boost to see what you are good at and be clearer in how you contribute.

Remind them you are on the same team

If someone has spent a lot of time in their life feeling different, or not good enough then it can really help to feel you truly belong and that others have your back and want you to do well. Where this shows up most is if the athlete with ADHD you are supporting also has Rejection Sensitivity (RSD). You may inadvertently say things that might trigger their RSD and get a strong emotive response. Being aware of this can help you to consider how you phrase questions or statements; reducing the opportunities for them to interpret neutral comments as negative or critical. It also becomes helpful for you to think about how you phrase feedback so that you can have a positive conversation about it rather than them becoming very defensive and emotional dysregulated. This might mean instead of saying something like 'You spent hours at the gym – you'd better not be going for so long tomorrow' you might phrase it as 'Seems like you did a great gym session today – does that mean you get more rest tomorrow so you recover?'

Value each others' values

One of the most helpful activities I do with any athlete as their sport psychologist is helping them to identify their values. There are 100 words below which cover a wide range of values that we might have as humans. The goal (and it isn't an easy goal) is to filter out from this group of words just three! These will be the values that feel at the absolute core of you. The ones that you feel completely drive you forward, but also, if someone violates them, will totally trigger your threat system.

Acceptance	Passionate	Intelligence
Community	Truth	Transparency
Connection	Certainty	Understanding
Equality	Grace	Learning
Security	Risk-taking	Logic
Harmony	Commitment	Quality
Spirituality	Dedication	Attentiveness
Teamwork	Determination	Charity
Accomplishment	Drive	Compassion
Capability	Conviction	Empathy
Effectiveness	Comfort	Generosity
Efficiency	Dignity	Humility
Excellence	Productivity	Thoughtfulness
Growth	Respect	Kindness
Effort	Freedom	Achievement
Patience	Discipline	Ambition
Persistence	Creativity	Recognition
Professionalism	Sustainability	Enjoyment
Balance	Diligence	Belonging
Power	Assertiveness	Mastery
Agency	Bravery	Autonomy
Self-reliance	Fearless	Purpose
Contentment	Honesty	Confidence
Control	Integrity	Process
Curiosity	Loyalty	Courage
Adventurous	Strength	Optimism
Empowerment	Enthusiasm	Insight
Independence	Energetic	Gratitude
Fairness	Innovative	Family
Accountable	Spontaneous	Health
Challenge	Prosperity	Joy
Consistency	Adaptable	Wealth
Decisiveness	Awareness	
Inspiring	Clarity	

When you have your three values, ask others in the household to identify theirs as well. Then you can have an honest conversation around how your values might at times clash, or also harmonize. It helps you see where you need to consider potential conflicts but also how you will sometimes be able to easily work in alignment.

Get specific

Find solutions for specific problems. Each issue that can show up in ADHD can cause stress and tension in a relationship and may also lead to misunderstandings and conflict. Considering each of the individual key symptoms of adult ADHD can help us reflect on where, as partners, we might be able to help and support.

Concentration and distraction	Help them develop an approach to maintain focus and attention. Do they need a space away from distractions when working or training? Do they like to do some of their training alone to focus or value the distraction from the boring elements? Discuss the best places and times for them to focus so they can do what they need to do and then have time for you and family.
Organization	Look together at some time management and scheduling apps . If those don't seem like they would be helpful then charts, lists or notes around the house to jog memory can help. The areas for athletes where organization is vital will be around day-to-day wellbeing, eating regularly, taking medication, having kit prepared and responding to key emails or messages. Where something is vital; ordering medication or showing up to appointments then put these into your own diary and offer reminders. For everything else rather than feel like you are nagging them, visual reminders can be helpful and less stressful than repeating yourself and annoying both of you. A kitchen white board or phone alarm schedules for timetables, shopping lists or medication timings can keep things less tense.
Energy levels	Try to get to know when their energy levels rise and fall. This means you don't get annoyed if they have their burst of energy (with a side of hyperfocus) at 10pm – may be this could be the time they do their S&C work, they get their kit ready for the next day or write their training plan.
Processing time	Allow additional processing time. If you can see your partner is emotionally overwhelmed or there are some sensory challenges around, give them space. We might really want to help or fix their stresses but giving them some time to process and calm down while the threat system subsides will mean we have a more constructive conversation afterwards.

Hyperfocus	Let them hyperfocus where it is safe to do so. When they are fully absorbed it might be frustrating if you are having to pick up the pieces but letting the continue with this hyperfocus and not breaking it will allow them to do their best work. So rather than interrupting (which will get a glare or a shout) ask when would be a good time to stop and catch up and then leave them to it.

Look after your own wellbeing

Finally, and probably most importantly, if you have a role in helping to support anyone with a neurological condition it is really important to look after your physical wellbeing, your other relationships and your mental health too so that you are in the best place possible to provide your contribution to your athlete's scaffolding. If you are depressed, having relationship issues, using poor coping methods or don't have your own support then you won't have the capacity to help your athlete with ADHD. Read about coins at the start of chapter five and think about how you spend your coins and how you can earn some back. Then also consider which people in your life you can lean upon when you need.

LOUISE'S STORY

Louise is the mum of an 18-year-old Netball player. Both she and her daughter have ADHD.

'My daughter walked very early at 10 months. She was swimming unaided before she was 3 and a half. She was riding a bike without stabilizers by about the same time. She was just constantly on the go, with boundless energy. I remember sitting in the garden, and she wanted constant interaction, things like: "right, set me an obstacle course" and time me and then she would want to keep going to try and beat her time. She had a pogo stick and she would pogo for hours. She had a little scooter and would just scoot backwards and forwards, backwards and forward.'

'She was never, ever disruptive or violent.'

'Her Year 1 teacher did remark on her fidgeting and said she needed to pay attention more, but because she was so bright nobody really thought about it. She sailed through primary education and her Year SATS showed that she had exceeded all the expectations of a year 6 pupil, so nobody ever picked up on anything else. She also did so much sport, my belief is that she pretty much self-medicated with the adrenalin and Dopamine that sport releases.'

'She was a county swimmer by the time she was 9. I think she loved the repetitiveness; constant back and forward of swimming was quite calming but eventually they wanted her training five or six times a week and she got bored with having to give so much time to one thing. From there she started doing triathlons and riding horses then as well and then she started Tetrathlon. From the minute she started doing it she was always in the top three in her age group.'

'She seems to have this natural affinity to sports and is good at whatever she tries with what appears to be very little effort. She also started playing netball – she joined a local club and within months she was a primary part of their age-related teams. She stayed that way all the way through Juniors also competing at regional level for 2 years playing all over the Southwest. Trialling for County though was a different story – she failed every single time, and we had no idea why. How could her ability at club level not translate or transfer to competitive trials. It really knocked her confidence and dampened her enthusiasm and motivation to keep improving.'

'She was doing really well with her club netball and pony club tetrathlon and then Covid hit. Overnight she went from doing 20 / 30 hours of sport a week to nothing – no sport at all. It was shocking. There were times where I thought we were going to lose her. She barely came out of her room for three months, she barely spoke. She just disengaged from us and her very limited Covid world.'

'I came home from work one day in July 2020 and as I walked into the house she was waiting for me. She said, "Mum, I want to be tested for ADHD." That saying "you could have knocked me over with a feather" well honestly, that! I tried to keep the shock off of my face and replied "Okay, why?" She told me "I've been doing some research. There just has to be something wrong. Life cannot possibly be this hard when it used to be so easy".'

'This was such a pivotal moment. I thought she was mad, because like many millions of other people my perception of ADHD was naughty little boys running around and causing havoc. But, I am a problem solver through and through, and I love my daughter very much, so I spent 48 hours immersing myself in the world of ADHD. I went from ADHD to ADHD in Girls, to ADHD in Bright Girls (2E / DME) and then to ADHD in Girls and Puberty / Hormones etc. It was very clear very quickly that she was right, and that sport had been a huge benefit for her and had helped mask her difficulties and barriers.'

'On the back of my journey with my daughter I have also been diagnosed; the amount of research I did in such a short time, and continue to do, is definitely courtesy of my ADHD hyperfocus.'

'I now know that bright girls especially manage to fly under the radar to such a degree that they often don't start to fail until they get to A Levels or university and sport seems to eek that out as they are basically self-medicating. As the requirement on my daughter grew in terms of executive function type tasks and concentration she started to struggle. Sport was definitely her friend and without Covid it might have been years until we finally realized.'

'She had the assessment, and it came back that she definitely had ADHD and they also diagnosed General Anxiety Disorder. A well-documented aspect of ADHD is masking to fit in and that mask had also covered all of the anxiety that she was feeling inside because, in her eyes, she was failing, couldn't achieve to the level she had before without having to work so much harder, and didn't understand why.'

'Some of the teachers at her school were utterly phenomenal. The head of academics will be forever in my heart, because he came on this journey with me. When she left the school he said to me, "I can't thank you enough, I can already see some of these traits in other kids, and now I know how to help them." She went from failing at school to leaving with all eights and nines in her GCSEs.'

'It took about eight months to get her medication right. It really impacted her appetite – even though she was still playing lots of sport. She was skinny. Her diet was, and is, appalling. She's picky and she has some sensory issues with food textures and smells. With so much training and her picky eating, her weight was a problem. Even if she won't change what she eats I would love her to just add a few things that will really pump up her energy levels.'

'Also, the meds that she takes make her sweat dreadfully, and she hates it. She knows that her meds make her smelly. Finding a balance between the benefits of meds versus things like sweating are hard to balance and it upsets her. I think there's been a definite realization in the last year that this is with her for life and I know that is something that bothers her.'

'Medication doesn't help her with sport, especially netball. They have a "dumbing down" effect that she says take away for energy and drive and the speed at which her ADHD brain works so trials remain a barrier for her.'

'My daughter has never been successful at a traditional "show up and play" trial. There are a number of factors that play into that like short match play periods on court, environments that she doesn't know that are noisy and chaotic, being on court with athletes of a lesser ability – all of these things (and more) make it really difficult for her to focus or find her place and that impacts her ability to show how good she is. She needs real challenge to step it up. I believe if you put her on a court with Super League players, she would really step up her game – she absolutely wouldn't be as good as them but you would see a very different athlete on court. She can pull it out of the hat when she needs to; her ability to read the game is so fast and being able to hyperfocus helps her work out the strategy of the game – she computes at an incredible speed. But if she's not challenged, she will coast and that is usually what selectors see – an athlete that isn't good enough, can't be bothered, or isn't paying attention.'

'If you want to see the best in her you need to consider how and where you test her. She is more than good enough to win on her own merit, but I do think there needs to be an understanding that she is being set up to fail if you don't have any understanding of the barriers she is facing.'

'We were given feedback relating to an old County trial that she attended after we got the ADHD diagnosis – the selector said, almost verbatim; "we just didn't feel that she was committed enough. She wasn't paying attention. She was fidgeting, she was dancing. She wasn't listening to us." Yeah, no shit, Sherlock.'

'But imagine if that selector had been provided with even minimal information about ADHD in Girls and how it might look – she might not have taken her trial on face value. If selectors were provided with some technical overview information from coaches that know the ND athlete beforehand and more in-depth knowledge of ADHD, outcomes for ND athletes may well improve. Imagine if that had happened for my daughter and she'd been getting the specialist coaching and stretch that she needed from 13 or 14 how that might have improved her current outcomes and her mental health.'

'The amount of time you get on court in a trial is difficult. If they have a formula that says they want to see everyone on court for two lots of 10 min then for someone with ADHD make sure that those on court sessions are back to back so she has time to settle on court and better still try and factor in 4 x 10 minutes in 2 sets. If you put her on and take her off, and then put her on half an hour later she will have disengaged, and it will be far more difficult to pull it back.'

'The one trial my daughter did get through was to play for her country in the national team. It was a trial that worked well with ADHD; a weekend trial and only girls who had been nominated by club coaches were invited to trial – so lots of time on court to settle and constant challenge because everyone was skilled. When she played for them, it really challenged her, and that's why she enjoyed it so much. She hates coasting. She hates not improving. What she really needs is a coach that will really, really make her work hard. As soon she feels she is improving she goes from strength to strength.'

'I still manage my daughter in terms of dates and times. I manage her in terms of information that hits her inbox. I don't do it for her. I did before but I am slowly starting to reduce the scaffolding I provide but it's hard because she still struggles. I refuse to take the scaffolding away completely though until I know she's ready because I'm not about to let her fail – it will be a gradual thing. I do things like make sure she's got compression socks, make sure that there's tape in the house just in case she needs to tape her legs. I make sure that we both get emails about all her netball stuff and I prod her to make sure she reads stuff. And I prod her to make sure she puts it in the diary. And I still sign up for trials for her and fill out forms for her. I try and make sure that she engages with deadlines before it's a real deadline to manage stress and anxiety. I do a lot of the nurturing stuff still because I'm her mum but I support her executive function barriers too.'

'Sport has been my daughter's safety net. Sport has supported her from the time she was a little dot. I may not have known it, but it has. More knowledge is needed in elite sport of how ADHD presents, the benefits of it in sport and the support that's needed to help the athlete achieve their potential is just so important because, in my opinion, there are huge benefits for sport especially elite sport, that can come from ADHD and sport is such a benefit to those with ADHD; there is good correlation between ADHD and the ability to excel in sport. When you're challenged, and when you enjoy something, the super focus of ADHD is such a benefit.'

Final reflections

This book was supposed to be 40,000 words. But when you really delve into ADHD in Sport and see how it helps and hinders, how there are many under-utilized strategies that can be effective, the impact of co-occuring conditions, the pros and cons of medication and the importance of brilliant scaffolding around the athlete, the number of pages multiplies. I also realized how valuable the knowledge of athletes with ADHD could be so their stories needed to be included too. While not undertaken as any type of academic analysis, and acknowledging that only eight athletes were interviewed, I think we can benefit from reflecting on the themes that arose in their stories.

It quickly became clear that the athletes with lots of external support; supportive, ADHD aware parents, coaches and teachers have found it much easier to navigate high level sport. A coach (like Jess), having an understanding of ADHD, how symptoms might manifest and how to mitigate for them seems to give the athlete confidence that they have someone on their side and their strengths will shine through. Additionally, a parent who facilitates your sporting life for you (like we see Louise doing for her daughter or Brooke's mum doing for her) means you don't miss important dates or information and you have the same opportunities for development as other athletes.

In the stories, it also became clear that the culture in a club clearly impacts whether an athlete feels they can talk to coaches about their ADHD. The fact that so many of the athletes used the word 'disclose' suggests they didn't feel comfortable mentioning it simply as part of who they are and felt some risk in talking about it. Even when some did explain their diagnosis, they were often brushed off by a coach who didn't understand how it might impact their sport.

Many of the athletes highlighted the unhelpfulness of the outdated stereotyped 'ADHD child' as a naughty, disruptive young boy which limits diagnosis in girls and those boys who internalize their struggles. They also felt it prevented athletes getting the support they need and deserve.

Finally, the athletes made it clear that self-awareness of what does and doesn't work for you makes a huge difference. You will always be your own best advocate and so, as an athlete, your job is to learn how to get the most from yourself. Understanding this, assessing it and making plans and strategies seems to be the best way to feel in control and reduce the risk of high stress, depressive mood or anxiety that can manifest as a consequence of undiagnosed, untreated or ignored ADHD.

I loved interviewing the athletes and I feel their stories really bring to life some of the struggles and successes that having ADHD as an athlete can bring. But I am incredibly aware that every athlete is different and everyone with ADHD is different so the stories are not for comparison or to copy,; but to see that athletes with ADHD are able to thrive and succeed in sport with the right support and strategies.

This book actually ended up at over 70,000 words but I hope the knowledge that is included, the strategies suggested and the stories from the athletes can help you to navigate your way through having ADHD in sport so you can thrive and be as successful as your talents and efforts deserve.

Glossary

9pm Zoomies	When you feel energetic at night just as others are winding down.
Adenosine	A chemical in the brain which can block dopamine release.
Alexithymia	When someone struggles to recognize and express their emotions.
Amgydala	A tiny part of the limbic region in your brain that plays a large role in your emotions. It is particularly focused on fear so it can act like an alarm system, constantly on alert looking out for things that could physically, psychologically or physiologically harm you.
Amygdala hijack	This is where the amygdala has been triggered (because it has noticed some sort of threat) and takes the lead in your brain, limiting access to the parts of your brain that will allow you to remain calm or logical.
Anorexia	When someone restricts their diet excessively to keep their weight as low as possible. They may have body dysmorphia (unable to see their body as others might), have a real fear of gaining weight, weigh themselves obsessively, restrict food and lie about what they are eating.
Anticipatory Anxiety	Where someone experiences increased levels of anxiety by thinking about an event or situation in the future that they are nervous about.
Anxiety	A feeling of apprehension or dread in situations where there is no physical threat and those fears are disproportionate to the situation.
Attention	The ability to focus on the right things at the right time.

(Continued)

GLOSSARY

Attention Deficit Hyperactivity Disorder (ADHD)	Persistent patterns of inattention, hyperactivity or impulsivity (or a combination) which causes significant dysfunction and challenges.
Autism Spectrum Disorder (ASD)	Where someone might find it harder to communicate and interact with other people, understand how others might think or feel, find sensory elements or lots of people overwhelming or stressful, get very anxious when things are unfamiliar or unpredictable and like to have routines in order to feel safe and secure.
Brain-derived neurotrophic factor (BDNF)	Plays a key role in the way the hippocampus (the area where your memory is stored) functions, creating greater long-term effectiveness of learning and memory and supports cell proliferation.
Behavioural inhibition	Someone's ability to control their responses to the things that happen to them.
Binge Eating Disorder	Diagnosed when someone has regular, recurrent binge eating episodes, consuming large quantities of food in a short amount of time, feeling like they are unable stop.
Bipolar	A mental health condition that affects your moods where they swing from one extreme (depression) to another (mania).
Body doubling	The practice of having another person present while you try to complete a task even if working towards your own individual goal in order to enhance accountability and limit procrastination.
Brain drain	A strategy to reflect and write down everything that is causing worry or threat in a forthcoming event.
Brain fog	A cognitive impairment affecting the ability to think clearly, focus, concentrate, remember and pay attention. It makes it hard hold a conversation, remember what you were doing, keep your train of thought or follow instructions.
Bulimia	Diagnosed when someone binges and then purges (through vomiting, laxatives or over exercise) to stop themselves gaining weight.
Burnout	Total and utter mental, physical or emotional exhaustion.

(Continued)

Cardio	Exercise (like running, jumping, dancing or cycling) that raises your heart and breathing rate.
Catecholamine System	Catecholamines are a group of neurotransmitters (Norepinephrine, Epinephrine (we know it better as Adrenaline) and Dopamine) that are responsible for our body's threat system responses as well as regulating movement, emotions and memories.
Chunking	Breaking down tasks into smaller sections to make them feel more manageable.
Circadian rhythm	The internal body clock that sets out when someone will fall asleep, feel hungry, thirsty, feel tired or alert and be able to focus.
Cognitive control	The thought processes which allow us to make the right choices at the right time to achieve our goals.
Cognitive flexibility	The ability to adapt behaviours and ways of thinking depending on the environment someone is in or the tasks they need to complete.
Cognitive functions	The different skills facilitating learning and problem-solving.
Concussion	A traumatic head injury where the brain twists or moves inside the head; stretching and injuring the nerves and blood vessels, causing chemical changes that temporarily make the brain stop working as well as it should.
Conduct Disorder	When someone has emotional and behavioural problems that will cause them to behave in socially unacceptable, harmful and sometimes illegal ways.
Controlled drugs	Drugs where the manufacture, procession and use is regulated by government because they can cause addiction or harm if misused.
Co-occurring conditions	Two or more medical conditions or disorders that can occur at the same time.
Coping mechanisms	Strategies that help people deal with difficult issues, situations or emotions.
Depression	A condition where someone has long lasting feelings of unhappiness and hopelessness and loses interest in things they used to enjoy.

(Continued)

GLOSSARY

Dexterity	The ability to perform an action skilfully and effectively with our hands.
Disordered eating	Irregular eating patterns that may not fit the diagnosis of an Eating Disorder but are still harmful to health or performance.
Disorganization	A lack of proper planning and control.
Distraction	Something that prevents someone from concentrating.
Dopamine	A neurotransmitter which is associated with motor control, reward, pleasure, motivation, attention and affect. It allows someone to think and plan, strive, focus and become motivated and spikes when we anticipate something good or significant happening.
Dopamine buzz	The positive feeling that comes when we have done something we enjoy or have achieved a goal we were working towards.
Dyslexia	A condition that causes issues with reading, writing and spelling.
Dyspraxia / Developmental Co-ordination Disorder	A condition that impacts movement and co-ordination making it harder to carry out tasks that need balance or physical skills like writing neatly or using small objects.
Emotional Dysregulation	When the threat system has been triggered someone will not have access the rational, logical decision-making part of the brain. The signals coming from around the brain (handling memories, emotions, input from senses, awareness of others) might feel overwhelming so they are unable to behave in the way they would desire.
Emotional Literacy	Widening the emotional vocabulary so someone can use more specific words to describe how they feel helping them communicate better and find the most effective coping mechanisms.
Endocrinologist	A medical professional who specializes in hormones.
Endorphins	Neurotransmitters released when you feel pain or stress and are designed to reduce those feelings (like a natural pain killer).

(Continued)

Epinephrine	Also known as Adrenaline, a neurotransmitter which plays a big part in the threat system keeping us both safe but also excited and driven.
Executive functions	The brain processes that help someone to problem solve (plan, organize and execute the things they need to do) so they can achieve their goals.
Explicit memory	The conscious retrieval of information (like facts and events).
Extroversion	Where someone gains energy (recharges their mental battery) by engaging with other people.
Fawn response	Where the involuntary response to a threat is to appease the threat by ignoring your own needs and pandering to others in order to increase your own feeling of safety. This is often used by those who have been bullied or abused at home or in school, work or sport.
Fight response	Where the involuntary response to a threat is to confront the threat with anger, rage or (most often in sport) lots of energy.
Fine motor skills	The tiny movements that someone will make with their hands, fingers, feet and toes.
Flight response	Where the involuntary response to a threat is avoidance.
Freeze response	Where the involuntary response to a threat is disassociation, numbness, shutdown and low energy, leaving someone fairly immobile.
Goal setting	Goal setting helps to turn intentions (outcome goals) into actions (process goals).
Graphomotor skills	A specific set of psychomotor abilities that enable drawing and handwriting.
Gross motor skills	Skills that use the whole body to make large movements.
Habit function	A virtual storage unit holding your values, skills, strengths and techniques to make automatic decisions based on pre-programmed thoughts and behaviours so that mental energy is reserved for activities that need more thought or effort.

(Continued)

Habit stacking	To develop a new habit someone will adds that action onto a habit they already have.
Heritable	A characteristic or condition that is transmissible from parent to child.
Hippocampus	A part of the brain involved in storing long-term memories that also plays a part in spatial processing and navigation.
Hyperactivity	A state of being unusually active. Often seen as constant fidgeting, excessive physical movement, excessive talking or not being able to take turns or show patience when needed.
Hyperfocus	A state of heightened, intense focus where someone is totally engrossed in a task.
Hypermobility	A connective tissue disorder where joints overextend beyond typical ranges, may dislocate easily, and may regularly move into awkward positions which fall short of full dislocations.
Hypervigilance	Increased alertness where your brain is constantly scanning for threats.
Implicit memory	Unconscious recall (like skills and habits).
Impulsivity	Acting before considering the consequences.
Inattention	When someone has difficulties in focusing and gets distracted easily.
Information processing	The way the brain gathers, manipulates, stores and retrieves information.
Introversion	Where someone gains energy (recharges their mental battery) by spending time alone.
Locomotor skills	The skills that help someone move from one place to another like walking, marching, running, jumping, hopping, galloping, skipping or climbing.
Locus of control	The degree to which someone feels in charge of their own life. Someone with an internal locus of control believes the outcomes they get will be down to their own skills and efforts. Someone with an external locus of control believes what happens to them is control by fate or by other people.

(Continued)

Logical decision function	The networks in your brain that helps someone make great choices, specifically those based in the pre-frontal cortex (involved in decision making, executive functioning, behaviours and planning).
Low frustration tolerance	When someone gets frustrated at seemingly minor issues and has a low level of resilience.
Magpie Syndrome	Someone constantly having their head turned by new (shiny) things or ideas.
Masking	Someone camouflaging who they really are to fit into someone else's expectations of how they should be.
Medication holiday	Where someone stops taking their medication for a few days to a few months.
Melatonin	Melatonin is a hormone that plays a role in managing sleep-wake cycle and circadian rhythm.
Meta-analysis	A process which pulls together the data from multiple studies in order to see patterns and make stronger conclusions.
Metabolic budget	A framework to describe the aspects of metabolism based on energy uptake, storage, and how different substances within the body are utilized.
Mono-identity	Having one thing in your life that is much more important than everything else.
Motivation	The force behind our actions and behaviours.
Motor skills	A function that involves specific movements of the muscles to perform a task. There are gross motor skills and fine motor skills.
Negativity bias	A tendency to focus on, learn from and use negative information more than positive information.
Neurogenesis	The process of creating new neurons in the brain.
Neuroplasticity	The brains capacity to change and adapt.
Neurotransmitters	Chemical messengers that send signals in the brain and body.

(Continued)

Norepinephrine	Also known as noradrenaline is it as neurotransmitter in your brain and spinal cord which increases alertness, arousal and attention and impacts your sleep-wake cycle, mood and memory.
Novelty seeking	To constantly persue new experiences.
Obsessive-Compulsive Disorder (OCD)	A condition where someone experiences obsessions (recurring, unwanted thoughts) or compulsions (repetitive behaviours) in an attempt to alleviate anxiety.
Oppositional Defiance Disorder (ODD)	When someone has regular and continuing patterns of anger, irritability, arguing and defiance towards anyone in authority.
Organization skills	The set of cognitive abilities which allow us to work towards our goals.
Overwhelm	Where tasks or objectives can feel too much due to lack of time, sensory overload, boredom, emotional stress or being asked to switch between tasks too quickly.
Performance goals	A specific goal (often times, distances or scores) by which an athlete will measure themselves.
Peripheral vision	The things you can see outside of your central vision.
Perseverance	Keeping going on a task even if there is a setback.
Physical threat	A risk of something harming your body.
Physiological threat	A risk of something inside our body harming us
Prefrontal Cortex (PFC)	The front of the frontal lobe within the brain which affects behaviour, personality and cognitive abilities.
Problem-solving strategies	Tools someone can use to think constructively about a problem so they can come up with flexible and effective ways to deal with it.
Process goals	The goals (usually behaviours, actions, strategies or tactics) that are required to make something happen.
Processing difficulties	An inability to effectively use the information gathered by the senses.
Information processing speed	How fast the brain can take in, assess and choose what to do with new information.

(Continued)

Procrastination	Putting off a task until later with the aim of protecting yourself from the potential physical (pain), psychological (boredom, risk of failure) or physiological (internal discomfort) of the activity.
Procrastivity	Where someone stays busy by doing less important tasks (because they fear starting the ones they really need to do) but still end up feeling unproductive and stressed because they haven't tackled the most important task.
Proprioception	The sense of self-movement, force and body position.
Psychological threat	A threat to someone's identity, their values or how they want to be seen by others.
Reaction time	The amount of time between noticing a stimulus and doing something about it.
Relative Energy Deficiency in Sport (RED-S)	When an athlete does not have enough energy to fuel all the exercise they are doing as the nutrition they take in is inadequate to cover the energy needed by their body.
Reframing	Proactively switching shaming, negative or unhelpful thoughts into helpful ones.
Rejection Sensitive Dysphoria (RSD)	A condition where neutral comments or actions are interpreted as critical or attacking and leads someone to feel rejected.
Response inhibition	Being able to hold back from inappropriate behaviours or saying inappropriate things in order to work towards long-term goals.
Risk taking	Choosing to do activities that have the potential to be dangerous or harmful and not considering the consequences.
Rumination	Repetitively focusing on negative thoughts and feelings.
Scaffolding	Tools and behaviours to help others feel supported and able to reach their goals.
Seasonal Affective Disorder (SAD)	A type of depression which is associated with seasonal changes; most commonly as the person heads into winter.

(Continued)

Self-esteem	Someone's confidence in their own worth or abilities.
Self-regulation	Someone's ability to control their behaviour and to manage their emotions in ways that are appropriate for the situation they are in.
Sensation seeking	The tendency for someone to crave new and different sensations, feelings, and experiences that are varied, novel, rich and intense.
Sensory sensitivity	When someone processes sensory stimuli and information overly strongly so they become overwhelmed at loud noises, too bright lights or lots of sudden changes. When the brain is unable to process all of this information, it can lead to feelings of confusion, anxiety, and even physical symptoms such as headaches or fatigue.
Serotonin	A neurotransmitter that plays a key role in brain and body functions as mood, sleep, digestion, nausea, wound healing, bone health, blood clotting and sexual desire.
Set shifting	Also known as task switching, it is the ability to unconsciously shift attention between one task and another.
Sleep debt	When someone gets less sleep than their body needs. Will result in sleepiness, less focus, lower cognitive functioning, impaired memory function, irritable and low mood.
Sleep pressure	The process of becoming tired throughout the day so we are ready to fall asleep at night. It comes from Adenosine (above) which builds up in our brain throughout the day attaching to the wakefulness centres to slow down their activity and attaching to the sleep areas to make them more active.
Social battery	The amount of energy someone has for socializing.
Social jetlag	The discrepancy between the timings within the body clock and socially acceptable timings (like needing to be at school, work or training at a certain time.
Stimulant medication	Drugs that increase activity in the brain.

(Continued)

Stress	How someone responds to a stressor if they don't believe they have the capability or capacity to handle it.
Survival function	Ways the brain helps to keep someone safe; helping them predict possible outcomes, body budgeting so the body runs efficiently, prioritizing negative memories and activating a threat system in emergencies.
Task switching	Also known as set shifting, it is the ability to unconsciously shift attention between one task and another.
The Twisties	A movement disorder caused by anxiety where the muscles get tight and tense and the athlete is unable to feel where they are in the air (the proprioception sense) so their body won't do the move they were attempting.
Threat response	When the brain releases adrenaline and cortisol after noticing a perceived threat prompting someone into a fight, flight, freeze or fawn response.
Threat system	The process by which the brain tries to keep someone safe – triggering in threat response in reaction to a perceived threat.
Time blindness	An inability to accurately perceive and manage time.
Therapeutic Use Exemptions (TUE)	A medical document that allows an athlete to use a prohibited medication to treat a legitimate medical condition.
Values	The things someone believes are important in life.
Vigilance	The action of keeping careful watch for danger.
Visual motor speed	The ability to integrate eyes and hands so they work together to complete a task.
World Anti-Doping Agency (WADA)	An organization tasked with developing, agreeing and co-ordinating anti-doping policies across sports and countries.
Waiting mode	Feeling unable to start any additional tasks when there is an event or appointment later that day.
Working memory	Our brain's short-term storage system allowing someone to hold onto the information they need for the current task they are working on.

Acknowledgements

Most importantly, I start by thanking the athletes who generously gave up their time to share their stories, and allowed me to share their stories with you: Jen, Tom, Olivia, Isla, Hannah, Rachel, Brooke and James, thank you. I am also incredibly grateful to coach Jess and mum Louise who gave their perspectives supporting athletes who have ADHD and also to Sonia Westcott for sharing her experiences.

I would like to thank Chris Chapman who commissioned me to create content on supporting athletes with ADHD for the UK Coaching resources. It was seeing the huge need for this content that gave me the initial idea to write the book.

A special thanks to Kate Walsh who found the athletes, arranged many of the interviews, transcribed the interviews and gave valuable feedback.

Thank you to all those researchers inside universities who spend their time studying and growing knowledge about ADHD so that we as practitioners can better support our athletes.

Andy Peart and all at Sequioa, thank you for taking a chance on this book.

Kathryn Meadows, Daphne Chan and Caragh McMurtry all very kindly read a draft of the book and gave some invaluable advice on improvements – so thank you.

Finally, a special thank you to my daughter Harriet who has lost out on 'hanging out together' time while I wrote and still doesn't complain when I practise new tools and strategies on her!

www.ingramcontent.com/pod-product-compliance
Lightning Source LLC
Chambersburg PA
CBHW051540020426
42333CB00016B/2018